SOME REMINISCENCES OF
WILLIAM MICHAEL ROSSETTI

William Michael Rossetti.
From an Oil-painting by Alphonse Legros 1864.

SOME
REMINISCENCES
OF
WILLIAM MICHAEL
ROSSETTI

Pensando il breve viver mio nel quale
Stamane era un fanciullo ed or son vecchio ·
PETRARCA

VOL I

AMS PRESS
NEW YORK

Reprinted from the edition of 1906, New York
First AMS EDITION published 1970
Manufactured in the United States of America

International Standard Book Number:
Complete Set: 0-404-05440-4
Volume 1:   0-404-05441-2
Library of Congress Number: 75-132386

AMS PRESS INC.
NEW YORK, N.Y. 10003

DEDICATED TO

MY WELL-LOVED DAUGHTER-IN-LAW

DORA BRANDRETH ROSSETTI

MY INFANT GRANDCHILDREN

GEOFFREY WILLIAM ROSSETTI

AND

IMOGENE LUCY CRISTINA MARIA ANGELI

AND THE NOW FEW SURVIVORS AMONG

MY OLD FRIENDS

CONTENTS

PAGE

I. EARLIEST YEARS I

II. MY PARENTS, SISTERS, AND BROTHER . . 16

III. SCHOOL 23

IV. FAMILY LIFE, 1839 TO 1844 30

V. THE EXCISE OFFICE 44

VI. HOME LIFE—MY BROTHER AND MYSELF . . 57

VII. THE PRÆRAPHAELITE BROTHERHOOD . . . 62

VIII. BEGINNINGS IN LITERATURE 77

IX. MY FATHER'S LAST YEARS 107

X. SOME SHAPING OF MIND AND CHARACTER . 118

XI. SOME ARTISTIC ACQUAINTANCES . . . 130

XII. SOME LITERARY ACQUAINTANCES . . . 163

XIII. THEATRICAL AND OTHER DIVERSIONS . . 185

XIV. DANTE ROSSETTI AND ELIZABETH SIDDAL . . 192

XV. FURTHER ACQUAINTANCES: BURNE-JONES, MORRIS,
SWINBURNE, AND OTHERS 201

XVI. THE BROWNINGS, LANDOR, TENNYSON . . 232

XVII. SOME PERSONAL AND GENERAL DETAILS . . 260

XVIII. CHEYNE WALK AND ENDSLEIGH GARDENS . . 271

LIST OF ILLUSTRATIONS

VOL. I

WILLIAM MICHAEL ROSSETTI . . . . *Frontispiece*
(From an Oil-painting by Alphonse Legros, 1864)

TO FACE PAGE

FORD MADOX BROWN. c. 1862 61

MS. OF DANTE G. ROSSETTI 79
(Sonnet written to Bouts-Rimés, c. 1848)

CARICATURE, BY DANTE G. ROSSETTI, OF MISS SIDDAL AND
HIMSELF 192
(Chatham Place, c. 1855)

ELIZABETH E. SIDDAL (ROSSETTI) 200
(From a Drawing by D. G. Rossetti, c. 1855)

ALGERNON CHARLES SWINBURNE 218
(Drawing by Dante G. Rossetti, 1860)

MRS. WILLIAM MORRIS 230
(By Dante G. Rossetti, 1861)

MRS. BROWNING 244
(The last photograph taken of her, 1861. Copy sent by Robert Browning
to W. M. Rossetti)

WILLIAM BELL SCOTT, JOHN RUSKIN, DANTE GABRIEL ROSSETTI 291
(Taken in Rossetti's garden, 1864)

PREFACE

I FIND little to state here by way of preface ; but may say that, as I have passed through life with few if any apparent enemies, so also I hope that I have given occasion for not much heart-burning.

Two things would have ill beseemed me in this work, and I trust I have avoided them both. The first is the offence of appearing as a self-praiser ; the second is the still graver misdemeanour of being ill-natured, or of decrying the men and women of whom I speak. What I thought praiseworthy in them I have praised ; to what I thought blameworthy I have felt it to be my right part to award only a thin modicum of blame, or mostly none. Some readers may opine that, although I speak of several important personages from my own know-ledge of them, I say little about them that is of much moment ; neither should I dissent from this allegation. But it does not follow that I know nothing beyond that which I write. In some cases I do know a good deal more ; but to cast a slur here or violate a confidence there would make me contemptible to myself.

For some matters I have a moderately fair memory— I might mention dates in particular. But there are two kinds of things for which my memory is decidedly bad

—the faces of people I meet, and the words of conversations. When a conversation is over, I am not long in forgetting even its definite purport, and more especially I recollect scarcely at all the precise words that had been used. Naturally therefore, when I come to write reminiscences, I can say little of the talks which I had, even with men of mark, and I could very seldom give a *résumé* of their actual phrases. To invent diction which would convey the same sense in a certain way is what I do not feel at liberty to do. The result is that these pages of mine are most rarely enlivened with a few words of remembered talk : which is a pity, but under the circumstances it cannot be helped.

The writing of this book was begun in August 1901, and was substantially completed in March 1903. Since the latter date several things have happened, entitled, on their own showing, to figure in my reminiscences. They are glanced at here and there ; but, so far as may be, I have left my text unaltered.

My life having been an eminently unadventurous and uneventful one, and perhaps of little import to anybody save myself and my immediate surroundings, I do not exactly propose to write my life, and I even take little or no notice here of some of the matters which most closely affected myself. But I have some reminiscences of personages and incidents not unknown to fame, and these I partly set down.

It may be as well here to say that I have already written and published various things in which my personal reminiscences, more especially as affecting other members of the family, are concerned. I shall have to recur to some of the same matters, but shall, so far as manageable, avoid repeating the same identical details. The writings in question are as follows :—

1. 1884. Notes on Works by Dante Gabriel Rossetti—Four articles in *The Art Journal.*

2. 1886. The Collected Works of Dante Gabriel Rossetti—Editorial matter. Amplified in the illustrated edition of his Poems, 1904.

3. 1888. The Portraits of Dante Gabriel Rossetti—Articles in *The Magazine of Art.*

4. 1889. Dante Gabriel Rossetti as Designer and Writer.

5. 1895. Dante Gabriel Rossetti : his Family Letters, with a Memoir by myself.

6. 1896. New Poems by Christina Rossetti—Editorial matter.

7. 1898. The Blessed Damozel, by Dante Gabriel Rossetti—Introduction.

8. 1898-1901. Prefatory Notes to The Poems of Dante Gabriel Rossetti—Siddal Edition.

9. 1899. Ruskin, Rossetti, Præraphaelitism—Editorial matter.

10. 1900. Præraphaelite Diaries and Letters—Edited and partly written by me.

11. 1900. Lenore, by Bürger, translated by Dante Gabriel Rossetti—Editorial matter.

12. 1901. The Germ, Facsimile Reprint—Introduction by me.

13. 1901. Gabriele Rossetti, a Versified Autobiography—Translated and supplemented by me.

14. 1902-3. Bibliography of the works of Dante

Gabriel Rossetti—Articles in *The Bibliographer* (New York), since republished and amplified as a pamphlet.

15. 1903. Dante Rossetti and Elizabeth Siddal—Article in *The Burlington Magazine.*

16. 1903. Rossetti Papers, 1862 to 1870.

17. 1904. The complete Poetical Works of Christina Rossetti, also a selection of them in the *Golden Treasury* series—Editorial matter.

There are also some minor writings, not here specified, bearing on the same range of subject.

It will thus be perceived that, even if I were now to write no more, I have contributed in some substantial measure to public information concerning relatives and associates more interesting than myself. But for several years past the reminiscent or autobiographic mood has been in the ascendant (I think it was Sir Henry Taylor who gave it the first re-impulse), and I may perhaps be excused for joining the goodly company—goodly in numbers and often in quality—of persons who will not keep their private transactions to themselves. "Interviewing" is one of the manias of the day—to my thinking, a noxious one. The reminiscents are persons who, whether interviewed or not by others, interview themselves. To me this seems, if an evil, at all events a minor one.

W. M. R.

London. *January* 1906.

SUMMARY OF THE SECTIONS

I. *Earliest Years.*—My birth in London, 25 September 1829—My parents, sisters, and brother—Restricted income of the family—My father's literary works subsidized by two friends, Frere and Lyell—The Street of my birth, Charlotte Street, Portland Place—My grandfather Polidori and his family—Their country-home, Holmer Green—We remove from No. 38 to No. 50 Charlotte Street—Family life—My early readings—Italian and a very few English visitors—Few works of art in the house

(pp. 1–15)

II. *My Parents, Sisters, and Brother.*—My father and mother towards 1834—My sister Maria—My brother—My sister Christina—My own demeanour in childhood *(pp. 16–22)*

III. *School.*—In 1837 I go to the school of the Rev. Mr. Paul, and soon afterwards to King's College School—A robbery in our house—My brother and myself at school—Two school-fellows—My laziness as a schoolboy after my brother had left—My masters from the same time—I leave school in February 1845 *(pp. 23–29)*

IV. *Family Life, 1839 to 1844.*—The Polidoris leave Holmer Green and resettle in London—Books read by my brother and myself—Polidori's private printing-press—I write two boyish tales—My brother's influence over me in writing, and its limitations—My father falls into ill-health and becomes nearly blind, 1843, and his professional employment fails—Many illnesses in the family throughout my life—My mother goes out giving lessons; and Maria becomes a governess, afterwards a teacher—Position of Christina and Dante Gabriel—Money affairs and death of my. grand-aunt Harriet Pierce—Narrow circumstances of the family—My father takes me away from school, and, through Sir Isaac Goldsmid and Mr. John Wood, I obtain temporary employment in the Excise Office *(pp. 30–43)*

V. *The Excise Office.*—My early days in the office—System of employing Excise officers there—Various officials with whom I came in contact—One of them tried on suspicion of matricide—The Chartist meeting of 1848—Business arrangements in the Inland Revenue—A. C. Lyster and his connexions—Herne Bay (*pp.* 44–56)

VI. *Home Life, My Brother and Myself.*—Our intimate association in daily life, reading, etc.—Persons whom I knew through my brother, such as Thomas Doughty, W. B. Scott, Madox Brown, etc.—Scott's *Autobiographical Notes*—General condition of our family (*pp.* 57–61)

VII. *The Præraphaelite Brotherhood.*—Formation of the Brotherhood, 1848, consisting of Holman Hunt, Millais, Dante Rossetti, Woolner, Collinson, Stephens, and myself—Details concerning each of the six— The closeness of intercourse between the members diminishes after 1850 —Collinson's engagement to Christina Rossetti and its termination—His death—Eventual dissensions between the P.R.B.'s—My own relation to this matter (*pp.* 62–76)

VIII. *Beginnings in Literature.*—Casual writings in boyhood—My early attempts in verse, gradually relinquished—*Bouts-rimés* sonnets written by my brother and myself, and a few by Christina—*The Germ*—My blank-verse poem, *Mrs. Holmes Grey,* intended for *The Germ,* but left unpublished until in 1868 it appeared in *The Broadway*—Some poets whom I knew from 1849 onwards : Patmore, Tennyson, Allingham—Woolner goes for a while to Australia—Officials in the British Museum : Garnett etc.—The Orme family—Miss Haydon and her connexions—Through *The Germ* I know Serjeant Cox, who engages me as art-reviewer in *The Critic*—Am afterwards similarly engaged on *The Spectator,* November 1870—The editor, Rintoul—Thackeray and others—Literary notices in *The Critic*—Meeting with Clough, Heraud, Marston, and others— Early baldness (*pp.* 77–106)

IX. *My Father's Last Years.*—We move from Charlotte Street to Arlington Street, where my mother and Christina open a school—Afterwards my father and mother and Christina settle at Frome-Selwood, Somerset, where another school is tried with little success—Death of Polidori and his wife—Maria and I move into lodgings in Albany Street, kept by R. P. Burcham—My position at Somerset House having improved, the family reunites at No. 166 Albany Street—My father's last illness begins on 16 April 1854, and he dies on 26—Details from notes taken at the time—His will and literary works (*pp.* 107–117)

X. *Some Shaping of Mind and Character.*—Divergences of religious opinion in the Rossetti and Polidori families—I early take a sceptical or agnostic turn, and in politics a democratic turn—Churches which I attended in boyhood—Feelings of my mother and sisters in religious matters (*pp.* 118–129)

XI. *Some Artistic Acquaintances.*—William Bell Scott and his wife—Through the Scotts I know the Epps family, Johannes Ronge, and others—Madox Brown and his family—Persons known to me through Brown : Cave Thomas, Mark Anthony, John Marshall, and others—Alexander Munro, Arthur Hughes, Walter Deverell, Charles Collins, G. P. Boyce, Edward Lear, etc.—John L. Tupper and his family—Some of his poems published in 1896 (*pp.* 130–162)

XII. *Some Literary Acquaintances.*—James Hannay and his associates—William North—J. F. McLennan—The Howitts—Mrs. Bodichon—Charles B. Cayley—Ruskin and his connexions—Details as to my relations with Ruskin (*pp.* 163–184)

XIII. *Theatrical and other Diversions.*—No turn for athletics or sports—Operas and theatres—Love of music thwarted by ignorance of the art (*pp.* 185–191)

XIV. *Dante Rossetti and Elizabeth Siddal.*—Miss Siddal known to Dante Rossetti through Deverell—She becomes engaged to Rossetti and eventually marries him—Swinburne's commendation of her—Six poems by her inserted (*pp.* 192–200)

XV. *Further Acquaintances: Burne-Jones, Morris, Swinburne, and others.*—Through Holman Hunt, on his return from the East, I know various persons—Robert Martineau and Michael Halliday—Little Holland House, tenanted by the Prinsep family and George F. Watts—Val Prinsep and Mrs. Cameron—Watts and his paintings—Leighton, Richard Doyle, Thackeray, and others—Burne-Jones's first knowledge of Dante Rossetti—His personality, and relative estimate of his paintings and Rossetti's—William Morris—Algernon Swinburne—His notes on pictures, 1868, and anecdote relating thereto—The firm of Morris, Marshall, Faulkner, & Co.—Spencer Stanhope and others—The Hogarth Club and some of its members : Street, Alfred Hunt, etc.—The families of Burne-Jones, Morris, and Swinburne (*pp* 201–231)

XVI. *The Brownings, Landor, Tennyson.*—Early readings by my brother and myself of poems by Elizabeth Barrett and Robert Browning—Browning's manner and conversation—I meet the Brownings in Italy in 1860—William W. Story and Landor—Mrs. Browning's admiration of Napoleon III and belief in spiritualism—Browning's disbelief and some manifestations at Kirkup's house—Landor and the flies—Mrs. Browning's appearance and manner—Her discussion with Madame Mario (White)—Browning's return to London and his social popularity—Tennyson—My meetings with him at Little Holland House and at Faringford—Details

of his talk etc.—Mrs. (Lady) Tennyson—Use of cork in influenza etc.
—Three anecdotes of Tennyson—The memoir of him by his son ;
(*pp.* 232–259)

XVII. *Some Personal and General Details.*—My first matrimonial
engagement, 1856, and its rupture, 1860—Sir Walter and Lady Trevelyan, Miss Boyd, etc.—Captain Ruxton gets up an American exhibition
of British art, for which I act as secretary—W. J. Stillman and his
Autobiography—The Lushington family—Meetings in the chambers of
W. S. W. Vaux—A visit to Bedlam (*pp.* 260–270)

XVIII. *Cheyne Walk and Endsleigh Gardens.*—Dante Rossetti leaves
Chatham Place and settles in Cheyne Walk, 1862, with Meredith, Swin-
burne, and myself, as sub-tenants—He takes to collecting furniture and
articles of virtù—Becomes acquainted with Japanese colour-prints etc.
—I buy various objects of this sort in London and Paris—Remarks
on the quality of Japanese art—Anecdote of an art-collector, Y. Z.—
Animals kept by Dante Rossetti : the wombat etc.—Meredith and
Swinburne in Cheyne Walk—Old friends who frequented the house—
On leaving Albany Street, 1867, I remove with my mother and sisters
to Endsleigh Gardens (*pp.* 271–295)

SOME REMINISCENCES OF
WILLIAM MICHAEL ROSSETTI

I

EARLIEST YEARS

I WAS born in London, 38 Charlotte Street, Portland Place, on 25 September 1829. Charlotte Street has, since I wrote these pages, been renamed as Hallam Street. I have spoken elsewhere in some detail about my father, Gabriele Rossetti, as a poet and constitutionalist in Naples, and a political refugee in England, and about his marriage to Frances Mary Lavinia, second daughter of Gaetano Polidori. Here therefore I shall take these antecedents for granted.

I was the third of four children, being preceded by Maria Francesca (February 1827) and Gabriel Charles Dante (or Dante Gabriel, May 1828), and succeeded by Christina Georgina (December 1830), all born in the same house as myself. The very bed in which we were ushered into life continued to be used by my brother up to almost the date of his death, 1882. After his decease it was sold with the other contents of his house. More by accident than by intention I failed to retain it as a family relic, and who may now be in possession of ft (if any one) I have no idea.

B

At the time of my birth and early childhood our family was not in anything to be called poverty, but its means were narrowly restricted. My father lived by teaching Italian ; he did likewise a large amount of literary work, but that hardly ever brought him in any payment at all. In fact, he would have been quite unable, in most instances, to meet the expenses of printing his books, and for this he had to depend upon the plan of subscription or the liberality of friends. A year in which he made a clear £300 was regarded as a very good year, and a rare one ; generally I suppose the income of the household may have been from £220 to £280 a year. He was professor of Italian in King's College, London : this only yielded him a few fees, and added to his income nothing worth naming.

I have spoken above of "the liberality of friends." These were the Right Honourable John Hookham Frere, living in Malta, whom my father had known there between the date of his escaping from Naples and that of his settling in London, and Mr. Charles Lyell, of Kinnordy in Forfarshire. Mr. Frere, the author of the poem in octave stanzas *The Monks and the Giants* and translator of Aristophanes, was a high-minded man, profusely generous, and having ample means to draw upon. His bounty, though unsolicited by my father, kept flowing freely while the latter was in London : every now and then an order for £50 or £100 would arrive. Indeed, I think it more than likely that Frere, when he encouraged Rossetti to migrate from Malta to London, had engaged to keep an eye on his affairs and not leave him in the lurch at a difficult moment. He does not, however, appear to have been so directly concerned as Mr. Lyell in financing Rossetti's

authorship ; nor, indeed, was he so keenly interested in
the theme on which Rossetti wrote, the systematic interpretation of Dante's books, and of much literature
besides, medieval and other. The first of my father's
London labours, Dante's *Inferno* with a *Comento Analitico*
(Analytic Comment), came out in 1826–7, and to this
Mr. Lyell was merely a subscriber ; but he must have
spent several hundreds of pounds upon the *Spirito Anti-
papale che produsse la Riforma* (Antipapal Spirit which
led to the Reformation) and upon the *Mistero dell'Amor
Platonico del Medio Evo derivato dai Misteri Antichi* (Mystery of the Platonic Love of the Middle Ages derived
from the Antique Mysteries). These two works, seven
volumes in all, were printed (the former alone *published*
in England) in 1832 and 1840. Mr. Lyell (father of the
celebrated geologist Sir Charles Lyell) was a great en-
thusiast for Dante, and was the author in 1835 of an
English translation of his lyrical poems. By spending a
small fortune on Rossetti's books he gratified his own
likings as well as those of the Italian critic ; but this in
no way detracts from his munificence, being only as much
as to say that he entertained and indulged a generous enthusiasm, further manifested in the scores or hundreds of
letters which he interchanged with Rossetti in discussing
such matters of literature. In his later years—he died
in 1849 — he receded somewhat from his belief in
Rossetti's system of interpretation, being, I think, a
trifle provoked at the extremes to which it was pushed,
and timorous as to the light in which he would himself
be regarded as its promoter.

Charlotte Street, which forms a cul-de-sac close to
No. 38, is one of the least-frequented streets in the
Portland Place vicinity. It is dingy, and in my time

was mostly unrespectable ; I fancy it is so still. Every
now and then the decorous section of the inhabitants
would make an effort to clear out offenders, but the
effort lapsed, and the offenders remained or resumed.
I remember the shop of a barber (at some little distance
from our own dwelling) who must have posed as the
local Figaro or Leporello, and whose shop-windows became increasingly conversant with coloured prints hostile
to the cause of decency. Of No. 38 I recollect not
much. It had a moderate frontage, with shallow inside
space. By the end of 1835, when I was six years old,
the family had outgrown the accommodation here existing, and we removed to another house, No. 50, at
an annual rent of £60. Here we remained until the
beginning of 1851.

My maternal grandfather, Gaetano Polidori—who, like
my father, was a teacher of Italian and also an author,
but not a political refugee—tenanted a couple of rooms
in Wells Street, Oxford Street ; and the aspect of his
sitting-room, in which I always observed a green-baize
tablecloth and a lamp with japanned shades, is more
present to my mental eye than anything in No. 38
Charlotte Street—if I except a curtain, veiling I suppose
a dressing-room, which excited a certain sense of the
unknown. My grandfather's family—wife, son, and
daughter, not to speak of others who had ceased to form
part of his establishment—did not live with him in
London, but in an inconspicuous country-house or
cottage-residence at Holmer Green, near Great Mis-
senden, Buckinghamshire. Polidori himself was often
there as well ; and, towards the same time when we
quitted No. 38 for No. 50, he abandoned London and
lived wholly at Holmer Green, relinquishing his work

as a teacher. This arrangement continued till 1839, when all the Polidori family returned to London, settling at No. 15 (now 30) Park Village East, Regent's Park. Much of Park Village East was demolished recently, but No. 30 has not been interfered with.

Some of my earliest recollections appertain to the cottage at Holmer Green. I was there not often—perhaps three times after the period of unconscious infancy —three or four weeks in each instance. It was the only sort of countrifying that I got; for my father, and therefore my mother, never made any holiday, at the seaside or otherwise. I can recall being mounted on a pony by the local medical man, Mr. Tallent—an effort of equitation too seldom repeated in my over-sedentary career : he took a fancy to me, and, being a childless married man, had some inclination to adopt me, but this was not at all in accordance with my parents' ideas. The pigs and the pigstye at Holmer Green were objects of interest, also the good-natured large spaniel Delta ; the spiders and earwigs and slugs in the garden were viewed with repulsion (though I was not brought up to have any foolish prejudices against animals harmless though possibly uncouth), and with some tremor the wasps which flitted about the parlour. My leading enjoyment was shared with Gabriel (he and I were, I think, only twice together at Holmer Green), and consisted of resorting to a pond in my grandfather's small grounds, and lying in wait for the frogs, and capturing and releasing them. I don't think I ever went far afield, but of course had some strolling acquaintance with the country in the neighbourhood. All this was before the era of railroads, and we used to go down and up by stage-coach to Uxbridge, Wycombe, Amersham, etc.

My last stay at Holmer Green may have been in 1839,
or perhaps 1838. I never revisited the spot till 1898 ;
when (in company with Mr. Mackenzie Bell, the biographer of Christina Rossetti, and under the obliging
escort of the then clergyman, Mr. Ffolliott) I found
out the old house, and realized to myself the fact that
a good deal of the country thereabouts is extremely
pretty and pleasing.

Polidori and his family lived at Holmer Green on
a modest though quite comfortable scale : there was no
pretence at the standing of a " country gentleman," and
very little intercourse with neighbours. The family
—besides Polidori himself, aged seventy-two in 1836—
was made up thus : his wife (who had been Miss Anna
Maria Pierce), of a proportionate age, always confined
to her bedroom or bed by an internal illness ; his son,
Philip Robert, who was weak-minded and " odd " (not
insane nor imbecile), and had never been able to take
up any vocation in life ; and the youngest daughter,
Eliza Harriet, constantly devoted to attending on her
mother and managing the household affairs. She was
a courageous, conscientious woman, not at all literary in
her leanings (though a very rapid reader of such books
as she thought entertaining), of strong character, by no
means pliable and only partially amiable, cheerful and
unconventional in habit of mind and address. She
survived all her brothers and sisters, and died in 1893,
aged eighty-three. Polidori had a good inkling of
country occupations, and after a while he bought, at
some small distance from Holmer Green, a piece of
ground, Stony Grove, which he looked after every now
and then. He worked with equal zest at literature and
at manual crafts : translating Milton in a forenoon, and

fashioning a table in wood-mosaic in the afternoon. One of the rooms in the cottage was made his carpentry. Here the smell of glue became very familiar to me ; varied by the smell of gunpowder, at moments when my grandfather, looking up from his cabinet-work, would see a wood-pigeon or other eatable bird within convenient range, and would point his gun out of a window at the mark. A loud bang ensued, and mostly—for he was not a bad shot—a bird at next day's dinner-table. He did not shoot game, not being either a licensee or a poacher. Often also he sent up two or three very savoury wood-pigeons to our London household. Polidori was a man alike solid in physique and in character, a scorner of all flimsiness and idle pretension, including some of the minor elegancies of life ; affectionate with his daughters, and quite as much so with his grandchildren. Christina was particularly fond of him : in fact I think she had more positive warmth of feeling for him than for her father. We four were the only grandchildren in those years ; later on there was a fifth, the daughter of Polidori's son, Henry Francis, a solicitor (or mostly a solicitor's articled clerk), who preferred to anglicize his name into Polydore. This change was projected mainly as a bait for clients, but the clients never came.

My reminiscences must now revert to the newly entered London house, 50 Charlotte Street. Like No. 38, it was a smallish dwelling, but it afforded the accommodation needed for our family of six — two rooms on the ground floor, two on the first floor (not much used in our life from day to day), and five or six bedrooms on the second and third floors. There was a small back yard, but nothing approaching to a garden ;

there was also the usual kitchen basement, with the characterless-looking railing so distinctive of the middle-class Londoner. Opposite us was a public-house, quietly enough conducted, and quite innocent of the flaring gaseous attractions of a gin-palace. Two or three "hackney-coaches" were constantly to be seen close to the public-house; possibly this indicated a "stand," but I think it was rather an adjunct of the tavern as a "house of call." The hansom-cab did not then exist; nor even was the term "cab" well acclimatized—my mother, in those early years, always said "a cabriolet." The hackney-coach of that epoch, sometimes a two-horse vehicle, was a lumbering and in the highest degree an unsmartened affair; its floor bare, or scantily supplied with musty or soppy straw. It rattled and jolted over roadways chiefly of slightly rounded stone and in a minor degree of the macadamized type; wood pavement, and still more asphalte pavement, were unknown in my opening years. Omnibuses (they were not then snipped into "busses" by ordinarily well-bred people) had come into use; we children were occasionally in an omnibus, but scarcely ever in other public vehicles, which counted as too expensive for the family pocket. I have seen such a personage as a watchman now and again, but the "new police" were already in activity as far back as my memory extends. Hats, not helmets, were for many years their head-gear. Of course, penny or halfpenny daily newspapers only came in long after the dates I am here speaking of. There were daily newspapers, but costing too much for us to take in. Our recourse was to a weekly newspaper, *Bell's Weekly Messenger*—of stiff Tory politics highly spiced with evangelical religion, sabbatarian and other.

The one room in the house which was constantly used by the whole family was the front parlour or dining-room. Here was my mother, with the four children, and, when he returned from his daily round of teaching, my father, with his books and manuscript. At times, however, he used the front drawing-room for studying and writing. Naturally my mother had in the earliest years a nursemaid for her child or children ; but I cannot remember any such person, nor any time when we were relegated to a nursery. Afterwards there was only one servant. The family life, within my recollection, was "one and indivisible" ; father, mother, and four children, with the very frequent addition of two or three Italian *habitués* in the evening. Such a domestic arrangement was no doubt well adapted for sharpening our wits and "bringing us on," though it would have been trying to most parents and unwelcome to most visitors. With our father we always talked Italian, and thus we picked it up from our earliest years, and the like when we spoke to other Italians. With our mother we talked English. My father could indeed speak English fairly enough when he chose, but he never did choose *en famille*. Polidori, though with a certain degree of foreign accent, spoke it perfectly—he had been in England ever since 1790.

Next to the front parlour (for we used not to call it the dining-room) the apartments which I most frequented in my waking hours were the back parlour and, at a later date, a small room on the third floor which had been my father's dressing-room (I pretty often saw him shaving there), but which was eventually assigned to Gabriel for purposes of study or leisure, and I consorted there with Gabriel. Of this more anon, for it has not

to do with my mere childhood. A recollection still
vivid to me is this. In the back parlour, close to its
single window, was a fixed basin with water-tap and
plug ; all covered over by a solid flap, which, when put
down, formed a seat amply wide enough for me to sit
upon with tilted knees. Here I would frequently seat
myself and read a book, neighboured by a squirrel in a
revolving cage. I would read a page or two, and then,
raising my eyes from the volume, watch the squirrel's
rapid evolutions, pondering whether he enjoyed them,
or merely couldn't help himself. Scott's *Ivanhoe* was
one of the books I thus read, and could not but be
an immense favourite ; there were very many others.
These perusals began some few months after we had
entered the house, which was at the Christmas of 1835 ;
for, not having proved a very apt or rapid acquirer of
the reading art under the loving tuition of my mother,
I was not at that date able to read currently, and had to
be coerced into the craft by my aunt Margaret Polidori,
a middle-aged spinster, extremely nervous, but not
wanting in rigour. Towards the middle of 1836 I was
fully coached up, and became, what I have ever since
continued, a voracious reader. Even before this date I
knew a good deal of the contents of several books,
either by clumsy reading on my own part or by hearing what my seniors read out. In manhood I far out-
stripped Gabriel as a reader, and still farther Christina.
Maria could not be easily surpassed : in her fifth year
she could read any ordinary book in English or in
Italian. Gabriel also was quick in learning to read ;
Christina more on the same level as myself.

Family life in No. 50 Charlotte Street was a simple
affair ; I will try to throw myself back in reminiscence

to the years 1836 and 1837. My mother, the most regular and self-postponing of women, always rose at seven in the morning (a practice which may have been prolonged up to 1880 or some such year); my father also, with the habit of most Italians, was an early riser. Soon after breakfast he went off to his lessons (the fee in private families was, if I recollect aright, half a guinea an hour), walking the greater part of the distances, and would often not return till the late evening. He then set to with his books and papers. Our dinner was at four, with or without my father as the case might be; a simple substantial meal, of good materials—for my mother knew that true economy favoured going to good tradesmen, and not to bad ones. My father, more of a vegetarian than most English people, often had some Italian dish of his own. In the evening Italian visitors dropped in, and kept up lively discussions—mainly patriotic and political, partly literary. We children were continually present throughout, for no one said us nay.

The Italian visitors were often three or four, sometimes more, in the course of an evening; of English visitors there was so little admixture that I might almost call it none. For my mother to pay or to receive a morning visit was a decided rarity. It did happen sometimes, the family chiefly concerned being that of Mr. Cipriani Potter, the principal of the Royal Academy of Music—a gentleman who had a particular regard for Rossetti, and became one of my godfathers. He lived to a good old age, dying in 1871. His wife, who was also a very competent pianist, had more the tone of a lady in society than any one else we habitually saw. There were four children, two sons and two daughters (as in our own family), of ages differing but little from ours ; these, and in addition the English children of another musical man, Signor Rovedino, were companions of whom we saw something, though not very much. No other family of children counted for anything in our opening years ; there was, however, Guglielmo Sangiovanni, the rather sickly son of an Italian father and American mother.

My father had, on first reaching England, been a good deal about in society, various members of the Bonaparte family being (among others) well pleased to see him. Some dwindling residue of this continued within my recollection ; but I might almost say that in my time neither my father, nor especially my mother, ever went out to any social entertainments—dinners, conversazioni, and the like. Even at home they had no amusements, unless the reading of some books not directly instructive is to be so called ; they did, indeed, amuse their children —my mother, for instance, by playing cards with us, and my father by teaching us (but this was later on) the game of chess. Although devoted to her home duties, my mother was not concerned in any such matters as cooking or making up or planning dresses, neither were my sisters at any period of life ; not that they were " above it," but it did not seem to come in their line. At home, then, did my parents live, each fully occupied in affairs of literature or of the household ; with the continuous addition, as already observed, of Italians coming in in a very informal way for chat and discussion, interspersed frequently by recitation of my father's verses, patriotic and other. These Italians were of all classes, men of high cultivation and others of very little; their political views (unless they happened to have none worth speaking of) were of the ultra-liberal and sometimes of the revolutionary kind. I may particularize in those early years Sangiovanni, Pepoli, Filippo Pistrucci, Ferrari, Janer (or Janer-Nardini) ; but this is a matter on which I have given some details elsewhere, and I do not here repeat them. There were odd characters, queer characters, shady characters, picturesque characters, high-minded and exalted characters, and some quite common-place ones as well. The one that I liked best was Sangiovanni, and next to him Pistrucci ; for Janer, who had a rather marked fondness for me, my liking was somewhat less. Amid these surroundings our parents passed their quiet and uniform life, with warm domestic affection, no bickerings, serious aims, assiduous exertions, cheerful content, no display and no wish for it, and no clear social ambition beyond the performance of duty and the exercise of ability in the appointed sphere. *Age quod agis* was a favourite axiom with my father, and he conformed to it.

Our house contained few objects of art or decoration. It may have been in 1837 that a Vastese painter of local distinction, Gabriele Smargiassi, came over and spent a few days with his fellow-townsman and old friend Rossetti, and gave my mother two small oil-paintings— one representing the maritime city of Vasto and the other the Blue Cavern at Capri. I could not aver that before then there was a single framed painting in the house. Soon afterwards came from my grandaunt, Harriet Pierce, a framed engraving, exceedingly popular about that date, of Queen Victoria in her opera-box. Then, perhaps in 1839, an Italian friend presented to my father a fair-sized oil-painting of *The Marriage-feast of Tobias*. The donor fancied it to be by Paul Veronese, but this to a well-trained eye is a manifest mistake, as the picture belongs to the Italianized Flemish school of some such date as 1560. It is a moderately good average specimen of that manner, and it hangs in my writing-room as I pen these words. I also retain the two works by Smargiassi. Two or three years afterwards Polidori gave my parents a portrait of the painter Wright of Derby, by himself. How such a thing had come into Polidori's own possession I cannot say—possibly from his old friend and housemate, Signor Giovanni Amedeo Deagostini, who likewise had been an Italian teacher, instructing among others the Princess Charlotte, heiress to the British crown. I presented this painting to the National Portrait Gallery in the early days of that institution, and there it continues, a rather popular work. It almost seems to me that the five examples here specified were the only framed works of art which figured on our walls up to the time (beginning of 1851) when we left No. 50 Charlotte Street. Another decorative object which we children, and our seniors too, viewed with bewildered admiration was an ivory card-case from China, elaborately carved all over its surface with figures, buildings, etc. This also, I apprehend, came from my grandaunt (who was fond of my mother and liberal of small presents) towards 1841 or 1842. It now belongs to my daughter Helen. My grandaunt's presents included several books which she, though the most precise and neat-looking of old ladies, had a habit of cutting open in a truly reckless or unsteady-handed manner. The mangled margins of various volumes still on my shelves bewray her inauspicious touch.

As to that picture of *The Marriage-feast of Tobias*, my eye seldom falls upon it without my recollecting one of those totally trivial circumstances which somehow linger in the memory when so much else, of incomparably greater moment, has passed into nothingness. Soon after the picture came into our house, an Italian acquaintance was looking at it, and opined that the action of a certain page in the group is wrongly represented : the page is pouring wine from a jar into a cup, and the Italian considered that, in the relative positions of the jar and the cup, the rillet of wine would never have reached the latter. This inaccuracy he rashly dubbed an "*anacronismo*" (anachronism). My father noticed the misuse of this term, and after the Italian had gone, mentioned it in my presence. I dare say I had never before heard the word *anacronismo* ; from that moment, I knew what it does *not* mean, and also what it does.

In the Rossetti family, and also in the Polidori family, there was very little craving for elegance of dress : no one (if I except Charlotte Polidori, who lived as governess in some distinguished families, and who more or less fell in with their habits) aspired to be "in the fashion." My father was more than ordinarily careless in such matters ; Margaret Polidori, and still more Eliza, would be found, in 1860, wearing "coal-scuttle bonnets" and other such things which had been obsolete in 1840. The costume of my mother and of my sisters, though not absolutely *outré* like this, was simplicity itself, and out-of-date simplicity to boot : Mr. Edmund Gosse, in writing something relative to Christina, has commented upon the point. Not indeed that any of the women in the family were slovenly, for that was far from the fact. Gabriel and I likewise grew up rather indifferent to such questions, but perhaps without offering much to be remarked upon.

II

MY PARENTS, SISTERS, AND BROTHER

I HAVE endeavoured to make my father pretty well known in two books—Nos. 5 and 13 in the list which appears in my preface. Here therefore I shall not attempt anything approaching to a full-length portrait of him. I will only, for the present, record the sort of impression which in childhood I received.

I remember him as a plump, fleshy man, age fifty-three in 1836, with hair thinned but still dark, brought in a sweep across the forehead—his stature a shortish middle height. He was extremely good-natured with his urchins : I cannot recollect his being even once " in a rage " with any of us, or seriously " put out." His temper and temperament were lively and ardent, not without excitability, yet essentially placid ; his habit was to work hard and then " take things easy." He was much addicted to bringing home lollipops and distributing them among us children : this did not please our mother, whose name for the lollipops was " trash." He would also pretty often take me (or one of us) on his knee and clap my hands together, repeating, with his Italian intonation and clear-cut delivery, the rhyme—

> Pat a cake, pat a cake, baker's man ;
> So I do, master, as fast as I can.

His excellently fine recitation of verse must evidently have formed an important though unprepense element in our training ; but he did not undertake any formal teaching of us, leaving all that to our mother. None of us felt timorous in his presence ; though we were from the first conscious of his being a man of mark, treated as such by all who approached him.

Fond as we were of our father in those early years, we were a good deal fonder of our mother, who was busied with us all day, and as tenderly indulgent as a reasonable regard for our right up-bringing would allow. I shall not enlarge here upon her solid qualities of mind, her high and unassuming consistency of character, and her warmth of heart, attested in the two books already referred to, as well by my father as by myself. *The Family Letters of Dante Rossetti* (the letter-section of No. 4 in my list) bear ample witness to the reciprocal love of the mother and son.

Every person has some defect. In my father the most obvious defect has appeared to me to be that sort of self-opinion which involves self-applause. My mother may have been a little open to observation in the contrary direction—that she hardly put herself adequately forward, but preferred, or took refuge in, the dignity of self-retirement, rather than that of mixing with and influencing others. 1 will admit that — possibly from maternal heredity—I sympathize very much with this bias of character, but it has its drawbacks too. My two sisters, and even my brother in a certain sense, shared the same heredity ; in this respect they were all more or less like my mother, and not like my father in the least.

I must have a dim sort of memory of some things which occurred before 1 was five years of age : one of

c

these things seems to be an illness of mine from intermittent fever or what not, when I kept seated in a dis-
consolate yet not querulous mood in a little chair, for
some two or three days, holding my hands pendent in
front of me, like those of a kangaroo. However, in
here speaking of my sisters and brother, I will assume
for myself the age of five, September 1834, or from five
to six. In September 1834 Maria was seven and a
half years old ; Gabriel, six and a half ; Christina, three
and three-quarters.

Maria was a precociously clever and thinking child,
though without any inventive turn : she learned easily
whatever was brought before her. In childhood and
early girlhood she was by far the most enthusiastic in
temperament of the four, and ran through a varied
gamut of fancies, from the British seaman to Napoleon,
and on to the swift-footed Achilles and Grecian mythology in general. Fancies of this sort were more
prominent in her, in mere childhood, than the religious
emotions ; but, before she was far advanced in girlhood,
she settled down into religion, and there she abode for
the rest of her life. In person she was strictly Italian—
according to my father, extremely like his mother (bearing the same Christian names), a Vastese of the Pietro-
cola family ; complexion more than commonly dark,
hair thickly curling and black, eyes large, dark, and
speaking. Her features were not more than moderately
good, nor was her figure advantageous. Her disposition
was loving, and developed into the most unbending
standard of rectitude and veracity. By nature, however,
she had in her character a strong spice of jealousy, which
was early conquered as a matter of principle.

Gabriel was much handsomer than Maria—with a

vivid, animated, and resolute look, which presaged to
the discerning that he might prove something remarkable. His eyes were of a bluish grey, his hair a bright
but not light auburn, his complexion ruddy and full-
tinted. In all these respects he got darker as the years
advanced, and I have heard his hair, in manhood, termed
black, though it never was that. On the two junior
children, Christina and myself, Maria exercised something like the function of an inspiriting Muse in a
pinafore (in our household " pincloth " was always the
word) ; while Gabriel was a familiar spirit—familiar but
fiery, and not lightly to be rebelled against. Apart from
his mental gifts—as to the force of which people are
tolerably well agreed nowadays—the quality most innate
in him appears to have been dominance : *Hoc volo, sic
jubeo, sit pro ratione voluntas.* In anything wearing the
garb of mischief he counted for all, and Maria for
nothing ; he was imperative, vehement, at times angrily
passionate ; but his anger was a sudden and passing
impulse, and to sulk or bear a grudge was not in him
at all. This placable spirit abode with him through
life, and even survived to a great extent the hypochon-
driacal twist of his closing years. In childhood there
was not much use in opposing him at the critical
moment ; after that moment was past, things resumed
their normal condition, and there was peace, with amity
and warmth of heart. Even when he dictated to me, he
did not bully me : leadership was in his composition,
but not hectoring. I must remember the earliest beginnings of his passion for drawing (in a sort of way)—
some of his subjects being such minor characters as
Falstaff, Hamlet, Macbeth, etc., and for colouring sheets
of theatrical prints : I am not sure that I realize to my-

self any time antecedent to these habits of his, or to his expressed resolve to be a painter. By his parents and their friends the boyish Gabriel was always discerned to be rather a "rum customer," with "a great deal in him" to work itself out, but not likely to prove very malleable in hands other than his own. He was more headstrong than obstinate, but obstinacy also was there. A semi-blind eye to some of his small escapades was more judicious treatment than a swingeing rebuff. Manual correction, I may here say, was eschewed in our family, except at rare intervals a so-called slap in the face from our mother, or still seldomer a nominal whipping by her. The whipping was really a mere farce ; but as the idea of it was held over us *in terrorem*, the patient may perhaps have made it a "screaming" farce. Gabriel and I were, from infancy to the fatal moment of separation, the very best of friends. He would hear reason from me on some occasions when it seemed apposite to present it to him ; but anything like a "preachment," as if delivered from a plane of moral perception different from his own, might have proved worse than useless.

Pretty little Christina—and very pretty some people considered her in those days—was the most "fractious" of the quartette : hardly less passionate than Gabriel, and more given to mere tantrums. This may have depended partly on the condition of her health, which was subject to greater disturbances and pains than that of the others. She had hazel eyes, bright hair, which however soon settled down into brown, a clear, good complexion, oval visage (Maria's was decidedly round), and a winning air of half-thoughtful *espièglerie*. To have a temper of her own was perhaps her right ; to be amiable and affectionate along with it was certainly her endowment. As Maria and Gabriel were comparatively big children when she was a little one, and were slightly inclined at times to treat her *de haut en bas*, she relied on me as a sort of intermediary—a fact on which I have often reflected with pleasure in later years. She was thus my chief "chum" in point of standing, while Gabriel was the like in point of sex, and of community of likings besides. Christina was a spirited, and also a lazy, small girl ; every now and then she would say something which was regarded as sprightly and piquant, and savouring of wit. If Gabriel was the more capricious in character, she was the more whimsical in turn of mind. My grandfather pronounced of Christina, at an extremely early age, the dictum, "*Avrà più spirito di tutti*" ;[1] and it turned out that he was not far wrong.

And now a word as to myself. I am afraid that I belonged to that unengaging though well-advertised type, the "good little boy." I was not noisy nor plaguy nor volcanic. Gabriel was certainly, in his way, a leopard or leopard-cub ; and he found in me something of a kid or goat to "lie down with." I shared all his occupations in the way of reading, colouring prints, and even to some small extent drawing ; but, as to the last, without any sense, on my own part or on that of others, that I had any vocation that way. At such an age one can hardly be priggish ; but one can be demure, and I was somewhat in that line. My temper was markedly equable ; my spirits not high, but seldom depressed.

My parents were entirely free from invidious favouritism : all the four children were treated alike, and that

---

[1] She will have more wit (or cleverness) than any of the others.

was kindly and judiciously. My father had possibly a certain predilection for Gabriel, and my mother for me ; the claims of the two daughters seemed to be about evenly balanced, by contrasting qualities. Not one of us ever felt, or was led to feel, any sense of unfairness in family life. Whatever sign of ability any of us may have shown in any direction, it was properly fostered, without being " cockered up."

III

SCHOOL

TO say much about my school life seems to me needless : the gist of what I could record is inserted in my *Memoir of Dante Rossetti*.

It was at the beginning of 1837 that I, at the age of seven, entered the day-school of the Rev. Mr. Paul, Foley Street, Portland Place. Here one of the pupils (I believe in my own time) was Henry Stacy Marks, who became a popular painter and a Royal Academician ; I have not any recollection of him as a school-fellow, but I had some slight acquaintance with him in later years. About the middle of August of the same year I proceeded to the day-school of King's College, London, the institution in which my father was professor of Italian. The college formed an outlying part of Somerset House, Strand ; the school, with a scanty playground, was on the basement. I was the youngest boy in the school—the regulation age being nine. Gabriel had both preceded and companioned me at Mr. Paul's, and he accompanied me to King's College School. We entered in the lowest class of all, the Lower First, and passed together to higher classes (Gabriel once or twice in advance of me by a term or so) until we were both in the Fourth Class. Then my brother quitted

school altogether, either in 1841 or 1842, but I think
the former, and began a regular course of study for the
painting profession. I remained behind, and gradually
reached the Upper Sixth.

Very soon after I entered the school, i.e. in December 1837, an untoward incident befell the family—the
theft of a sum of £30 (to ourselves a rather large sum)
and various articles of linen etc. belonging to my
father. The culprit was an Irish carpenter, named
Mullins, whom we frequently employed—a good work-
man, and supposed to be otherwise commendable, married and with a family. He was detected when he tried
to pass some bank-notes; and I can still well recollect
the bustle and rumour of his being led by policemen
into our hall-passage. My father commiserated Mullins,
and addressed the police magistrate, trying to withdraw
from a prosecution; this was not allowed, and the
offender was sentenced to some years' transportation,
and dispatched to Australia. What became of him
there? Did he possibly settle and make a fortune?
I know not.

There were two sequels to this disagreeable affair.
First, that, although some money and some goods were
recovered and in the hands of the police, my father
never succeeded in getting anything back—a fact viewed
by us all as a very odd specimen of juridical procedure.
Second, that years afterwards, say 1856, a youth who
used to attend our house delivering greengroceries
avowed himself to be a son of Mullins, with whose
doleful story he was familiar.

Some men seem to remember their school days with
a sort of fondness which they bestow upon no other
period of their lives. Such is not the case with my-

self, neither was it with Gabriel—far from that. We both found a grievous descent from the tone of feeling and standard of conduct which we had witnessed at home to that which we experienced at school—especially with respect to veracity, which had been constantly enforced upon us, not less by example than by precept. We deteriorated, and were conscious of deteriorating. At Mr. Paul's most of the pupils were, I suppose, sons of local tradesmen ; at King's College School the sons of professional people may have been in the majority. To say that I was unhappy at school would be an exaggeration, for I was well enough satisfied with my treatment, and the daily routine of life ; with myself I was less satisfied. I had few of the tastes of an English schoolboy, and cared not at all for vigorous physical exertion, or for athletics of any sort. The idea of playing cricket, for instance, never occurred to me ; and to this moment I do not rightly understand what the game consists of. To be asked to join in a "sweepstake" on the Derby Day merely teazed me ; I would much rather have spent the money upon buying Skelt's *Theatrical Characters*, or some new numbers of the illustrated *Gil Blas*—or (for the matter of that) upon a nice "tuck-out" of three-cornered cakes or Banbury cakes. I am well aware that this indifference to sports of whatsoever kind will not be counted to my credit ; I state it because it was and is a fact.

My aptitude for the school studies—which consisted of little beyond Latin, Greek, and French—was nothing conspicuous ; but it was good rather than bad, and I was generally near the head of a class. For Latin, and also French, I found my knowledge of Italian to be a potent help. There were classes for writing, arithmetic, drawing, German, algebra, and singing (on Hullah's system), and some faint inkling of scripture history and geography. To all of these classes I resorted, either early or late in my school course. As to the algebra, I attended (much against the grain) in the classroom, but I wholly shirked the science ; a book was on the desk before me, but no sort of vivâ voce instruction came my way, and I never understood what the book was about. I might say nearly the like of Euclid, whose problems were presented to my consideration in almost the same mode. In the algebra class about the most proficient pupil was William Henry Millais, brother of the celebrated painter whom I was destined to know not long after leaving school.

Apart from the school attendance I made some acquaintance with some few of the boys, but nothing which amounted to a close intimacy at the time or to a permanency in my after-years. Those who were known to my brother as well as myself have been named in my *Memoir of Dante Gabriel Rossetti,* and are omitted here. After he had left I consorted most with two boys— Edward Nussey, a son of the Queen's Apothecary, and Felix Moscheles, a son of the eminent pianist. Nussey, who was an Albino, went to Oxford, and I believe, entered the Church. Moscheles, younger than myself and in a lower class of the school, became my companion in going to and from the building, because his father (though hardly or not at all known to my father) called upon him and asked that the boy might be allowed to receive my valuable patronage and protection to this extent. As I was never of an expansive turn, and always preferred being left to myself in any such matter, I rather disliked the arrangement ; but I submitted, and (let me hope) with a tolerably good grace. Hence I came to see a little—it was by no means much—of the Moscheles family : the pianist, his agreeable wife, and one or two daughters. One of these married a deservedly esteemed French professor—Antonin Roche—who later on was acquainted with my sister Maria. Of Felix Moscheles, who became a painter, and of late active in the good cause of international peace, I saw nothing for long years following my school days. At some such date as 1885 I re-encountered him in society, and have met him once or twice since then.

By the time when my brother quitted school I knew Latin and French pretty well (in proportion to my age), and Greek in some measure ; and up to that period I had been, if not specially studious, still moderately diligent in preparing my lessons and so on. But soon after my brother's departure I changed very much in this regard, and became as audaciously lazy a schoolboy as one could easily find. I scarcely made even a pretence at preparing my lessons, trusting to my existing small smattering of knowledge and to the chapter of accidents for keeping up appearances and wriggling out of scrapes. The habit of the master, as for instance in the Greek class, was to take the prescribed passage from Herodotus, Homer, Sophocles, or other author, and fix, without premonition, upon any particular boy to begin by construing the first sentence ; then, in regular succession to the boy in question, those stationed below him had to take up the ensuing sentences. I was always in trepidation lest the master might fix upon me as the boy to make a beginning ; but, strange to say, this happened hardly ever, or perhaps not at all, and thus, being able to compute pretty nearly which would be the sentence to come to me,

I, by hook or by crook, managed to vamp up some sort of notion as to the meaning of that sentence and to scramble through it when my turn came. I was pretty well known to be a perfunctory scholar, but was never so thoroughly exposed and soundly rated as my indolence would have deserved. I hardly know, on retrospect, *why* I became so lazy as all this. I always preferred to be occupied somehow, and school lessons would have been the right occupation—possibly that was the very reason why I shirked them. Another principal reason may have been that, being still in daily companionship with my brother, who was released from school and mainly free to choose his own intellectual pabulum, I followed his example, took up such books and mental exercises as I fancied, and drifted far aside from the school course. I might add that not any of the schoolmasters took any particular pains to make the classical authors at all interesting to the boys. One had to read glorious stretches of verse by Homer, Euripides, Virgil, or Horace, as so much " dead language," with very little encouragement towards looking into the whole thing as a literary and emotional masterpiece, with a general bearing and a finely balanced sequence.

The masters under whom I came after Gabriel's departure from school were the Rev. Mr. Edwards, Mr. Hayes (brother of the Rev. Mr. Hayes who had instructed us in the Lower First), and the head master, the Rev. Dr. Major. The last, I conceive, was not at all partial to me and my limp habits as a pupil. I however respected him, and still remember him as a man worthy of genuine regard. He was a trifle irritable, but in essentials obviously just. The algebraic master, from whom I did not derive and did not try to derive any benefit, was Mr. Hann. Dr. Bernays was the German master. I was in his class for a very short time, having previously learned something of German at home from Dr. Adolf Heimann, of University College, who had lately become known to our family generally, and proved a very kind and pleasant friend of our adolescent years.

My stay in King's College School lasted up to February 1845, when I was well turned of fifteen years of age. Since then I have had no sort of scholastic instruction; and I am sorry to say that I have not pursued either Latin, Greek, or German, with any such steadiness as to enable me to know these languages better than I did in 1845 : German, however, I did at one time take up with a little persistency, turning a few small books into English. I can read a Latin book tolerably well; not as I do an Italian or French author, but so as to see the general sense, and, with a little reflection, most of the precise meaning. Greek remains, optically, as easy to me as when I was at school (the reverse was the case with my brother); and I retain a number of words, phrases, and grammatical details, so that I am not wholly abroad when I take up a book. But to peruse a Greek work currently, as literature, is beyond my power—a grievous deficiency.

IV

FAMILY LIFE, 1839 TO 1844

I HAVE already referred to the fact that in 1839 the Polidori family quitted their ruralizing in Buckinghamshire, and resettled in London, Park Village East. There was, as before, Polidori, with his bedridden wife, Philip, and Eliza ; to these was added Margaret, who about this time laid aside her work as teacher in one or two households (succeeding to regular engagements as a governess), and lived at home with the others. Thus the family ties with my mother and the rest of us, always strong, were still further riveted. Day by day, with only casual intermissions, my mother went to see her relatives ; Maria and Christina were along with her continually, and Gabriel and I were frequently in that house. My grandfather, who had at one time owned a rather large number of books, still retained a good many ; more perhaps than were possessed by my father, whose bookshelves, loaded with the *libri mistici* which subserved his studies on Dante, were not on the whole alluring to boys on the prowl for romantic or other entertainment. Polidori's books were always open to our inspection. In his library-room we looked constantly through an *Ariosto* illustrated with French engravings of the eighteenth century ; and hence we flitted to Philip's small apartment, and battened on *The Newgate Calendar*, Hone's *Every-day Book*, and a collection of stories, verse and prose, of ghosts, demons, and the like, called *Legends of Terror*. The house also contained a complete set of the Waverley Novels.

In my *Memoir of Dante Rossetti* I have given some particulars as to books which he read in early years, specifying the Bible, Shakespear, something of translations from Goethe and Schiller, Walter Scott's poems and some of his novels, the *Arabian Nights*, Keightley's *Fairy Mythology*, poems by Monk Lewis, the ballad of *Chevy Chase*, Carleton's *Traits and Stories of the Irish Peasantry*, *Robinson Crusoe*, *Gulliver*, Gay's *Fables*, Dumas's *Pascal Bruno* (translated), numerous fairy tales, and yet some other things. The *Iliad* and Byron came a little later than these, but still long before my brother was out of his boyhood ; and in the memoir I have named, as proper to that rather later period, several other books, which I need not here repeat. In all these readings I kept pace with him. I must have then given to reading much the same amount of time that he did, with somewhat less of initiative in choosing the books and less ardour of temperament in gulping them down, but with a like kind and degree of pleasure. There was moreover one class of books that I was fond of, but to which Gabriel paid very scanty attention ; books which convey a certain modicum of positive information, biographic or other. I had for instance a volume about distinguished and eccentric characters, with portraits of Sir Humphry Davy, Elwes the Miser, and so on ; likewise a book on *The Seven Wonders of the World*, and James's *History of Chivalry;* and easy books on natural history, such as that of Peter Parley, were greatly to my taste.

As I progressed a little in years, nothing, if one sets poetry aside, gave me so much pleasure as biography—more especially that class of biography which involves historical subject-matter.

Non cuivis contingit to have as servant the widow of a man who was murdered. This *was* the hap of the Polidori family, who employed as charwoman, and not long afterwards as servant, a young and very quiet-mannered widow, Mrs. Catchpole. She said that her husband, a respectable working-man, had been found dead under extremely suspicious circumstances, pointing to murder by two of his mates who were known to have some grudge against him. Her tale was never called in question in our household; though, as I think over the case, it seems strange that the alleged offenders, men perfectly well known, were not made accountable for such a crime. They were not put on their trial, nor even (I think) kept under provisional arrest. Mrs. Catchpole, to whom Eliza Polidori in especial became much attached, remained as her servant up to a comparatively very recent date (1885), when age and infirmities compelled her retirement on a weekly allowance paid by Eliza.

At the back of my grandfather's house was a moderate-sized garden sloping down towards Regent's Canal. I often strolled or sat there, but was more generally under cover. Spiders and snails were partial to the garden, and a Sicilian compositor, Privitera, was partial to the snails, and picked them up *passim* to make soup in his own domicile—not a little to the scornful indignation of Eliza Polidori. This Privitera was employed by my grandfather to assist him in working a private printing-press which he set up in a shed in the garden. Here were printed many of Polidori's own works, including his translation of Milton ; in 1841 Maria's blank-verse rendering of a short Italian poem in memory of Gwendalina Talbot, Princess Borghese ; in 1843 Gabriel's ballad-poem *Sir Hugh the Heron;* and in 1847 Christina's *Verses.* Of my own there was nothing to be printed, though I had in 1840 begun a " romance of chivalry," *Raimond and Matilda,* and in 1843 indited a larger portion of another story, *Ulfred the Saxon, a Tale of the Conquest.* In both these important enterprises I was set going by Gabriel, who was producing at the same dates romances of his own named *Roderick and Rosalba* and *Sorrentino;* but, beyond supplying this incitement, Gabriel was not asked for, nor did he afford, any assistance to my pen, still less experienced and still more inexpert than his. This was characteristic of our relations throughout our joint lives. If it had not been for him, I might perhaps never have attempted anything in the way of literature, art-criticism, and the like ; but in pursuing the attempt I relied entirely on my own resources, not consulting him at all as to how I should fashion the work, or what code of opinions I should adopt or set forth. His mind was inventive, mine uninventive ; from him ordinarily came the impulse, from myself the development and execution. By people who have cared to form any opinion on so subordinate a subject, this point has, I conjecture, been often misapprehended; it may have been supposed that I was the mere mouthpiece of my brother's conceptions, including sometimes his fancies. As, for instance, in the years when he was a " Præraphaelite " painter I was a Præraphaelite critic ; but I did not criticize in a certain tone at his dictation, or to subserve his opinions, but because

I myself entertained the views which I expressed. My performances throughout were no doubt very small ones in comparison with his, and the leadership was his continually; still those performances were genuinely my own. There was a natural, a congenital, sympathy of mind between him and me, which made us both see many things—not *all* things—in much the same way. He gave effect to his conceptions in an inventive form, and I to mine in forms of inferior import.

Ulfred the Saxon was "a tale of the Conquest," and comprised a description (and what a description!) of the battle of Hastings, which no one then called the battle of Senlac. I was a partisan, not of the Saxons, but of the Normans; and Ulfred was intended for a character more or less bad. I rather piqued myself upon concocting a name which does not exist—Ulfred; sufficiently Saxon-seeming to suggest "Alfred," but with something of an ungainly twang about it. In those days I was wont to be on the side of that party which appeared to me to have some prescriptive right to show for itself, and I thought that William of Normandy had some, and Harold none. Similarly, at a still earlier date when I read Shakespear's *Henry VI.* over and over again, and enjoyed it even more than any of his other dramas, I was a pronounced Yorkist, opining that the true hereditary claim appertained to the house of York. The very relevant question—which of the two claimants was favoured by the nation at large—did not, in either instance, present itself strongly to my mind.

I do not think that I made the least attempt at verse-writing in the days of my mere boyhood—perhaps not until I was turned of sixteen.

The fortunes of the Rossetti family—never other than

most moderate, as I have already said—declined markedly
from the year 1843 or thereabouts. My father's health
got seriously impaired towards 1842, and, after some
troubles of a different kind, he was victimized by
bronchitis in a severe and painful form. His professional
affairs were then going on well, possibly better than in
any previous year; but in the summer of 1843 he had to
lay them all aside, and, by medical advice, he proceeded
to Paris with his wife, believing himself to be practically
under sentence of death. In Paris, however, he rapidly
improved, and about the beginning of the autumn he
returned to London as good as cured. But these
illnesses were only the beginning of his disasters.
Before that year had finished he totally lost, in a single
night and without any forewarning, the sight of one eye,
and the other eye grew dim and risky. Soon absolute
blindness seemed to be closely impending—the worst
period being perhaps in 1846 and 1847. On this
however I will not enlarge; for in fact he never was
blind, and, allowing for variations from time to time, his
eyesight rallied to a certain extent, and served him—
badly, it is true—up to the close of his life in 1854.
I need not say that this alarm of impending blindness
cast a thick mantle of gloom for months and years, not
only over my father's own feelings, but over those of the
entire family. Originally his sight had been of singular
acuteness, and I have more than once heard him say that
he had won some wagers on the strength of it. Some
of his handwriting in my possession (done, I infer, soon
before he came to England) is astonishing for minute-
ness and precision; and, although he had had to use
spectacles for several years preceding 1843, there had
been nothing to suggest any serious damage to his eye-

sight. After the loss of one eye he continued giving lessons for a year or two, but soon this became no longer possible, and, apart from receiving some very few pupils in his own house, his professional occupation was gone, and with it the family income. One of the pupils thus received was a student in King's College, Mr. Charles Bagot Cayley, who some years afterwards produced a remarkable translation of Dante's *Comedia* in the original *terza rima*. Another was Mr. Joseph Sebag, known later on as Sir Joseph Sebag-Montefiore. In 1847 Rossetti had to resign his professorship in King's College ; so far as income was concerned, this made hardly any difference. He had wished to be succeeded by Antonio Gallenga, the author of the so-called *Mariotti's Grammar*, and afterwards well known as a *Times* correspondent in Italy, and by other literary work. This however did not ensue, for a son of our old friend Filippo Pistrucci was elected—not regarded by Rossetti (spite of his attachment to the family) as by any means a right choice.

Is there any trial greater or more wearing than that of ever-recurring illnesses and deaths among the persons near and dear to one ? Certainly I can see that there are some trials still more formidable, as especially those which involve grave self-reproach or public dishonour, merited or unmerited. But in my own life I have found nothing more afflictive than long-continued illnesses among close relatives or connexions, followed by death. Of these my experience has been large ; whereas, so far as my own health is concerned, I have had, spite of occasional and not insignificant upsets, much to be thankful for and very little to repine at. My father's health from 1842 onwards, along with the state of his eyesight, gave incessant anxiety. Christina was more or less an invalid, often in a truly distressing form, almost all her life. Gabriel's health broke down towards 1868, and more grievously in 1872, and he died prematurely in 1882. My wife was a severe sufferer, with few partial intermissions, for the last nine years of her life, and she died, still more prematurely, in 1894. My father-in-law and dear friend, Ford Madox Brown, had few fairly healthy intervals between some such date as 1872 and his death in 1893. I will not dwell here upon the deaths of my sister Maria, an infant son, and my mother, as these were not preceded by maladies of long duration ; nor upon the numerous and sometimes severe illnesses of my other four children, or of my son-in-law Antonio Agresti, all happily alive as I write ; nor upon the illness and death of another son-in-law, Gastone Angeli. Old friends and familiar acquaintances have been mowed down by the score—they still get mowed down month by month as I write the pages. Of this a man long turned of seventy years must not complain, but he can feel it none the less. When one reflects upon the sorrow of mind caused by events such as I am speaking of, the sudden alarms and tremors at crises of disease, the interruption to one's own settled course of life and projects of work—not to name that very real though comparatively unheeded evil, the unceasing drain upon one's resources in various instances—it may be admitted that a man who has been greatly tried by this form of misfortune has suffered a marked diminution of what otherwise might have been the happiness of his life. Not to be sensitive in full to the diminution would be to confess oneself callous and an egoist.

When the income forthcoming from my father's exer-

tions was sensibly dwindling—and not long afterwards
it was wholly extinct—it became necessary to cast about
for some other means of subsistence ; so my mother,
who was very well versed in Italian and French, and had
been a governess before her marriage, laid herself out to
obtain some pupils.   This may have begun as early as
1844, or clearly not more than a year or so later.   She
got a few pupils—one that I recollect was daughter of
a banker, Mr. Barnard ; and thus she managed to keep
things going, though in a very meagre way.   Maria
attained in 1844 the age of seventeen.   She had been
educated wholly by her mother with a view to her
becoming a governess, and towards that year she pro-
cured her first situation in the family of the Rev. Lord
and Lady Charles Thynne : the present Countess of
Kenmare was her pupil.   Lord Charles was a brother-in-
law of the Marchioness Dowager of Bath, in whose
house my aunt Charlotte Polidori was then governess,
and after her tuitions had come to an end she remained
very many years (up to 1885 or so) as companion to this
peeress.   Not long after 1844 Lord Charles Thynne
joined the Church of Rome.   My sister Maria had left
the Thynnes even before that occurrence, and Christina
had in some minor degree succeeded her.   Maria was
afterwards in the family of Mr. Read, in or near Fins-
bury Pavement.   Here she, and also Christina who
became known to the inmates, were very highly appreciated.   The " Bessie Read " of those days, who married
a well-known physician in Hereford, Dr. Bull, wrote me
soon after Christina's death in 1894 some letters replete
with kindly feeling and memory.   This was, I think, the
last resident governessing done by Maria.   She always
had a great preference for life in her own family, and on

returning thither (which may have been towards 1848) she continued teaching in several houses with much acceptance, but without living away from home. This went on till 1873.

Christina, who was also taught entirely by my mother, was in childhood assumed to be likely to adopt the family vocation and become a governess; but, her health being infirm even in girlhood, she never did this—the nearest approach to it being that in one or two instances (such as that of the Thynne family) she passed a week or month or so with some acquaintance, conversing in Italian, and so bettering a knowledge of that language among the young ladies of the house. In 1851 she began assisting my mother in a small day-school; of that anon.

In the year 1844 (which is the latest year of which I am here particularly speaking, though I go beyond it at moments) Gabriel could not add in any sort of way to the family income. He was a student of art in Bloomsbury Street under Mr. F. S. Cary—the so-called "Sass's Academy." He therefore cost something and earned nothing.

Under the will of her maternal grandfather William Pierce my mother was entitled to a certain sum of money—I believe it was £2000—contingent upon the death of her own mother, Mrs. Polidori, whose strong constitution, spite of her permanent and disabling illness, held out until the spring of 1853. This sum therefore, which would have been a godsend to us in those days, Mrs. Rossetti could not touch; but I presume she obtained some advances upon it from one or other member of her family, and thus the amount which eventually came to her was sensibly curtailed. I should not omit to add that all the Polidoris were most willing to aid Mrs. Rossetti in her straits, if only their circumstances had allowed of their doing so to any purpose ; but, while they had enough for living upon in reasonable comfort, they had no more than that, and were unable to perform acts of generosity on any noticeable scale. The one who had readiest command of money, in a mild way, was Charlotte Polidori, the most affectionate of sisters to my mother (the two were sometimes called " Substance and Shadow ") ; but neither had she anything considerable to produce at trying moments—and moreover my mother was the last sort of person to hold out the soliciting palm. There was another relative, her aunt, Miss Harriet Pierce, from whom my mother had well-founded expectations ; and in effect this old lady, who died in 1849, did leave some money to Mrs. Rossetti, and made her residuary legatee. This bequest amounted to a substantial sum ; but it turned out that Miss Pierce had not conformed to the legal requirements as to the mode of witnessing wills. So the bequest totally lapsed, except that Mrs. Rossetti came in for something, according to her degree of relationship to an intestate. Another relative, of whose very existence we were unaware, had to be ferreted out and satisfied. This was a lady of the Pierce family, married to a solicitor, Mr. Kincaid. Gabriel eventually saw something of this couple ; the rest of us also knew them, but not much.

I can most truly say that, under the condition which I have been describing, I know what it is to be " hard up," and to see all those around me hard up—pinched and pinching. Various small details dwell in my memory ; I will mention one. I was invited, perhaps in the autumn of 1844, to pass a day at the house of my school friend Edward Nussey, in Cleveland Row, close to St. James's Palace ; his family were very well off—I dare say opulent. I had only one blue cloth jacket possible to put on for such an occasion. The elbows of it were whitened by wear ; so I took some of the Prussian-blue water-colour paint which I was wont to use in colouring woodcuts, and daubed upon those elbows, in the hope—mainly a vain one—of making them less unpresentably white. On the same occasion maybe my father (to whom the Prussian-blue experiment was not reported) made use of an expression which also lingers in my thoughts : that, if only he had the means, he would send me to my appointment "*vestito come un principino.*"[1] I felt grateful to him for the fatherly remark, though my jacket grew none the handsomer for it.

The condition of the Rossetti family may be very accurately defined in the classical phrase *res angusta domi.* It was not absolute poverty, and, owing to the good management of my mother, it never involved us in any debts nor left a tarnish on our self-respect—though to outsiders we may have looked "in a bad way." It consisted in a perpetual sense of the difficulty of "making both ends meet," and in the struggle to "keep our heads above water"—not "to keep up appearances," for that had never formed an element in the family ideals. This state of things was hardly at its worst in 1844, and it continued, with some fluctuations in either direction, up to the middle of 1853 ; after which we found ourselves tolerably secure, though in circumstances the reverse of easy. Were we unhappy because we were

[1] Dressed like a princclet.

poor, or on the verge of poverty? I answer no. We all had our occupations, our intellectual interests, our single-hearted endeavours to stem the current, and we were thus preserved from being mopish and faint-spirited. It is a fact too that we never wanted for the requisites and the primary conveniences of life. In all those years the threatened blindness of my father, followed by various forms of illness including paralytic shock and enfeeblement, saddened our thoughts far more than did the material straits of our position. With what is called " genteel poverty " one ought clearly to sympathize to a certain extent ; but my experience in my own family tells me that the sympathy should not be unmeasured, and that it lies with the sufferers themselves to meet their difficulties in the proper spirit.

In 1844 my father, seeing that every available family resource ought to be brought into play, most wisely resolved that I should remain no longer at school, if only any suitable employment could be obtained for me. He spoke to an old and valued acquaintance, Sir Isaac Lyon Goldsmid, a very wealthy Hebrew stockbroker in whose family he had taught Italian, asking him to bear me in mind if any opportunity should present itself. I can remember the look of this worthy gentleman, whom I may truly call my benefactor, pretty well : a rather short, compact figure, with a face perceptibly but not strongly Jewish, and a composed, intent air. He lived in St. John's Lodge, Regent's Park ; and I was more than once there in childhood, eagerly scanning the designs in Lane's *Thousand and One Nights*, while in another room my father gave his Italian lessons. Sir Isaac, who was on the Council of University College, London, mentioned the matter to one of his colleagues

there, Mr. John Wood, who was Chairman of the
Board of Excise, and Mr. Wood undertook to see
about it. This resulted in my receiving notice, in February 1845, that I could attend at the Excise Office and
find employment there.

V

THE EXCISE OFFICE

BEHOLD me then on 6 February 1845, aged about fifteen and a half, launched on my life's work. Throughout my uneventful career I have had only two occupations, fitly to be so called : official work in the Government office, and literary work wholly apart from it.

To become a Government clerk had not been in the least my wish. My earliest and merely childish fancy had been to go to sea ; but as I advanced a little into boyhood I thought no more of this, and would have liked the medical profession. There was however very little appearance that my family would ever have means for meeting the expenses of that calling ; and, as circumstances had dictated my entry into a Government office, I decided to make the best of it, though rather considerably against the grain for the first year or so. Not that I particularly disliked the actual work on which I was engaged ; but I disliked the notion of being in an office, occupied upon details of a routine or quasi-mechanical kind, while all my associations had to do with intellectual matters, literary and artistic. I am glad to reflect, however, that I never neglected my official duties ; I always performed them with much assiduity and persistency, and was soon recognized in the office

as competent for whatever I was set to do, and not unlikely to "get on."

My work in the Excise Office—or the Inland Revenue
Office, as it was called from about 1849 onwards—never
had anything to do with accounts, which I should not
have much relished : up to 1867 it was essentially in
the nature of letter-writing, varied to some small extent
with the custody etc. of official documents. In 1845 it
consisted principally in filling-up printed forms of letters
relating to sick and private leave in the various branches
of the Excise Service, and soon there was letter-writing
of a less strictly formal kind. I was in the first instance
an extra clerk, or "officiator" as the office phrase ran,
and the probable duration of my employment was
dubious. My pay was quite as good as could reasonably be expected at so early an age, £80 a year : a sum
which (I need hardly say), moderate as it was, told for
not a little in our stinted household. Thus I continued
until late in 1847, when I was "put on the establishment," i.e. appointed permanently to a clerkship. My
future was thus assured ; for, setting aside misconduct,
I could not be turned adrift nor dropped out of employment without a proportionate pension, accruing at
the end of ten years' service. In case however of a
voluntary resignation on my own part, I should not have
been entitled to any pension. I had not to undergo
any sort of examination prior to the temporary appointment nor yet to the permanent appointment, a matter
which is quite altered now. In the latter instance I
had to take some "oath of office," declaring myself (if
I remember right) "well affected to the present Government," which must have been a relic from the times of
George I, or possibly of William III or Charles II.

The Excise Office of that date was in Old Broad Street, a little farther east than the Royal Exchange, an old-fashioned building, claiming in all likelihood more interest than I took in it. The edifice was pulled down after the amalgamation of the Excise with the Stamps and Taxes and the concentration of both staffs in Somerset House ; the site is now occupied by the so-called Palmerston Buildings.

I was employed in a branch of the Secretary's Office, termed the English Correspondent's Office, the business of which was to correspond with members of the Excise Service in England and with traders paying Excise duties, but not with the "upper classes," Government officials, Members of Parliament, etc. The Secretary, with whom I hardly came into contact in the first three years or so of my service, was a gentleman of some social position, Mr. John Clayton Freeling, son of Sir Francis Freeling who had been Secretary to the Post Office. From Mr. Freeling to his subordinates there was (allowing for the exception of some few who could also be accepted as gentlemen in the popular sense of the term) a great gap in social standing. Most of them had been Excise officers, or what the public dubs "Excise-men"; for it was a peculiarity of the Excise Service in my time (or the Excise Branch of the Inland Revenue Service) that numerous positions in the Chief Office were filled in this way from what we called "the Out-door Branch." Towards 1853 this system extended to the Secretary himself, and so it remained up to the close of 1893, the year preceding my retirement. I am far from saying that this plan was wholly unjust, for superior merit in the Government service, in whatever grade of the establishment it may appear, ought to be noticed and rewarded ; but the plan necessarily caused some heart-burnings among clerks who had been appointed direct to the Chief Office, and it entailed some inequalities of treatment, especially since the fusion of the Excise with the Stamps and Taxes, in which latter section no such rule was applied. I do not scruple to say that I myself was subjected to more than one grievance in this respect.

It would not have been easy to get together a more observable assemblage of "odd fishes" than I found in the English Correspondent's Office, supplemented by the Scotch and Irish Correspondent's Office and the Secretary's Office. I do not apply this remark to the head of the first-named section, Mr. George Foster Ross, who was a well-mannered, pleasant man, not at all captious or exacting, and to myself always kindly. He was succeeded by Mr. Edgar Eldred, afterwards Collector of Inland Revenue in Dublin ; he was a stricter disciplinarian, but not any less willing to give full credit to all who acquitted themselves well ; he was indeed an excellent official. The second in position under these was a Mr. William Trent, a wizened, cadaverous-looking, little elderly man, still habited in knee-breeches. He always went to see a criminal hanged—a practice which occasionally made him, though the most punctual of clerks, some minutes late at the Excise Office. His memory seemed to be infallible upon two subjects : (1) the names, dates, and offences, of men and women who had been hanged, perhaps including (but of this I am not certain) their last dying speeches and confessions ; and (2) the names of all sorts of towns and villages in England, with their counties, and the Excise "districts" in which they were situate. Spite of his taste for the gallows and gallows-birds, I never found Mr. Trent other than an estimable and obliging business man. Not long after my entering the office—it may have been early in 1847—one of Mr. Trent's and of my colleagues, Mr. W. S. S., ran a considerable chance of being himself hanged—not a little to the consternation of the entire staff. This was a dissipated-looking young man, of what was then termed the "gentish" type, who had always been decidedly distasteful to me, though I had no complaint to make of him on my personal account. He was arrested on a charge of murdering his mother by poison, and was brought to trial and acquitted. It was recognized, in newspaper comments and otherwise, that although some circumstances of suspicion had arisen, there was nothing approaching to plain evidence. When S. was acquitted, the question arose of what could possibly be done with him officially. Assuredly none of us wished to welcome him back as a colleague; still there is such a thing as justice, linked or unlinked with the verdict of a British jury, and I felt at the time, and still feel, that S. was treated with the very opposite of justice. The evidence at the trial had shown that he was not a man of strictly temperate or correct habits, and the Board of Excise, taking advantage of this plea, "superseded" the unfortunate man, or in effect dismissed him, without retiring allowance or compensation of whatsoever kind. His petitions and protests were numerous; but they were not listened to by either the Board of Excise or the Treasury. What became of S. after this I never knew; there seemed to be very little chance of his obtaining in any quarter the bare means of living.

Another curious incident of a semi-judicial kind took

place in my early official days—perhaps in 1849. A leading personage in the office was behindhand with his accounts—some money which he ought to have paid into the revenue was unpaid. The sureties of this gentleman, I believe, produced the money. He himself bolted to Edinburgh and took sanctuary in the precincts of Holyrood Palace. No one could touch him there; there he lived for some years, and there, if I mistake not, he died. Does such an antiquated immunity still exist? If it does, it seems to be an instance of "the survival of the unfittest."

In the Scotch and Irish Correspondent's Office I recall, among others, an Irishman, Mr. Bartholomew Simmons, who had published a volume or two of poems (minor verse of the usual kind, not at all worse, I assume, than other specimens of that class), and who seems to have been the only man in the Correspondents' Office having any literary affinities. He died in early middle age. Another Irishman was Mr. W. B.—a truly typical example of the impecunious but still vivacious Hibernian, with a quite scanty salary, and an overcrowded quiverful of children, say a dozen. There was an anecdote—more than sufficiently tickling to the official mind—that the Chairman, Mr. Wood, who barely knew Mr. B. by sight, happened to meet him one day in one of the corridors of the building, and was addressed by him with a profuse exposition of his domestic sorrows, owing chiefly to the fatal fertility of his wife; and he capped the narrative with the phrase, "And would ye belave it, Mr. Wood, she's in that way again!"

In the Secretary's Office—of which, as aforesaid, the two Correspondents' Offices were dependencies—there was an assortment of originals not less curious; some of them appeared to have been appointed to their posts rather because they were unfitted for anything else than because they were fitted for them. The chief clerk—and he was efficient enough in that capacity—was Mr. C. H. Corbett, a very red-faced gentleman with reddish hair and red beefy hands, singularly puffed out with gout or what not. He was a very zealous member of the Established Church, in its Evangelical section, and would go round the rooms every Saturday distributing small tracts. Not many of them came my way—perhaps not any until, at the beginning of 1848, I passed from the English Correspondent's Office (abolished at the same date) to the Secretary's Office ; if I received few tracts, I read still fewer, and Mr. Corbett mercifully abstained from inquiring how I liked them. Strictly " Low Church " though he was, he had a great antipathy to dissenters, and seriously maintained that he always knew a Wesleyan by the smell. Mr. R. S. C., coming from " the North Countree," was well known to be at intervals insane ; on one occasion (but this was before my time) some motiveless motive filled him with fury, and he raised on high a heavy ruler to smite on the head, and too likely to kill, an unsuspecting half-sightless colleague, Mr. W. E. B. ; luckily his hand was stayed by a third party. This Mr. C. was a fairly tall, lean man, his demeanour quiet (so far as I ever saw), but rather stiff and unfamiliar ; his performance of duty was fully up to the mark. The Mr. W. E. B. just mentioned was the more odd of the two in externals. Like the previously named W. B. (with whom he had no relationship), he was the father of a large family, and grievously low in cash. He was about the most short-sighted man I ever knew, with prominent gooseberry eyes ; and, setting his nose almost on the paper, he wrote with the most stumpy and sputtering of quill pens the least steadfast of manuscript. He was amicable and kind-natured; but so unaccountably touchy that, almost at the same moment when he was tendering you a companionable pinch of snuff, he would bounce out of the room in a pet of which it would have been vain to ask the explanation. Mr. W. E. B. might be regarded as labouring towards efficiency, with the scantiest natural endowments; but Mr. R. H. made no effort and no pretence at efficiency; indeed his inaptitude showed so glaringly that scarcely anything was given him to do. If he could write his name, he could certainly not write an endurable business letter. He was a broken-down fox-hunting squire from Norfolk, his visage fiery with big pimples, which seemed to mark him for a drinking man, though I never heard of his indulging in any excess; when his means failed and he could hunt no more foxes, "my Lords" of the Treasury, or some ministerial patron, fastened him upon the public and the Excise Office. I will not omit saying that the poor elderly gentleman was as inoffensive as he was incapable.

A more attractive Norfolk man was Mr. Joseph Crome, son of the deservedly famed painter "Old Crome." He was a tall and rather well-looking man, a young widower when I entered the service. I did not at that date know much about the Norwich School of Painting, though one distinguished member of it, John Sell Cotman, had been my drawing-master at King's College School. In process of time I got clearer notions about it, and appreciated the interest attaching to Mr. Joseph Crome. I liked him moreover, finding him friendly and conversable. As his years advanced—he must have been well turned of fifty when he died at some such date as 1865—he became somewhat eccentric and less regular in business ; the reason for this may have been plain to others—to me it was a mere rumour.

There was yet another Norfolk man, Mr. William Browne Ffolkes, brother of a baronet, and descended from Sir Martin Ffolkes, who was Secretary of the Royal Society in the seventeenth century ; he was principally employed as private secretary to the Chairman, Mr. Wood. Mr. Ffolkes was a pleasant, good-humoured, and rather off-hand young man, noticeable as having a very high-pitched voice which at moments made a sudden drop. His position in society and in the office lured him into taking now and again some liberty at which we clerks would have scrupled ; and I remember my surprise at seeing one day under a written order of the Chairman, " Acquaint the magistrates " so and so, the note in Mr. Ffolkes's handwriting, " Beaks acquainted."

The 10th of April 1848 was an abnormal sort of day in the Excise Office. A great Chartist demonstration had been fixed to take place on Kennington Common, and the governmental and " respectable " classes were sufficiently flustered. Multitudes of people were sworn in as special constables. All or most of the Excise clerks were sworn in, myself included. I was invested with a constable's staff, but as it turned out I was not detailed for service in the streets ; indeed, the whole day passed off quietly, and the demonstration became a fiasco. We garrisoned the office throughout the night. If I had had to break a Chartist's head with my staff

I suppose I should have tried to do so, but as a matter of opinion I was considerably in sympathy with the Chartists, and had no inclination for breaking of heads, theirs or my own.

I recollect many other men who were in the Excise Office when I entered it, and necessarily a great number who joined at later dates, for I was in the Excise and Inland Revenue very nearly half a century—February 1845 to August 1894. I shall not however attempt to pursue the subject further for the present. From Old Broad Street we removed to Somerset House towards 1851. Thus I was a denizen of that building almost all my life, first while in King's College School, and afterwards while in the Inland Revenue. The personnel of the office improved about 1848, when some examination test for candidates was established, and after many years (towards 1870) the officials were separated into "Upper Division and Lower Division"— a change which might have worked well for both economy and efficiency if only the diversity of employ had been strictly fixed and stringently applied. Such was not the case to any adequate degree in the Inland Revenue Office, and I was never myself in favour of the change, which introduced invidious distinctions and some unfairness in practice. Many of the Lower Division men perform work which cannot be discriminated from that of some in the Upper Division, and I may be permitted to doubt whether even the highest employments in the Upper Division demand qualifications of intellect or training which could not be found among the best men in the Lower. To be a good Government clerk in the higher seats one requires business capacity and some amount of talent ; but neither

high talent nor a wide range of educational acquirements
is needed for the posts which I knew in the Excise
Branch of the Secretary's Office of the Inland Revenue,
and few indeed were those of which I did not know
something.   I may as well add that, taking my own
office as the criterion, it is quite a mistake to suppose
that Government clerks have " nothing to do."   All of
them have something to do, and many of them more
than enough.   I was myself often overworked, especially
in the second half of my service.   Piles of papers, many
of them requiring diligent reading, careful thought, and
rapid decision, came loaded down upon me.   Without
a turn for system, or without prompt resolution, they
could not have been got through.

I formed not any private intimacies in the office.
Occasionally—very seldom—I was in the house of one
or other official, and was out again without its leading
to anything.   Many men however I both esteemed
and liked.   Of some of these I purpose to speak in the
sequel.

There was indeed one private intimacy with an
official ; but this arose from the fact, not that I encountered him in the Inland Revenue, but that he was
the nephew and adopted son of our old family friend
Mr. Thomas Keightley, author of *The Fairy Mythology*,
The Life of Milton, etc.   I am speaking of Mr. Alfred
Chaworth Lyster, who entered the office at the beginning
of 1848, and who, at Mr. Keightley's instance, at once
made himself known to me.   Mr. Lyster was not cut
out by nature for a Government clerk, neither had he
his uncle's literary turn.   His tastes were rather in the
direction of country sports and manly recreation—matters
for which I, by nature and habit, had no sort of

aptitude. He and I nevertheless became the best of friends, and at one time saw plenty of one another, not alone in the office. Along with more solid qualities, he had—or I should rather say has—the easy pleasantry of an Irishman ; and I have often had occasion to prize his genial spirits, friendly goodwill, and accommodating temper.

Soon after knowing Mr. Lyster I was invited down to the country - house, near Newbury in Berkshire, then occupied, along with some four hundred acres of land, by Mr. Keightley, who had permanently quitted his native Ireland. It was a patriarchal (or matriarchal) establishment, such as one seldom sees in England. Mr. Keightley was the owner ; but his mother, infirm but still bright at the age of ninety or little less, was in a sense at the head of the establishment. There were three maiden daughters of hers, one of them very intent upon matters of religion (Protestant) ; also a second son, with his wife, and an adopted daughter not directly related to the family ; of course too Mr. Lyster himself, who escorted me. All this changed very much two or three years afterwards. The venerable mother was gone, the second son and his wife were in Australia, and the others domiciled in a suburb of London, moving afterwards a little farther off. Except Mr. Lyster, I have not at any time known in strict intimacy any man who did not belong more or less to the literary or the artistic class.

I may here mention that my first sight of the sea was in 1846, at Herne Bay. Since my grandfather relinquished Holmer Green for London, in 1839, I had been very little out of town ; in 1846 I joined at the seaside one or two others of the family. I was (let me confess it) rather "disappointed" with the sea, having heard Maria very enthusiastic on the same subject ; but indeed Herne Bay can easily be outrivalled for marine majesty and grandeur. Having thus got to understand what the sea is like, or may be like, I soon, in after-experience, learned to be other than "disappointed" with it.

VI

HOME LIFE—
MY BROTHER AND MYSELF

NO two brothers could be more constantly together,
or more uniformly interested in one another's
doings, than Gabriel and I. Until he quitted school
we were hardly at all apart, for we slept in the same bed.
We rose, talked, walked, studied, ate, amused ourselves,
and slumbered, together. Divided though we ultimately
were so far as study was concerned, all the rest remained
as before. We read the same authors, coloured prints
in the same book, collected woodcuts for the same
scrapbook. All books were in common between us;
and I still possess various volumes, the relics of the old
time, where the inscription (more generally in *his* handwriting) is simply " Rossetti," as the initials of either
would have been out of order. Poetry was our chief
reading: Byron was succeeded by Shelley; he by
Keats, Tennyson, Mrs. Browning, Philip Bailey; these
by Browning. There were also a large number of
romances — English, such as Scott, Bulwer, Dickens,
Maturin, Thackeray; French (from about 1843 onwards) still more numerous — Lesage, Hugo, Sue,
Paul de Kock, Dumas, Soulié. I regard the reading
and re-reading of Shelley, which began in the summer of 1844, as an epoch in my life. I revelled in

his glorious idealism ; and got confirmed in those general tendencies of opinion, on matters of faith and polity, to which I was already drifting. My French readings moreover were of much service to me. My knowledge of the language, as acquired at school, was fair ; the readings familiarized me with the tone and idioms of it ; and I believe that, when I first went to France, in 1853, I was about as well able to express myself in French as I have been at any subsequent date.

I have said before that, "if it had not been for Gabriel, I might perhaps never have attempted anything in the way of literature, art-criticism, and the like." The same statement holds good as regards acquaintance-ships. Being of a very retired and self-poised character, addicted to certain occupations, and not feeling the need of communicating them or myself to other persons (except indeed to Gabriel), and being from boyhood in a line of life—the Government office—in which I did not find a genuine comradeship of mind, I should presumably have made hardly any friendships, or even familiar acquaintances, if left to my sole resources. It was almost invariably through Gabriel that I got to know people, to like them, and sometimes to love them.

Emerging from Sass's Academy, and passing through an ordinary period of probation, my brother, in July 1846, became a student of the Royal Academy, and soon his circle of acquaintances was in one or other degree mine as well. I do not consider that he had any of that aloofness from picking up with Tom, Jack, and Harry, which marked myself in an exceptional degree. He would indeed summarily reject Jack and Harry, because he happened not to like them ; but Tom, though not specially congenial to him *au fond*,

would be consorted with, according to the dictate
of circumstances and the habit of encounter. Tom, in
this instance, really happens to have been Tom—
Thomas Doughty, an American art-student—to whom
I have referred in my memoir of my brother. And,
because my brother associated with him, he became
about the first young man who was my own familiar—
towards 1846, 1847, and 1848. I prized his rather
bluff good-fellowship, and saw in his company a little—
a very little—of the outskirts of "life." Dr. Adolf
Heimann (already mentioned) and his wife were our
most constant and kindly family friends in these years,
well known to the entire household. Then, through
my brother, I knew Major Calder Campbell, a retired
officer of the Indian army and a light *littérateur* of some
general acceptance. Next, late in 1847, Gabriel, greatly
admiring some poems he had seen by William Bell
Scott—by profession a painter, and master of the
Government School of Design in Newcastle-on-Tyne—
wrote off to him, enclosing verses of his own ; and
soon Scott called upon us in London. We all took
to him most cordially, and he to us ; and this I say
without any modification or misgiving, although it is
true that in his published *Autobiographical Notes*, compiled partly before and partly after my brother's death, he
said some ill-natured things about him—ill-natured past
doubt, and, though containing several grains of truth,
in detail very inaccurate. None the less I am sure that, up
to a late date in Gabriel's life, Scott both prized his powers
and sympathized with himself. With me, I am satisfied,
he sympathized still more; fully sensible of the difference
in our aptitudes and performances, but relishing me
personally the better of the two. Indeed, he was

always a most affectionate friend to me, until, in advanced age and broken health, and wholly withdrawn from London, he may possibly have conceived some minor amount of soreness against me, along with a much greater (and equally motiveless) amount against various others—Dante Gabriel Rossetti first and foremost. I will take it upon me to record here my real belief as to Mr. Scott's leading incentive towards writing about the latter in a spirit of detraction. I regard it as twofold. First, an honest desire to treat a man of mark without any of those disingenuous glosses and smug compromises which are often applied to such persons, and thus to strip him of any adventitious prestige and write truths about him—if disagreeable truths, all the more consonant to the biographer's plan. I know as a fact that Scott considered almost all biographies untrustworthy, as ignoring or misrepresenting matters of importance ; and he aimed at compassing a contrary result. Second, a jealous or invidious feeling arising after my brother's death, when a great amount of matter—sometimes highly laudatory, but not by any means exclusively so—got published concerning him. It might be expressed in the unpraiseworthy yet intelligible utterance : " Why all this outpouring about Dante Rossetti ? If he was a painter and a poet, am not I the like, and did I not precede him in both functions ? And who sounds the praises of William Bell Scott ? " Such is the opinion which I entertain on this to me rather repugnant theme.

Soon after he had secured the acquaintance of Scott, my brother, on the look out for some one to give him practical guidance in the processes of painting, wrote in March 1848 to Ford Madox Brown, also unknown to

FORD MADOX BROWN.

c. 1862.

him ; Brown responded, and the two were soon on a
footing of friendship, and indeed of intimacy. I too,
after a little while, became known to Brown, my senior
by nearly eight years.

Thus four of my earliest friendships—with Doughty
(who towards 1848 returned to America), Calder Campbell, Scott, and Brown—came to me through the
medium of Gabriel. The like was the case with some
other friendships which ensued from time to time.

I am here getting on towards the period of the Præraphaelite Brotherhood, or P.R.B.— September 1848.
Of the other members of the family I need only say
that their position up to that date continued to be such as
was sufficiently indicated in my fourth section. My father
seriously ailing, half blind, and incapacitated for any
active professional exertion, but not for writing in verse
and prose, which he diligently persevered in. My
mother teaching in one or two families, with only
scanty profits, and keeping the family together by her
unintermitting pains. Maria was either still a governess or (I think by this time) living at home and going
out as a teacher, both of Italian and of other branches
of education ; in this capacity she was seldom quite un-
employed, and gradually she made her way. Christina
living at home ; known in the family to be showing
unusual promise and some performance as a poet, appreciated on these and on all grounds by a very few
intimates, otherwise quite unknown. Gabriel, although
he had not yet succeeded in producing any art-work of
a paying kind, was tolerably well understood to be a
clever young fellow who would not remain for ever
obscure. My salary, in the middle of 1848, may still
have been £80, and was certainly not more than £90.

VII

THE PRÆRAPHAELITE
BROTHERHOOD

THE formation of the Præraphaelite Brotherhood
has been so often detailed by various writers, myself not the hindmost, that I will here assume it as an
accomplished fact. William Holman Hunt and John
Everett Millais, both at that time competent and even
able exhibiting painters, were the first to moot some
desire for a new movement; Gabriel Charles Dante
Rossetti added to the impetus and aided in giving it a
name, being then a mere tiro in handling the brush.
The sculptor Thomas Woolner, the domestic painter
James Collinson, and (with more of real ardour towards
something that could be termed "Præraphaelite")
the art-student Frederic George Stephens, were enlisted,
spontaneously or under persuasion. Stephens and
Rossetti alone had as yet exhibited nothing. Here were
six members. Clearly five of them can at the first
have had no wish for me as a seventh, but Gabriel
had; no one (so far as I ever knew or supposed)
raised the least objection, and so I was installed as
P.R.B. No. 7. Being once installed, I was treated
with the heartiest frankness and confidence, and indeed
affection, by all my "brethren"; no distinction was
made between me and the others, except that (after the

subsiding of some shadowy idea that I might become a professional painter) I was not expected to produce any works of art, and I was fixed upon as Secretary to the P.R.B. This post was more nominal than burdensome. However, I did such writing as was needed for convening meetings, etc., and I kept the *P.R.B. Journal*—a large proportion of which has by this time seen the light of publicity (No. 10 in my preface).

In these Reminiscences I have hitherto spoken of my brother as "Gabriel," that being his first Christian name, and the one by which he was to the very last called in the family, and by some other persons as well. But, as he adopted the form "Dante Gabriel" soon after entering upon professional life, I shall, from this point onwards, mostly use the name "Dante."

Let me try to give some idea of the members of the Præraphaelite Brotherhood, such as I knew them when the association was formed in September 1848. I say nothing here of Millais in his character as a baronet and P.R.A., nor of Woolner in his capacity of an R.A. who left a fortune of £64,000. Of the seven, the eldest was Woolner, born in December 1826 ; the youngest myself, born in September 1829. I will take them in the order of their seniority.

Woolner, the son of a letter-sorter in the Post Office, a Suffolk man, can have had but very scanty advantages of schooling. At an early age he had been introduced into the studio of William Behnes, the sculptor chiefly of busts. I scarcely know whether he was at that time definitely intended for the sculptural profession—always a very uphill calling for a youth without means or connexions. However this may be, Behnes took some note of him, and trained him in carving and modelling ; and (as I have often heard Woolner say) Behnes was a great expert in rendering the surface and qualities of flesh. My friend also got some instruction in the schools of the Royal Academy. By September 1848 he might be regarded as fairly launched upon his profession : he had exhibited two or three things, which had passed—and had well deserved to pass—not wholly unobserved. I am not sure that he had succeeded in selling anything or in getting any positive commission, and his financial outlook was of the dimmest, not to say the darkest. Woolner was of middle height, sturdily built, with a strong, animated look—dark eyes, rather short nose, and a fine crop of ginger-yellow hair. His manner was frank, decisive, self-confident, and full of warmth to persons whom he liked. I was indisputably numbered among these. His talk was somewhat varied, for he always took an interest in several matters outside the range of his art : it was entertaining, pointed, often incisive, and well stored with observation and reflection. He knew how to say a sharp thing sharply. He talked rather one-sidedly, in this sense—that he rated cheaply the abilities and performances of most men in his own branch of art, and indeed of several men in all departments of affairs, and where he disliked he was very ready to denounce. Notwithstanding any scantiness in his education, he had read amply (in English alone), and was a vigorous admirer of fine things in poetry, and in literature generally. He was a steady smoker ; in other matters very moderate, or even abstemious. He was too manly to " keep his family dark "—father, stepmother, and several children—on account of their undistinguished social position ; but I very seldom saw anything of them, my meetings with Woolner being constantly in his studio, a well-sized but not very cheerful one. Of all the P.R.B.'s, Woolner was perhaps (with the exception of my brother) the one of whom I saw the most in 1849 and 1850. I took to him at least as well as to any of the others, but for all of them I had a genuine and even affectionate regard.

Next to Woolner in point of age must have come Collinson. He was the son of a bookseller (deceased) in Mansfield, Nottinghamshire, and had a slightly provincial pronunciation. In person he was small and rather dumpy, with a thick neck ; his face intelligent enough, but in no wise handsome. He talked with good sense, but did not come out in conversation ; his manner was subdued and somewhat timid, and the same was the case with his art. He was a domestic painter ; and would, I assume, never have tried any other line of work but for his association in the P.R.B., whereby he was induced on one occasion to experiment in a historic-religious subject, *St. Elizabeth of Hungary*. Collinson was brought up in the English Church ; and (as it happened) he used, before I knew of him as an artist, to attend at the place of worship frequented by my family, Christ Church, Albany Street, where he was remarked by my female relatives for his heedful and devout bearing. After a while he came under the influence of Cardinal Wiseman, and joined the Roman communion : this was, it seems to me, very shortly before the formation of the Præraphaelite Brotherhood. Collinson was not the sort of man to excite ardent emotions of friendship ; but a P.R.B. was a P.R.B., and as such he was regarded by me with the utmost goodwill, and something more than that ; and this even apart from some family circumstances which brought him very near to me, and of which something will be said further on. He lived in lodgings in Somers Town, upon a moderate allowance made by his family, in addition to what he might succeed in earning as a painter. He was thus tolerably comfortable, but had to be economical, and indeed showed no propensity to expensive habits. I have seen it stated—I suppose with accuracy—that Dante Rossetti was the promoter of Collinson's admission into the Brotherhood, although Millais and Holman Hunt considered him "not strong enough for the place"; and they were right, as the event proved.

Holman Hunt (he, Stephens, and myself, are now the sole survivors of the P.R.B.) is the son of a warehouseman employed by a City firm; he himself published in 1886 an account of his early and most manful struggles to obtain a training in fine art, and to conquer the position which was due to his remarkable endowments, so I need not enlarge upon that matter, nor will I enter into details as to the personal appearance of my living friend. If the other P.R.B.'s had had to pass a vote as to which of their colleagues they admired most, they would all, I conceive, have named Holman Hunt, while he himself would have named Millais. We thoroughly admired him for his powers in art, his strenuous efforts, his vigorous personality, his gifts of mind and character, his warm and helpful friendship. Not indeed that we should have ignored the more than co-equal claims of Millais as a pictorial executant; but he had not had to fight a savage fight— Hunt was still fighting it, and under very severe pressure, in 1848–50—and Millais had obviously not the same force and tenacity of thought. To manage

to work without enduring privations in the process
was not in those days the lot of Hunt; he endured
them in tough and silent magnanimity, being ambitious
no less than resolute. In conversation he was sagacious,
anecdotical, and, within certain limits, well informed,
with a full gusto for the humorous side of things. Like
Woolner, he was a reading man according to his moderate opportunities, with perhaps rather less turn for esti-
mating books critically. Some of us, off and on, called
him "the maniac"; I never much saw why, for few
young men could be less maniacal, though most of
them might be freer from those elements of character
which, upon occasion, go to make a fanatic. Some
arbitrary oddities of manner there may have been, yet
nothing which could rightly be dubbed eccentric. Towards the date of the formation of the Brotherhood,
Holman Hunt took a studio in Cleveland Street (near
Howland Street), which Dante Rossetti soon afterwards
shared with him. Thus I saw him very frequently
indeed, and with a degree of intimacy and of affection
which left little to choose between the two men. Hunt
had already—in his picture exhibited in 1848, *Porphyro
and Madeline leaving the Castle* (from Keats)—shown
some tendency in the "Præraphaelite" direction. His
first picture, as a defined Præraphaelite, was *Rienzi
swearing revenge for his brother's death*, begun as soon
as he entered the Cleveland Street studio. Here my
brother sat for the head of Rienzi, and I for that
of the young Colonna. I possess a very interesting
drawing of my brother's head, made as a preparatory
study.

Stephens's father had been (as I understood) an official
of some kind in the Tower of London. With him

and with the rest of the small family my Præraphaelite
Brother lived in a house in a main road of Lambeth.
Their means were evidently restricted, and Frederic
Stephens—an art-student who had not as yet advanced
to the point of painting any picture adapted for exhibition—was unable to add to their resources. He had an
attractive person and a face (still not very greatly impaired by the inroads of age) so thoughtful and picturesque as to be well adapted for the Ferdinand of
Millais in his painting of *Ferdinand and Ariel*, and
for the Christ of Madox Brown in his picture (now in
the National British Gallery) of *Christ washing Peter's
feet*. Stephens is a man of firm and settled opinions
and of character far from supple—even rather unbending—but none the less with a certain quality of personal
diffidence which tells in his conversation. As a painter
he produced in the early days two or three good portraits on a small scale, but nothing else of note. He
then withdrew from painting, and acted as an art critic
on *The Athenæum* for a long series of years and an art
instructor in University College School. I was from
the first fond of Stephens, and do not scruple to say
that he—at least as much as any other man alive or
dead—has always been and still is fond of me—the
kindliest and most persistent of friends.

Of my brother, whom I have constant occasion to
mention in the course of these Reminiscences, I need say
little here. He was very active in giving shape and
tone to the P.R.B., and was generally recognized as
holding the primacy in an intellectual, though not
in the pictorial and practical, relation. Shortly before
the formation of the Brotherhood he had, under Madox
Brown's guidance, first begun to exercise himself steadily

in oil-painting; and as soon as the association was started he commenced his first subject-picture, *The Girlhood of Mary Virgin*, exhibited in 1849. It had been preceded, in 1848, by a small head-portrait of Christina (still in my possession, and a very fair piece of painting for a beginner). This was followed by a life - sized bust - portrait of our father, begun perhaps a little later than the religious picture, but completed sooner. It was commissioned by his godfather, Mr. Charles Lyell, who paid a rather liberal price—the first that my brother pocketed. In the *Mary Virgin* picture Rossetti worked under the direct eye of Hunt, and profited hereby.

Lastly I come to Millais. He, as we all know, had been a student of art in the Royal Academy from a very early period of boyhood, had won various academic honours, and was, before the formation of the Brotherhood, a clever, promising, and well-accepted exhibiting painter. Those earlier productions of his had nothing "Præraphaelite" about them; i.e., they evinced no tendency to a new movement in art, whether in idea or in execution, and, though quite competent works for a student who was fast becoming a proficient, they bore no evidence of a minute and solicitous study of nature. As soon as he proclaimed himself a Præraphaelite, Millais altered his methods entirely, and set to work upon the rather extensive composition, of which he made an admirable picture, *Lorenzo and Isabella*, from the poem by Keats. I sat to him for the head of Lorenzo—presenting only an approximate resemblance to me; the head of Dante Rossetti appears in the background, and more prominently another head which I take to be that of Stephens. Millais lived in comfort,

but not in anything to be called affluence, in a well-sized
house, No. 83 (now 7) Gower Street, Bedford Square,
along with his father, mother, and brother (my old
schoolfellow). His father was a native of Jersey, a
musician, professional or semi-professional—principally,
I understood, a flute player ; a rather fine-looking, easy-
going, hearty, and very good-natured man. The mother
was a much more energetic and active character, and
obviously took the lead. Before marrying Mr. Millais,
she had been (as I heard) the widow of a tailor, Mr.
Hodgkinson, having two sons by her first union. Mrs.
Millais, when I knew her, had the remains of good
features, without much amenity ; she was decisive in
manner and voice, brisk and rather jerky in gesture.
She always wore a cap ; it was not always a smart one.
To myself she was uniformly kind, and I remember
her with regard. Millais was a very handsome, or
more strictly a beautiful, youth : his face came nearer to
the type which we term angelic than perhaps any other
male visage that I have seen. His voice hardly corresponded to his countenance ; it was harsh rather than
otherwise. In talk he was something of what one calls
"a rattle"; saying sprightly things in an off-hand way,
but not entering into anything claiming the name of
conversation. He sometimes started a subject, but
never developed it. We all entertained the highest
estimate of what he had now set about doing, and what
else he was certain to achieve in a short time. In this
sense he led us all, and moreover we had a genuine
personal liking for him : yet I do not think that
Millais, as "a man and a brother," ever stood quite
so high with us as Holman Hunt did. He was
the only P.R.B. who had some notion of music as an

art : he enjoyed it much, and could speak of it with intelligence.

It will be apparent from what I have been saying that all the members of the Præraphaelite Brotherhood belonged to the middle or the lower-middle class of society. Not one (if I except my brother and myself) had had that sort of liberal education which comprises Latin and Greek, nor did any of them—not even Millais, though connected with Jersey—read or speak French. Faults of speech and of spelling occurred among them *passim*. Of any access to " the upper classes " through family ties there was not a trace.

The Præraphaelite Brotherhood was a thoroughly informal association, and yet the link of comradeship was close among us. We had monthly meetings at the houses, successively, of all the members — meetings which consisted of good-fellowship, talk, and ventilation of projects, the consideration of any works of art which the host of the evening might be minded to show, and a very moderate allowance of refreshment, and of tobacco for those who smoked. About matters of this kind I have said, in my *Memoir of Dante Rossetti*, nearly as much as I find any occasion for saying. The whole of 1849 and the first half of 1850 may be regarded as the period when the Brotherhood, in this aspect, was most active. Soon the necessities of work, each man in his own groove, the distances between our houses, the not infrequent absence of one member or other from London, and other considerations of this order, interfered with fixed or numerous meetings ; and we were rather friends united by some common ideas in work than adherents of an organization.

There is one matter, partially connected with the

Præraphaelite Brotherhood, which I had never mentioned explicitly until I wrote the memoir of my sister Christina, published with her *Poetical Works* in 1904. James Collinson, about the time of the formation of the P.R.B., was introduced to Christina, then aged seventeen, in our family circle, and he immediately fell in love with her—as well he might, for in breeding and tone of mind, not to speak of actual genius or advantages of person, she was markedly his superior. He explained his feelings to Dante Gabriel, who, with perhaps too headlong a wish to serve the interests of a "Præraphaelite Brother," represented the matter to Christina and advocated Collinson's cause. Collinson was at this time a Roman Catholic; and Christina, though not indisposed to his suit on general grounds, was unwilling to marry a member of a religious communion other than her own. She therefore declined his offer. I do not rightly know what was Christina's precise point of view in this matter. She had certainly no strong prejudice against Roman Catholics; she considered them to be living branches of the True Vine, authentic members of the Church of Christ, although in error upon some points. I surmise that she was chiefly influenced by the consideration that difficulties, and trying cases of conscience for herself, would be sure to arise if there were offspring of the marriage. Collinson, upon receiving this refusal, set about considering whether he really was so firmly a Catholic as to be unable to revert to his original membership in the Church of England; he thought he *could* do this, resumed attending an Anglican place of worship, and renewed his suit to Christina, as being no longer a Roman Catholic. Hereupon he was accepted; the date was probably in mid-autumn of 1848.

There was no expectation of an *early* marriage, as Collinson was in a struggling position as regards money, and Christina had no means whatever. I will not suggest that Collinson was unconscientious in these proceedings—indeed, I consider he was not; but it is clear that, swayed by his desires, he misconstrued the true attitude of his mind in matters of faith. After serving this second apprenticeship to Anglicanism, he harked back to Catholicism. I forget what the precise date may have been—perhaps much about the time, May 1850, when *The Germ* came to a conclusion. As Christina had only accepted Collinson's suit on the understanding of his being an English Churchman, so, when he redeclared himself a Catholic, she revoked her troth. This she did with deep sorrow and reluctance, and only at the bidding of a supposed duty. I cannot say that she was in love with Collinson in any such sense as that she would, before knowing him to be enamoured of her, have wished him to become so; but having received his addresses and accepted them, she had freely and warmly bestowed her affections upon him, and would never have dreamed of withdrawing them, if only the conditions leading up to the engagement had been observed on his part. Being of a highly sensitive nature, and feeling keenly for him as well as for herself, she suffered much in forming and maintaining her resolve. A blight was on her heart and her spirits, and the delicacy of health which had already settled down upon her increased visibly. I remember that one day—it may have been within four or five months after the breaking-off of the engagement—she happened to see Collinson in the neighbourhood of Regent's Park, and she fainted away in the street.

The painter's after-career may be briefly summarized as follows. Soon after the termination of the engagement he severed his connexion with the P.R.B., on the ground (as his letter put it) that he thought it inconsistent with his obligations as a Roman Catholic. At the beginning of 1853 he entered a Jesuit College as a "working brother," but he soon left again, resumed his profession as a painter—he never rose to any real eminence in the art—and married a sister-in-law of the painter John Rogers Herbert, himself a Catholic convert. He had, I think, only one child, a son who may be now living. I happened to meet Collinson once many years after all these occurrences, and found from his conversation that his religious zeal had then very greatly abated. Whether this was only a passing mood, or one which abode with him to the last, I am unable to say. He died in 1881.

Considering that the Præraphaelite Brothers were all very young men, it is a little remarkable that only two women can be named as rather closely associated with their early proceedings. One was Miss Elizabeth Eleanor Siddal, who became Dante Rossetti's wife in 1860, and of whom more anon. The other was Christina, and this I say not only on the ground of her engagement to Collinson, but also because of her general mental gifts and sympathies, and especially her contributions of poetry to *The Germ* magazine. It has been said (but only, I think, of late years) that Christina went among us by the name of "the Queen of the Præraphaelites." This, as I have stated elsewhere, appears to me to be a mere invention *après coup ;* but certain it is that she might without much unreason have been so called, and that no one else could, in the dawning P.R.B. days, have disputed that title with her. She saw Holman Hunt, Woolner, and Stephens, frequently ; Millais much seldomer.

It is a sad and indeed a humiliating reflection that, after the early days of *camaraderie* and of genuine brotherliness had run their course, followed by a less brief period of amity and goodwill, keen antipathies severed the quondam P.R.B.'s. I here omit Collinson, who, after having voluntarily retired from the band, was practically lost sight of by the other members, though none of them took a serious dislike to him. Woolner became hostile to Hunt, Dante Rossetti, and Millais. Hunt became hostile to Woolner and Stephens, and in a minor degree to Dante Rossetti. Stephens became hostile to Hunt. Dante Rossetti became hostile to Woolner, and in a minor degree to Hunt and Millais. Millais, being an enormously successful man while others were only commonly successful, did not perhaps become strictly hostile to any one ; he kept aloof however from Dante Rossetti, and I infer from Woolner. In all these instances I know something about the causes of alienation, and in my memoir of Dante Rossetti I have stated the facts concerning him and Woolner ; but it is no business of mine to expound the details here, nor to endeavour to apportion acquittal and blame. I will however avow my belief that, with a moderate spirit of conciliation and of making allowance for diverging points of view, most of these acerbities would have been avoided or healed.

The reader may have noticed that I have not set myself down among the P.R.B.'s who exchanged friendship for enmity, or who fell under the ban of others. I could not do so with truth. I have always, on the contrary, remained on very good terms with every P.R.B. It is true that towards 1854 I began to see little of Millais, and after some years further I never met him unless by chance. When these casual encounters occurred he was always pleasant and cordial. My only reason for not courting more frequent meetings with him was—along with my general and ingrained disposition for keeping much to myself—the fact that he moved in one sphere of work and society while I moved in another ; he was also very often absent from London, chiefly in Scotland. It is likewise true that of Woolner in his later years (he died in 1892) I saw nothing. The reasons were nearly the same, with the addition that the feud between him and my brother had introduced a certain degree of awkwardness in our intercourse. But even so I never broke with Woolner in any sense. With the two surviving members of the Brotherhood, Holman Hunt and Stephens, I continue on terms of genuine friendship. I have not, indeed, happened to see Hunt of late years, but this (as in some other cases) is merely fortuitous. The fact is that, being of a disposition the extreme reverse of quarrelsome, I never felt in the least inclined to fall out with any P.R.B., nor indeed with any of those multitudinous acquaintances towards whom my feelings have never been so warm as they were to my " Præraphaelite Brothers." I know that a strictly pacific temperament has its congenital defects — defects possibly as serious as those which attend the contentious temperament. All that I can say as to this is that my temperament is the pacific one, with whatever consequent defects. I can " get on " with almost all people, and I conceive the frame of mind which recognizes merits, whatever these may amount to, to be a more agreeable one than that which concerns itself with the analysis of blemishes.

VIII

BEGINNINGS IN LITERATURE

AFTER the boyish period of *Ulfred the Saxon* I do
not appear to have had, for some while, any steady
inclination to do anything in the way of writing.
Dante Gabriel, as usual, set me going at odd moments.
In more instances than one he started the idea of a
family magazine, to which we were all to contribute in
manuscript ; one of these magazines was in being as far
back as 1843. To contest the fiat of Dante Gabriel
in such a matter was not in me ; so I produced something or other. I suppose there was some prose ;
certainly there was some verse of a kind, but this would
have been later than 1843.

I never found much difficulty in writing in verse.
On the other hand, I never discovered it to be my
natural form of expression, which with Dante Gabriel
and Christina it clearly was, and so also with my father.
My verse-writing, as I advanced a little in years, was
not, I think, exactly commonplace ; but it had neither
the impulse which abolishes stiffness of phrase nor the
fluidity which ensures verbal music. It appears to me
(but there may be some presumption in saying so) that,
if I had persevered with verse, I should have produced
some very passable work, rivalling that of various accepted
versifiers ; but, as professing to be poetry, it might

after all have proved "most tolerable and not to be endured." To be a quasi-poet, a pleasing poetaster, was never my ambition ; I felt that in the long run I should prefer to stay outside the arena of verse altogether. And so, after making some few experiments, I did.

It may have been in 1846 or 1847 that I first attempted verse ; for anything in the way of prose fiction I have from first to last (after dropping *Ulfred the Saxon*) never felt any inclination or vocation whatever. There were some half-dozen sonnets, and one or two other small pieces. In 1848—aiming I suppose at one of the family magazines before mentioned—I produced a poem in eight or ten stanzas called *In the Hill-Shadow*. It purported to be the utterance of a sorrowing father who had buried a beloved child-daughter among the hills. Why did I select a subject so extraneous to my experiences ? I know not, but such was my performance. In October 1848, almost contemporaneously with the starting of the Præraphaelite Brotherhood, I offered this composition to *The Athenæum*, then under the editorship of a gentleman quite unknown to me, Mr. T. K. Hervey ; he accepted and printed it, and wrote to me in rather strong terms of commendation. To me, aged just nineteen, this seemed a surprising as well as encouraging incident ; it is also singular that I, who was so much less capable and less productive in poetry than my brother and Christina, should have preceded them both in getting some verse published, and published under advantageous conditions. Maria however had anticipated me ; having a verse-translation printed in 1841 (as well as a small religious prose allegory in 1846), both of them semi-published rather than published. In some quarters *In the Hill-Shadow* got prized

13. The Sin of Detection

She bowed her face among them all, as one
By one they rose and went. A little scorn
They showed – a very little. More forlorn
She seemed, because of that: she might have gone
Proud else in her turn, and have so made known
What she well knew — that the free-hearted corn
Kissed by the hot air freely all the morn,
Is better than the weed which has its own
Foul glut in secret. Both her white breast heaved
Like heaving water, with their weight of lace;
And her long tresses, full of musk and myrrh,
Were shaken from the braids her fingers weaved,
So that they hid the shame in her pale face.
Then I stept forth, and bowed addressing her

G.

MS. OF DANTE G. ROSSETTI.

SONNET WRITTEN TO BOUTS RIMÉS, c. 1848.
(*Hitherto unprinted.*)

higher than it deserved to he, being republished in a volume (compiled by Serjeant Cox) named *Beautiful Poetry*, and afterwards in another (compiled by Mrs. Valentine) named *Gems of National Poetry*. I was not deluded into supposing it to be either a beauty or a gem. After my success with *The Athenæum*, Christina also sent some poems thither—not exactly good ones, but showing more native gift than mine ; two were published, others declined. Mr. Hervey held them to be infected with Tennysonian mannerisms.

About this time a practice grew up between my brother and myself of writing sonnets to *bouts-rimés*. We produced a considerable number of them, probably each of us some fifty to seventy. The chief scene of this exercise was the small room on the third floor of No. 50 Charlotte Street which (as mentioned in my first section) had originally been our father's dressing-room, but had been assigned to Dante Gabriel in his student days. It was a very bare apartment, with little if any carpeting, and my brother made it a littery one as well. I will admit that *cimex lectularius* was at times a co-tenant with him and me. There were a small fireplace, a shabby table, and two or three more or less unpresentable chairs. We managed however to make ourselves quite comfortable there, according to our unexacting standard of those days ; and any persons who happened to be calling for my brother or for me had mostly to seek that chamber up three flights of stairs, and there settle down into such accommodation as they could find. Here did Dante Gabriel write out the rhymes for me, and I for him ; and we polished off the sonnet at a rapid or even a breakneck pace. I still possess a minor proportion of these performances. Those of my brother

have spirit, some picturesque fervour of idea and expression, and even something approaching to subtlety.
What they want—and this must be necessarily wanting
in a *bouts-rimés* piece—is backbone ; diction has to come
as it can at the bidding of the moment, and the meaning
embodied in the diction has to come as it can. My
brother's *bouts-rimés* sonnets were done a little faster
than mine, and they approached more nearly to a true
poetic standard : as regards backbone or continuity of
purport I surmise that mine were often not inferior to
his. The year 1848 saw this practice of ours in fullest
force ; it may have begun in 1847, and must have lasted
through the better part of 1849—hardly later than that.
Christina indulged only a little in the same hobby ;
chiefly in the summer of 1848, when she and I were
together at Brighton. As she had more turn for whim
and sprightliness in writing than either of her brothers,
I apprehend that some of her *bouts-rimés* sonnets must
be the best of the batch, for a writer who is whimsical
need not be close-knit. That this practice with *bouts-
rimés* is a good exercise for versifiers, simply as an
exercise, can scarcely be denied. It compels rapidity of
thought and writing, and helps one at moments to
ingenious turns of expression. It bears some analogy
to the system of improvising, so familiar to Italians (my
father was a renowned improvisatore), so alien from
English people. It is however much less trying, and
less showy as well.

In the early autumn of 1849 the members of the Præraphaelite Brotherhood were preparing for the publication of their magazine *The Germ*. I have written already
so much about *The Germ* (see Nos. 5, 7, 10, 12, and 14,
in my preface) that I shall here cut it short. While

I was enjoying a brief holiday in the Isle of Wight, in September 1849, I was appointed to be editor of the forthcoming magazine. Woolner and my brother took it upon them to make this appointment, acquiesced in, if not expressly authorized, by all the others. Just before receiving notice of my new berth I had begun a blank-verse narrative poem of some moderate length, ultimately entitled *Mrs. Holmes Grey;* it was swiftly completed while I was still in the Isle of Wight, and was intended for *The Germ,* but that short-lived periodical expired before any fair opportunity offered for publishing the poem. *The Germ* aimed to be the exponent of the Præraphaelite principle of strict naturalism—the treating of a subject in all its details in exact conformity with the rationale of that particular subject, and thus excluding (in literature) exalted descriptive matter from any speech which professed to be a speech uttered in ordinary real life ; and I planned my poem upon the same model. *Mrs. Holmes Grey* purports to be a story of contemporary life ; the groundwork being given simply as a narrative, but all the more essential and passionate elements of it coming out in the form of conversation, and more especially in that of a newspaper report of a coroner's inquest. I tried to adhere to these conditions, and to make my newspaper report very much what it would really be in a newspaper, allowing of course for the fact that it assumed the form of blank verse and not of prose. My brother, who saw the poem soon after its completion, thought that I had met my self-imposed conditions, on the whole, very efficiently. Other intimates were of like opinion ; not indeed that they ignored any defects of abnormality in the story or want of elevation in the personages. As this com-

position could not be used in *The Germ*, and as I neither
found nor tried to find any other medium of publication, it remained by me several years, uninspected and
to all practical intents forgotten.   Towards 1861 I got
to see something of Mr. George Meredith, already
pretty well known to my brother, and I found to my
surprise that he expressed a very high opinion of *Mrs.
Holmes Grey* (which Dante Gabriel had shown him), and
he more than once urged me to publish it ; the like was
the case with my brother and my too generous friend
Mr. Swinburne.   I however, having by that date given
up any thoughts of figuring as a poet, staved off these
suggestions, and allowed the matter to drift as before.
Later on I was invited to contribute to a monthly
magazine, *The Broadway ;* and, nothing else being on my
hands to be offered, I bethought me of *Mrs. Holmes Grey*,
which saw the light accordingly in 1868, nineteen years
after it had been written.   Swinburne, the most munifi-
cent as well as magnificent of eulogists, continued more
than gracious to it ; and, were I to reproduce here the
praises which he accorded to the poem in more letters
than one, some readers might be apt to raise their eyebrows, and I (if age allowed me to do so) should assuredly
be bound to blush.   Another poet, James Thomson, the
author of *The City of Dreadful Night*, thought highly of
Mrs. Holmes Grey when he read it in 1874, and wrote to
me to say so.   A critic who afterwards became my
valued friend, Mr. Harry Buxton Forman, reviewed the
poem in *Tinsley's Magazine* in an article forming one of
a series which now makes a volume, *Our Living Poets*.
His estimate was moderate, mingling some praise with
a solid amount of stricture.   I have always supposed
that he came nearer the mark than Mr. Swinburne did,

although, if I *could* think the contrary, I should naturally prefer to adopt that alternative.   A woodcut illustration to *Mrs. Holmes Grey* in *The Broadway* was supplied
by Mr. Alfred Boyd Houghton, an artist of conspicuous
power, of whom I saw a little once and again.   I should
have liked to see more of him.   He suffered from very
defective eyesight, involving at times colour-blindness,
and he died in middle age.

The Germ gave me a good deal of occupation, from
late in 1849 till well on in 1850, in the way both of
writing contributions and of editing the magazine as a
whole.   The other contributors were all, or nearly all,
friends of mine.   We acted with a desire of mutual
accommodation, and I never found that the exercise of
my editorial powers, of which I did not make a nullity,
entailed any decree of soreness.   As I have acknowledged
in another instance, most of my own pieces in verse—
not all of them—were *bouts-rimés* performances.

The first distinguished poet whom I knew (I do not
here reckon William Bell Scott, who, though in some
essential respects a true poet, never achieved public
distinction) was Coventry Patmore.   Woolner made his
acquaintance in September 1849, and very soon afterwards I and other Præraphaelites were introduced to
him.   He was full six years older than myself.   His
only volume of poems as yet published was the first,
containing *The River*, *The Woodman's Daughter*, and two
or three other narratives ; my brother and I had read
and re-read it towards 1845, and delighted in it much,
and we came to Patmore fully primed to believe in and
admire him.   He contributed some prose and a little
verse to *The Germ*.   Patmore was a tall, rather thin
young man, with a protrusive nose and a large mouth,

and a general aspect more suggestive of a wit than of a
poet. He had a trick of blinking his eyes and smiling
a smile in which some self-opinion spiced a predomi-
nance of sarcasm. In manner he was a little dry, but
always pleasant and friendly within my observation.
His views upon matters of poetry and literature were
matured, and were very freely expressed. They were
received by the P.R.B.'s with much respect, but often
without acquiescence. Upon religion his views also
appeared to be matured ; but they were in fact, as the
event proved, only tentative and preparatory. He was
a strict Protestant and anti-Catholic Christian ; several
years later he became a fervent Catholic. Towards 1850
the religious book which was most in his favour, and
which he fruitlessly advised me to read, was *The Kingdom
of Christ*, by the Rev. Frederick Denison Maurice. Not
long before we first knew him, Patmore had married
Miss Emily Andrews, daughter of a dissenting minister
who had given some guidance to Ruskin ; she inspired
his poem *The Angel in the House*. There seems to be a
prevalent opinion, or a tradition, that Mrs. Patmore was
very beautiful ; we of the P.R.B. never thought so.
She was a slim and somewhat delicate-looking young
woman (indeed her state of health soon became subject
for grave anxiety), with dark hair and eyes, and a noticeably high nose ; polite and self-possessed in address, and
eminently gentle in demeanour. The mutual affection
of the pair was unmistakable. They lived in a small
house in the Camden Town district, upon slender means
(Mr. Patmore being at that time an assistant in the
British Museum Library), yet with an air of great propriety, not devoid of elegance. Afterwards they
removed to a rather retired dwelling near Highgate

Rise, which (as it happened) had previously been tenanted by my uncle Henry Polydore. At one or other of these houses I met once or twice my host's father, Mr. P. G. Patmore, author of the book entitled *My Friends and Acquaintances*.

Coventry Patmore showed himself very willing to give the P.R.B.'s any lift he could in the way of literary associations. He was well acquainted with several leading authors—among others, Tennyson. He invited some of us, or possibly all, to meet Tennyson at his house on 7 December 1849; this was not very long before the illustrious poet's marriage. I was impressed with Tennyson's massiveness, both intellectual and physical. He did not on that occasion come out much in conversation, and said perhaps hardly anything on matters of literature. The only point that I recollect in his talk is that he expressed an opinion that the abolition of the Corn Laws, and the Free-trade system, had been pushed on somewhat too hurriedly—it would have been better to achieve the same result by more gradual stages. He consented to sit to Woolner for a medallion-head, which proved a very good work of art. This, and some other employ obtained in Patmore's circle, formed a first beginning of Woolner's successes. There was still however a long interval before they could be brought to a head; he continued very scantily employed, and in July 1852 he made his way to Australia —trying gold-digging in the first instance, but soon afterwards resuming his sculptural profession in Melbourne. This again did not last long, and he returned to London, only a little better off than when he had quitted it.

Another poet whom we knew through Patmore was

William Allingham. This young Irishman, born in 1824, began corresponding with Patmore before knowing him in person ; he afterwards came on a short visit to London, and met the several members of the P.R.B. Patmore, I remember, entertained a very high opinion of the specimens which he saw of Allingham's verse ; but, for one reason or another, he did not like him as a man. I speak here solely of what I heard at that early date, towards the spring of 1850 ; for it may be (I am not competent to say one way or the other) that at a later period the two poets were on cordial terms of friendship. Allingham was a well-built man, hardly up to the middle height, with a thoughtful countenance, fairly regular features, crisp hair, and, under black eyebrows, a pair of very dark blue-grey eyes which I have rarely seen equalled. The " Celtic glamour " was at full in them. One could see him to be an Irishman, but in his speech there was only a faint trace of this. His voice was remarkably pleasing—distinct, low-pitched, deliberate, and in monotone, with a certain seeming air of slightingness or indifference. I have known more than one Irishman with a voice of this character. His talk was intellectual, with some sprightliness and some tartness, for he was far from inclined to take all the men he met, or whose writings he read, at their own valuation. My brother and I thought highly of Allingham's poems, or at least of the better specimens of them ; we liked his company and valued his friendliness. His marriage was a matter of much later date ; it was only about that time that I became acquainted with the delicately accomplished painter Mrs. Allingham (Miss Helen Paterson).

Through Patmore I also knew—but this was later on,

towards 1855—my excellent friend Dr. Richard Garnett, very youthful when I first met him and his fiancée. Dante Gabriel, I infer, did not see much of Dr. Garnett, nor indeed did I until some years afterwards. Some other Præraphaelites were perhaps unacquainted with him. Besides being remarkably accomplished and successful in verse, Dr. Garnett is renowned as a man of widespread knowledge, and one who has done the State not a little service as an official in the British Museum, and the daring adventurer of its printed catalogue. No man is easier to get on with than Dr. Garnett ; one never meets him in any other than a cheery humour, more than willing to do one any literary or personal service, big or small. Between him and me Shelley has moreover formed a bond of union ; and there seems to be in Shelley, more than in other poets, something which binds his sympathizers closely together. Just as I was writing this paragraph, I happened to see in *The Daily News* a notice of the death of Dr. Companyo, formerly head physician to the Suez Company. "He had a phenomenal memory," says the newspaper. "The late Khedive of Egypt offered to create a richly salaried post for him, that of ' Universal Remembrancer.' Ismail's idea, borrowed from Roman antiquity, was that, instead of resorting to dictionaries of dates, encyclopædias, and other such books, he should simply refer to Companyo, who would be sure to make him at once a satisfactory answer." If King Edward the Seventh had wanted a Universal Remembrancer, Dr. Garnett would have been the man for him. *Experto crede.* When in 1891 I was preparing for the Clarendon Press of Oxford an annotated edition of Shelley's *Adonais*, I wanted to ascertain which was the flower with inscribed petals

known to the Greeks as the hyacinth—for clearly the
inscribed petals have no application to our English
hyacinth. By mere chance I met Dr. Garnett in the
street, and to him I propounded my question. "Go,"
he replied, "to the British Museum Library, and get
out the *Georgics of Virgil with an English translation by
John Martyn*, 1755 ; you will find a long and lucid note
on the subject. Martyn with a y." He gave me the
number of the *Georgic*, and I am not sure but that he
gave me the page of the edition ; these I (who am not
a Garnett) have forgotten. I went to the Museum, and
found everything as he had said. Let me here acknowledge that the friendship of Dr. Garnett and his cultivated family has proved in later years as grateful to my
wife and children as to myself it has always been. They
were known to the Madox Brown family, including my
wife, before her marriage. The death of the amiable,
kindly Mrs. Garnett in 1903 came as a blow to all
of us.

There were two other officials of the British Museum
Library with whom Mr. Patmore brought me acquainted.
One was Mr. William Ralston, an uncommonly tall
young man, whose family had a long-pending lawsuit
which, if settled in their favour, would have made them
extremely rich ; ultimately it went against them. Mr.
Ralston was a Roman Catholic, and at one time a zealous
one ; he also in youth took personal part in works
of beneficence, acting as a sort of district visitor. The
Museum business did not suit his health ; he resigned,
and earned some repute as a translator from the Russian
(Turguenief, Tolstoy, etc.) and a lecturer on Russian
literature. The second of these Museum officials died in
early middle age, and I only met him once or twice—

Mr. Thomas Watts, a very ordinary sort of man to look at, with a puffy face. His memory was of the most surprising kind. I am not now clear whether (like Dr. Garnett's) it extended to literary matters in general, but it was specially conversant with the details of public libraries. He would tell you off-hand (so I was informed, and no doubt with truth) not only where a particular book—let us say Giolito's edition, 1555, of Dante's *Divina Commedia*—was to be found in the British Museum, the shelf, position on the shelf, press-mark, etc., but also the like particulars regarding the same book in the libraries of Paris, Vienna, and what not.

Mrs. Patmore had two or more sisters—one of them married to Mr. Orme, a prosperous rectifying distiller in London. The family—a large one—resided in Avenue Road, Regent's Park. It was not through the Patmores directly, but through Woolner, that I became acquainted with the Ormes. Mr. Orme was a sensible and hospitable man, not at all literary ; his wife however, a lady then not much turned of thirty, of rich physique, with luminous dark eyes, had a refined taste and a great liking for the society of writers and artists, and Mr. Orme seconded her with all goodwill. I was indebted to this family for much and constant kindness between some such years as 1850 and 1858, and have only myself to blame if later on I saw little of them. Here I met several well-known writers, and a few artists as well. David Masson, who was Professor of English Literature at University College, London (afterwards in Edinburgh University), editor of *Macmillan's Magazine*, and now Historiographer for Scotland, and who married the eldest Miss Orme ; Dr. Charlton Bastian, who

married another daughter ; Hepworth Dixon, whom
I knew otherwise as well ; and in a minor degree
Spencer Baynes, Alexander Bain, Andrew Findlater,
James Stansfeld, Mr. and Mrs. Peter Taylor, Douglas
Jerrold, Herbert Spencer, Frederick Tennyson, and his
sister Mrs. Jesse, who had been betrothed to Arthur
Hallam. This was a very lively little brunette lady, outspoken and full of character. She saw Christina once
or twice at Mrs. Orme's, and seemed to take a marked
fancy to her. The opportunity of meeting however
soon passed away, and nothing came of this. It may
also have been at Mrs. Orme's that I first met George
Henry Lewes ; at all events, I met him somewhere
in these early days, but I merely saw him casually on
and off. The only artist whom I particularly recollect
seeing here (beyond Woolner and some others of my
own set—Dante Gabriel was seldom present) was John
Brett the sea-painter, in his own line unsurpassed ; he
was a man of rather downright self-centred tone, in
some way related to the Ormes. He died not long
after I had written this sentence, and it surprised me to
observe how very scanty was the attention then paid
to his decease and to his performances in art, for there is
no one to succeed to the precise place which he occupied
with distinction.

A lady whom I encountered in the Ormes' house
pretty often was Miss Mary Haydon, daughter of the
celebrated painter who, wearied out at last with the
blows of adverse fortune, had in 1846 committed
suicide ; she it was who first found him lying dead and
bloodstained. She was a dark, handsome girl, with fine
features and dignified carriage, and was as modest and
sweet as she was attractive. A shadow seemed to hang

over her young life—either it was so or one fancied
it so. Soon her health gave way, and she died of a
decline, hardly (I presume) aged thirty. At a far later
date—1879—I saw something of her brother, Frank
Scott Haydon, when I was preparing to revise in the
Encyclopædia Britannica the article concerning the painter.
I decidedly liked this son—an official in the Record
Office. He was manly, with a decisive but far from
unconciliating address. After a while his mind seemed
to get unhinged (I know not the details), and, like his
father, he committed suicide. I have also spoken with
the other son, Frederic Wordsworth Haydon, who
brought out in 1876 the *Correspondence and Table-talk*
of the painter—a truly observable book. Benjamin
Robert Haydon had been a figure of much interest
to my brother and myself for some two or three years
before his death. We admired the intellectual and
elevated qualities in his pictures without supposing them
to be entire executive successes, and we thoroughly
sympathized in his gallant " alarums and excursions " in
the cause of " high art," and in his attacks upon many
attackable points in the constitution and management
of the Royal Academy. I attended the sale, ensuing
upon his death, of his remaining works and effects, and
thus saw the house he had dwelt in.

At the time when I was introduced to Mrs. Orme,
and for some while preceding and following, I was
a grievously shy youth. Anything in the way of self-
exhibition—whether I had to take my part in a dance,
or to read some short poem (I do not mean my own)
to the small company, or whatsoever else it may have
been—abashed me. And, indeed, some remnant of this
sort of shyness has stuck to me all my life. Shy

though I then was, I may have been not exactly back-
ward in speaking my mind, where perhaps self-effacement would have more beseemed my youth. I recollect
that on one occasion Mrs. Orme, walking with me in
her garden, told me in a tone of some slight displeasure
that on the last occasion of our meeting I had been
" sarcastic."   I did not seem well to know whether I
had really been sarcastic or not ; but I perceived that
I must somehow have laid myself open to observation,
and I reflected that, in that hospitable home at least,
I might as well in future keep my sarcasm to myself.
Sarcasm however is one thing, and an open, unrestrained
avowal of opinion and feeling is another.   I have always
liked plain speaking in other persons, and should feel
myself in the wrong if I had not, as a rule, practised it
on my own part.   In my special circle of P.R.B.'s and
others every one said very much what he liked.   There
was a common understanding that each person could
express himself with freedom without being misconstrued, and could be answered with freedom without
being annoyed.

I must now revert to *The Germ*, and to some acquaintances I made in connexion with that magazine ; more
directly in connexion with it than had been the case
with Coventry Patmore and his circle. My good friend
Major Calder Campbell, who contributed a sonnet to
The Germ, showed the magazine to Mr. Edward William
Cox (afterwards Serjeant Cox), who, besides being a
thriving barrister, was editor of more papers than one.
Among these was *The Critic*, a weekly review of much
the same class as *The Athenæum*, but far from competing
with it in point of popularity or circulation.   Mr. Cox
was a rather short man, not yet of middle age, with an

intelligent, agreeable face; he had married a daughter of
Mr. Fonblanque, the editor of *The Examiner*, whom I
met in the house once or twice. At a later date Serjeant
Cox became an assistant judge at the Middlesex Sessions,
and was prominent besides among the believers in
spiritualism; but of all this I saw nothing, as he had then
passed out of my ken. At his house I was introduced
to Mary Howitt, and her daughter Anna Mary, who
soon afterwards published a clever book, *The Art Student
in Munich*, and attained a very promising position as an
oil-painter. She also went off into spiritualism; dropped
painting in any form other than that of " spirit-draw-
ings "; and married Mr. Alfred Alaric Watts (son of
the better-known Alaric Alfred Watts), who happened
to be a colleague of mine in the Inland Revenue Office.
I did not meet at the Coxes' any other persons whose
acquaintance counted for anything in my after-years;
but I remember conversing there with the Rev. Robert
(commonly called Satan) Montgomery, author of the
poem of *Satan* which Macaulay made a laughing-stock.
He seemed to me agreeable enough. Mr. Cox was well
pleased with *The Germ*, and wrote in *The Critic* two very
laudatory articles upon it; he also at once invited me
to undertake the reviewing, in his paper, of picture-
exhibitions etc. I gladly closed with Mr. Cox's offer,
as it gave me a prospect, not only of doing some
practical work of a congenial kind, but more especially
of championing the cause of the Præraphaelite painters
at a time when every man's hand was against them, and
the abuse of their performances had reached a singular
excess of virulence. *The Critic* was at that period too
poor to pay for my contributions, so I had no inducement of money profit; not long afterwards its fortunes

rose considerably, and pay would have been forthcoming, but by that time I had transferred my services
to *The Spectator*. The chief cause of the advance of *The
Critic* in popularity was, I think, that it had published
long extracts from the *Life-drama* of Alexander Smith,
who was soon regarded as a protagonist of the so-called
" Spasmodic School" of poetry. As I had for years past
haunted the Royal Academy exhibitions, I took up my
task on *The Critic* with some fair current acquaintance
with British oil-painting,—with water-colour painting
much less. I soon fell into the way of forming and pronouncing an opinion upon works of art of all sorts ; it
was only the opinion of a youth of twenty, but it met with
acceptance from the editor of *The Critic*, and I surmise
from its readers as well. I was allowed a free hand,
and expressed myself with frankness to correspond. I
am afraid that some of my early articles (which I remember very imperfectly) must have been more aggres-
sive than was warranted by my years and experience.
Indeed, my object was not that of being civil to artistic
big-wigs, but rather of bringing forward the just claims
of younger men, some of them roundly abused, and
others but little noticed.

As I have come here to the beginning of my critical
career (or in fact it began even a trifle earlier, with some
literary reviews in *The Germ*), I will venture to say for
myself that I have never been an unconscientious critic.
I always looked carefully at works of art, and read books
heedfully and throughout, making notes as I proceeded.
I always endeavoured to form an unbiassed opinion, and
I always expressed it such as it was. For a little tartness of tone to artists or writers in the opposite camp,
or (what is still more difficult to avoid) for a little

smoothing down of edges when friends had to be dealt with, I ought perhaps to apologize, and so I do ; but I can honestly assert that, beyond this narrow margin, I never paltered with my personal perception (which may have been accurate or inaccurate) of the strict truth. If all my old critiques were to be reprinted (a chance which, if possible, would be formidable, for they might fill some stout volumes), and if I were to re-read them, I do not believe that I should in a single instance be compelled to confess to myself, "There I said what I knew to be neither true nor fair ; a bad personal motive was at the bottom of it." I may add that I should always have preferred, very much preferred, to sign my name to my criticisms, for I dislike the anonymous system in journalism and reviewing. I know that there are some plausible and even fair arguments in defence of it, but I regard the counter-arguments as far the more forcible. Very generally however I had no option in the matter, and by compulsion I wrote anonymously. At a later date, in *Fraser's Magazine*, *The Academy*, etc., I was free to sign, and I did so.

I have occasionally been asked what was the principle upon which I proceeded in framing my criticisms. I am not clear that there ever was any principle extending much beyond what I have just stated—the endeavour to form and to express an unbiassed opinion. There was however one rule—more a safeguard than a principle—upon which I constantly acted ; it is a convenient one for the critic himself, and I think it works well in the long run. This is the rule that, if one has to take up a many-sided subject—let us say, one of Ruskin's books, or a book treating of Dante, and works of both these kinds passed through my hands at times—the best thing is to deal with those aspects of the subject which one already knows something about, and to leave other aspects of it for the most part alone, instead of either trying to vamp them up in a hurry or expressing an opinion of no weight because not embodying any sound understanding of the matter. True, the critic who adopts this plan abstains from pretending to figure as omniscient ; but then he *is* not omniscient, and he had better not affect to be so. There must always in such cases be plenty for a critic to say from those points of view in which he possesses some competence.

My career as art-reviewer of *The Critic* only lasted from February to November 1850. I then, as already intimated, joined the staff of *The Spectator* in the like capacity. And thus it may be said that my connexion with *The Germ*, brief and inconspicuous though it was, exercised, by leading on to *The Critic* and *The Spectator*, a considerable influence upon my after-proceedings.

In 1850 the art-critic of *The Spectator* was Mr. William Smith Williams. It may be that Mr. Williams was in his younger days the author of some book or books, but of this I know nothing : he is best remembered at the present day as being the " reader " for the firm of Smith & Elder, and as having persuaded that firm that Charlotte Bronte's *Jane Eyre*, which had gone a-begging in vain to other publishers, was fully deserving of publication—with what result we know. The art-reviewing of Mr. Williams had in 1850 got *The Spectator* into some trouble, as a water-colour painter upon whom he had written an adverse critique resented this, and raised an action for libel against the publisher, and the jury had condemned the latter in damages. If I ever knew the details of this affair, I have long forgotten them. Mr. Williams consequently was about to resign his position on *The Spectator*, and in October was looking out for some writer whom he could recommend to the editor as his successor. One evening he was at the house of Mr. Lowes Dickinson, a portrait-painter well known and valued in my circle, afterwards a son-in-law of Mr. Williams. The latter was conversing on this topic; Madox Brown was present, and with his usual friendliness he brought my name forward. This was characteristic of Brown, not only as a friend, but also as a man inclined, at all periods of his life, to have confidence in *young* men, and to advocate their claims for employment. He thought that in many such cases the only thing wanted was opportunity; indeed, he had himself made a very early and efficient beginning with most matters—matrimony as well as painting. Thus it is a fact—and I acknowledge it with gratitude—that Madox Brown, if he set Dante Gabriel going in oil-painting, set me also going in the work of writing otherwise than gratis. Immediately after this I called upon Mr. Williams, whom I found living, with a very large family, in a very small house at Campden Hill, Kensington. He may then have been well turned of forty years of age, a pleasant-spoken man, with an open countenance and a fine crop of grey hair. I showed him some of my reviews in *The Critic;* he handed them to the editor of *The Spectator*, Mr. Rintoul. I was next invited to write, as for *The Spectator*, a notice upon some art subject of the day; and it happened just then that Sir Charles Eastlake was elected as President of the Royal Academy and Mr. Hook as an Associate. These formed my theme, my article found favour with the editor, and I was appointed.

I.—H

It was a matter of some surprise to me—and the surprise has increased as I grew older—that this appointment should fall to my lot. I was only just of age, had done but little writing of any kind, and in the way of art-criticism still less. What I had written in this line was favourable to the cause of the Præraphaelites, to whom *The Spectator* had as yet been hostile ; it had also been hostile, rather than otherwise, to *The Germ*, speaking of the poetry there as being an imitation of Tennyson, " pushed to an exaggeration of the master's exaggerations." Mr. Rintoul, who was proprietor as well as editor of *The Spectator*, was known to be one of the most capable journalists and editors in London, jealous of the character and repute of his paper, and well able to command, for any department of it, the services of able and accredited writers. Why he should have so readily closed with the proffer of a youngster, unknown to fame, and barely to be discerned as connected with the best-abused artists in the country, is anything but obvious. It might at least have been surmised that, having got hold of such a personage as art-critic, he would be disposed to dictate as to the tone of writing to be adopted ; but from this he entirely abstained. He left me at full liberty to form any opinions I liked, and to insert them in his paper, and he hardly ever interfered even as to the shape or diction of my articles. However, he did not pretend to any personal knowledge of fine-art matters, or to any particular interest in them, and it may be that he was not disinclined to try his chance with a new writer who, whatever else might be objected to him, bade fair to make something like a fresh start.

My salary on *The Spectator* was £50 a year, paid in

instalments now and again as best suited my convenience. With this moderate annual ' sum supplementing my salary in the Inland Revenue (which may now have been something like £110), I figured almost as a capitalist among the P.R.B.'s. Millais perhaps alone made more than this in the course of a year ; most of the others, much less or hardly anything. And with all of them the gains were precarious, not (as in my own case) settled and certain to come in. It should be understood however that I never used my small income as if it were so much pocket-money proper to myself ; it was treated as a part, and by this time a leading part, of the slender household resources.

Mr. Rintoul was a short, sturdy man, with a large head, well moulded, and full of character and resolution. He was a Scotchman, the architect of his own fortunes, and spoke with the rich Scottish intonation, but un-marked by provincial peculiarities—an intonation which I have always regarded as very superior to that of southern Englishmen. He belonged to the old school of Philosophical Radicals, and the tone of his paper was, rather than otherwise, in advance of the Liberal opinion of the day ; there was not however anything in it of the mere demagogue, but an air of dignified leader-ship and impartiality. *The Spectator*, founded by Mr. Rintoul, was the dearest weekly paper in London, nine-pence a number. By him and his I was treated with the most abundant kindness, and I found myself almost as much at home in his house—rather small apartments forming the upper storeys of the publishing office in Wellington Street, Strand—as in my own. Mr. Rin-toul's character and demeanour were energetic, and some people may have thought them a little severe ; he commanded respect. I gave him this, and affectionate regard as well.

The only important author whom I met in this house was Thackeray—and that (I think) only once. I may have seen and spoken to him on half a dozen other occasions, but cannot profess to have been known to him in any full sense of the term. I was a great admirer of his writings, from *Vanity Fair* (and indeed from several of his works earlier than that) to *The Book of Snobs*. In the little that I saw of him, I thought Thackeray, as a man, eminently genial and kindly-natured ; if there was aught of "cynicism" about him, I descried nothing of that. Much oftener than Thackeray, I saw in the same house Mr. Hogarth, the musical critic of *The Spectator* and father-in-law of Charles Dickens. This latter (I may here mention) I never encountered in society, but I just saw him two or three times—once as an actor, and a very forcible one, in Wilkie Collins's drama of *The Frozen Deep*. Mr. Hogarth was an affable, simple-mannered elderly gentleman, free from anything stiff or self-assertive. His daughter Mrs. Dickens was well known to the Rintouls (not at all to myself, though I believe I saw her once). When Dickens separated from her, I heard the matter canvassed in this family, and the verdict went dead against him. The principal literary authority of *The Spectator* was Mr. George Brimley, a Cambridge man and resident. I made his acquaintance in Cambridge in 1854, and saw him once or twice in London. He was of a more ' ionnish " order than most of my literary familiars, and I remember that he and I differed *toto cælo* about the Crimean War, then beginning, which he upheld rather ardently and I detested. We were on very good terms, how-

ever, for the little that I saw of him. Browning dubbed
him "George Grimly," on account of a not very well-
mannered observation about Mrs. Browning which Mr.
Brimley had put into print. The latter, a man of pale
countenance with a very tall forehead, was in poor
health ; he died towards 1860, in early middle age.

After I had discontinued the fine-art notices for *The
Critic,* in consequence of my engagement on *The Spectator,*
I took up, in the former paper, some general literary
reviews, principally of poems, and still without any pay.
A full number of very bad poems came to me, and a few
good ones. The reviews which I most recollect were on
the first volumes of Allingham and of George Meredith,
Beddoes's *Death's Jest-book,* and Bailey's *Angel World*
(now embodied in the reissues of *Festus*). There was
also a review of James Hannay's first novel, *Singleton
Fontenoy.* With much enthusiasm had my brother and
myself read and re-read *Festus,* towards 1847–8. *The
Angel World* appeared to me to be a manifest descent,
and I regretted afterwards to find it decanted bodily into
Festus, already an overbrimmed vessel of a most generous
vintage. This book-reviewing in *The Critic* may have
lasted for a year or so. I hardly recollect why I eventually discontinued it, but probably I judged that all
work and no pay had ceased to suit my interests, and
that I had quite enough to do otherwise. The art-
reviewing, when I dropped it, had been taken up by my
Præraphaelite Brother, Frederic Stephens. He and
Mr. Cox were not always at one on the subject, and he
left off after no very long experience.

I have here been following out my literary associations
and engagements consequent upon the action taken by
Major Calder Campbell in introducing *The Germ* to Mr.

Cox's notice. But this was not the only current of literary society into which that ill-fated serial led me.

One of the critiques which I wrote in *The Germ* was upon Arthur Hugh Clough's "Long-vacation Pastoral" in hexameters, *The Bothie of Toper-na-fuosich*, which I treated from a very admiring point of view. Dr. Heimann, who, as being professor of German in University College, knew something of Clough as principal of University Hall, showed him the review, and afterwards introduced me to him at a soirée; this was the only occasion when I had a little talk with Clough. He was a bulky man, with a rather hesitating way in talking; not the sort of figure that one perceives to conform to the poetic or literary type. He treated his youthful critic with much courtesy, but our interview closed without my feeling that I had gained any great additional insight into his personality.

John Abraham Heraud was in those days a poetic writer of some name. He was chiefly known by a long poem entitled *The Descent into Hell* (i.e. Christ in Hades). I have not read it, but suppose it to be a Miltonic experiment of some force. There was an anecdote that Douglas Jerrold had once been accosted by a friend with the inquiry, " Have you seen Heraud's Descent into Hell ? " " No," replied Jerrold, " I only wish I had." To Mr. Heraud (as to Mr. Cox) *The Germ* was produced by Major Calder Campbell. Heraud thought extremely well of it, and asked me, as the editor, to pass an evening in his house. The house was, I think, in Pentonville or Islington ; there were no signs of affluence about it, for Heraud was anything but a prosperous author. Several guests were present, and sat down to a hospitable though not *recherché* supper.

Heraud, I understood, had been a diligent acolyte at the shrine of Coleridge in the poet's latter days ; some one now asked him to deliver a Coleridgean oration, and he did so, not a little to my bewilderment.   This rhetorical feat did not seem to be regarded by the company as a joke, only as an animated " take-off."   I have quite forgotten what it was about ; and indeed I could not at the moment have defined such a point, for to me it seemed to have neither head nor tail, and only a very vaporous middle.   Here I met Hervey, the editor of *The Athenæum*, for which Mr. Heraud at this time acted as dramatic critic ; James Westland Marston the dramatist (his principal work as yet produced may have been *The Patrician's Daughter*) ; and Miss Glyn the actress. Miss Edith Heraud, our host's daughter, was then training for the stage.   While we were in the front room, she, in the unlit back room, recited the monologue of Juliet on her wedding-night ; the main object being to obtain the benefit of Miss Glyn's opinion as to her qualifications as a dramatic elocutionist.

A few words about these various new acquaintances. Mr. Heraud, then I conjecture getting on towards fifty, was a man under the middle height, with long dark hair ; there was some suggestion of Judaism in his face, but this may have been fallacious.   Mr. Hervey was one of the unsightliest little men that I ever saw : short, stumpy, and podgy, with unchiselled features. Dr. Marston was of a good height and fairly well-looking.   I immediately afterwards went round to his house by invitation ; and soon I saw there his small son Philip Bourke Marston, afterwards known as " the blind poet "; it was then already more than suspected that his blindness would be total and lifelong.   I was also

introduced to Miss Muloch (Mrs. Craik), who had
published something, and who became the highly
popular author of *John Halifax, Gentleman*, and other
novels. Miss Glyn, who was a member of Phelps's
celebrated Shakespearean company at Sadler's Wells
Theatre, had earned great renown in the characters of
Cleopatra, the Duchess of Malfi, etc. She had an
ample form and fine presence, and a face which, though
not specially intellectual, was handsome and gracious.
Both my brother and I admired her very much in some
parts, but not when she attempted lightsome characters
such as Shakespear's Beatrice. I felt it a privilege to
make her acquaintance, and was permitted to call at her
apartments, where she introduced me to the veteran
Charles Kemble, who had superintended her stage training. He was a fine old gentleman, of stately politeness,
partially deaf.

Miss Glyn appears to be nearly, though not absolutely,
the only theatrical personage, of either sex, that I ever
knew a little in private society. I will confess—it is
one of my weaknesses—that I have always had a certain
abstract distaste for theatrical people, and for all persons
whose vocations or propensities induce them to make an
exhibition of themselves in public. This, it may be
said, would include lecturers; but I, however untrue
herein to my colours, have since 1875 been in a few
instances a lecturer myself. This sentiment of distaste
must be inherited by me, more definitely, from my
mother and her father Polidori; but even my father,
although in his youth closely connected with stage-
doings, had a touch of the same feeling. He could
almost have echoed, with regard to dramatic and musical
artists, the vigorous utterance of the great painter

David, that if one were to cannonade all the artists in one solid squad not a single patriot would be slain. Of Miss Glyn (afterwards named Mrs. Dallas-Glyn) and Dr. Marston I continued to see something up to nearly the close of their lives, though at long-separated intervals ; much more did I see of Philip Bourke Marston when grown up. Of Mr. Heraud and Mrs. Craik I lost sight ; Mr. Hervey died within a few years ensuing. I also knew Mr. Edward S. Dallas—whom Miss Glyn married, but the union did not continue long. She used to address him as " Hal "—to suggest (I presume) some analogy between him and the brilliant young Prince, afterwards Henry V, in Shakespear's dramas. He was a singularly handsome man, a Scotchman, but one might almost have taken him for a Spaniard or Italian at first sight. He was as stately as a sculptured king from among the Ninevite marbles. Dallas came to London from Scotland, and joined the staff of *The Times;* a book called *The Gay Science* (on the art of criticism) was his principal work, but it remained uncompleted at the date of his comparatively early death. He wrote some poems, with which I am not familiar.

Another poet who expressed himself pleased with *The Germ* was Richard Hengist Horne, author of *Orion*, which used to be termed "the farthing epic," owing to a freak regarding its published price. I sent him a copy of the magazine, and he acknowledged it in handsome terms, adding his very reasonable conviction that it would not sell. I saw Mr. Horne once or twice—a sturdy, rather short man, not of prepossessing physique. I do not seem to have been introduced to him, nor to have spoken with him at all.

I will here introduce a personal detail, though it has

nothing to do with my "beginnings in literature."
Some people undergo mishaps which raise a smile rather
than a compassionate sigh. I am one of them. In boyhood I had an uncommonly thick crop of black hair;
but towards 1848 it began thinning, and by June 1850,
before I was of age, this process had reached such a pass
that I was advised to have my head wholly shaved as
the most likely method of retrieval. I acquiesced, and
wore a wig for a year or so. The wig was eventually
¹iscarded, but the hair was not recovered. Thus I have
been a baldish or bald man throughout my adult life.
This, in youth, was anything but pleasant to me. In
particular, I used to dislike entering a theatre or other
public place with my hat on, looking, as I was, quite
juvenile, and then, on taking off my hat, presenting an
appearance more like a used-up man of forty. People
who knew little of the facts were wont to tell me that
my baldness must be due to overstudy or (according to
some) to premature dissipation. But the truth is—and
I have already confessed it—that I had not studied half
enough; and I had dissipated not at all—unless the
mere habit of keeping late hours at night is to count as
dissipation. I could never myself divine why I had
become bald, except indeed that my two maternal
uncles had been in the like case at an early age, and
perhaps therefore baldness ran in that line of the family.

IX

MY FATHER'S LAST YEARS

ABOUT the time when I joined *The Spectator*, November 1850, the family were arranging for a removal from the house we had so long inhabited— 50 Charlotte Street, Portland Place. The main object must have been to pay a rather lower rent, and with this was combined a project that my mother, assisted by Christina, might open a little day-school in a fresh neighbourhood. Towards the beginning of 1851 we removed to No. 38 Arlington Street, Mornington Crescent (it is now merged in Arlington Road). The house may have been somewhat inferior to the one in Charlotte Street, but it sufficed for our immediate requirements, and possessed the advantage of a garden, which, small though it was, proved often welcome to my father for a little pacing up and down. He no longer went out of doors to any extent worth mentioning. The day-school was set up, and was certainly very well conducted by my mother, diligently seconded by Christina. It was not however in any sense a paying success. The pupils were a few daughters of neighbouring tradesmen, the hairdresser, the pork butcher, etc. I cannot remember that there was even one daughter of any professional man. The whole family were housed in No. 38 Arlington Street, including Dante Gabriel. He had a studio

elsewhere, and in November 1852 he removed wholly
to Chatham Place (No. 14), Blackfriars Bridge ; and
thenceforth his address was always separate from ours.
By the opening of 1851 he was already a painter of some
little note, having exhibited (not in the Royal Academy)
two oil pictures—*The Girlhood of Mary Virgin* in
1849, and *The Annunciation* now in the National
British Gallery, in 1850.   He was, besides, known
to town - talk as a member of the much - canvassed
and bitterly decried Præraphaelite Brotherhood.   The
former of these paintings he had sold readily to the
Marchioness Dowager of Bath ; the latter remained
unsold in 1851, but it found a purchaser early in 1853.
In this year (1853) my brother executed the pencil
drawing of our father, showing his surroundings in
Arlington Street, which has been reproduced in my
Memoir of Dante Gabriel Rossetti ; it is both accurate and
characteristic as a likeness.

As the day-school in Arlington Street barely paid its
expenses, Mrs. Rossetti, still unflinching, cast about for
some other means of keeping things afloat.   She and
her daughters, but more especially the daughters, were
now in sympathy with the High Church or " Puseyite "
section of the English Church.   A very High Church
clergyman, Dr. Bennett, had recently been ousted from
St. Barnabas Church, Pimlico, and had then been forthwith presented by the Marchioness Dowager of Bath to
the living of Frome-Selwood, Somerset.   It was thought
that, under the wing of Dr. Bennett, there might be a
better chance for a Rossetti day-school in Frome-
Selwood than in Camden Town ; so in the spring of
1853 off went my mother and Christina to the Somerset
town, and my father followed soon afterwards.   This

was grievous to all of us. To divide the family party between two such remote localities was the very last thing that my mother, in especial, could have tolerated, save at the clear call of duty and the bidding of hard necessity. They three settled in Brunswick Place, Fromefield, Frome, and there a new day-school was started. I never learned that Dr. Bennett did much to promote it, and, like its predecessor, it did not promote itself. It may possibly have turned out rather the less unsuccessful of the two. The pupils were, I take it, of much the same class as in Arlington Street—daughters of local tradesmen or farmers ; not one whose means or prospects in life courted the full range of cultivation which that particular schoolmistress and her assistant would have been well able to impart. Frome was then, and perhaps still is, a countrified sort of market-town with steepish streets to go up and down, and a good deal of pleasurable ruralism in the immediate neighbourhood. This latter feature was attractive to my mother and sister ; my father was beyond the chance of profiting by it.

My mother was of a placid, uncraving temperament, with a great trust in Providence ; a woman who, as long as she felt conscious of doing her duty according to her opportunities, was not likely to fret much as to the field in which such duty was exercised. Christina likewise was ready to undertake any sort of educational drudgery to which circumstances might relegate her, and to perform it unrepiningly ; still she was not at all unconscious of her poetic powers — amply proved to all discerning eyes by her contributions to *The Germ ;* she chafed at the separation from her sister and brothers ; and, having previously had more than enough standing cause for low spirits, she was anything but happy at Frome. She tried while there, rather less at haphazard than at other times, to do something in the way of drawing and water-colouring. Although she clearly had not any special vocation to fine art, and did not even possess, at any period of her life, that instinctive perception which enables one to say with assurance, "This work of art is good and that is bad," she now sketched one or two likenesses which were not amiss; and I suppose that, taking the necessary pains, she could have managed that moderate average of attainment which is within the reach of so many experimenters in art. Both Madox Brown and Dante Rossetti had a rather favourable opinion of her powers. Manifestly she had more ideas and more fancy than a large proportion of beginners. However, Christina's aspirations never pointed in the direction of being "pretty tolerable" in any intellectual or artistic pursuit—as for instance in music, for which she had no genuine gift. She did not afterwards continue, even with the same zest as at Frome, her attempts in drawing, and soon she dropped them altogether.

While still settled at Frome, my mother lost both her parents. Her mother, so long an invalid, died in April 1853, and her father in December. They were both octogenarians; he very nearly a nonagenarian. His faculties were not seriously decayed even at the last.

As I have already intimated, my father's health was quite broken for years before he quitted London. He had more than one stroke of paralysis. This did not permanently bereave him of the use of his limbs nor of speech, but it impaired his physical powers, and told to some extent on his mind. Not that he was in any con-

dition trenching upon senile dotage ; the numerous
poems, religious, patriotic, and political, which he continued inditing in profusion almost up to the last, attest
this sufficiently.   It had been hoped that residence in
country air might improve his health ; no definite result
of this kind ensued, and week by week it became increasingly apparent that he had not long to live.   He
bore his troubles and his banishment from London with
patience, but he would have much preferred reunion in
London for the whole family, had circumstances permitted it.

When my father and mother with Christina removed
to Frome, Maria and I had to shift for ourselves.   We
remained in the house in Arlington Street up to the
close of our tenancy, Christmas 1853.   We then took
lodgings over the shop of a chemist in Albany Street,
Regent's Park, near the Euston Road end of the street.
Here we were comfortable enough in our small way.
The chemist was a Norfolk man, Mr. Robert P. Burcham, who, as it turned out, was a water-colour amateur
of no small merit, in the line of still-life, flowers, mossy
hedges, etc.   He was well acquainted with the great
master in this class of art (and not in this alone),
William Henry Hunt, of the Old Water-colour Society,
and I now possess a portrait of Burcham done by Hunt,
which the former bequeathed to me.   He died towards
1894, at a good old age.   He moreover bequeathed to
Christina an example of his own art.   She had always
kept up acquaintance with him, and also with Miss
Bowen, a lady of advanced age who, at first a lodger in
his Albany Street premises, had removed with him to
other quarters, where they kept house together.   Mr.
Burcham was truly an estimable man, modest and un-

pretending, and rather shrinking from coming forward in any way. In his section of the Albany Street house I first encountered the physician Dr. Jenner, afterwards Queen Victoria's physician, Sir William Jenner, Bart. He was for many years, up to the date when he retired from professional practice, the doctor whom Christina consulted in any serious illness ; my brother also in some few instances sought his advice. Besides having my lodging in Albany Street, I was frequently along with Dante Gabriel in Chatham Place ; there I often passed not only the evening but the night, and was not less at home than himself.

The secession to Frome continued not long, barely a year. About the end of the summer of 1853 I received notice at Somerset House that I should soon be promoted to a higher post, with a salary of £250 and annual increments ; the promotion came to effect just before I was twenty-four years of age. With this salary, supplemented by what I received from *The Spectator*, and with the small income which my mother possessed consequent upon the death of her parents, and with that which Maria made from teaching, I saw that we could all manage to get on in one household in adequate comfort ; providing for my father's closing days, and relieving my mother and Christina from moiling, and moiling unremuneratively, at a semi-vitalized school. I made and enforced the proposal ; my mother, lovingly stipulating to safeguard my personal interests present or prospective, assented ; and by Lady Day 1854 we were all reinstalled in London. I took a house, No. 45 Upper Albany Street, not far from the Horse Guards Barracks ; after a few years it was re-numbered as 166 Albany Street. This continued to be our residence up to Midsummer 1867. The house presents a rather dejected appearance outside, facing the back entrances of a terrace-row which overlooks Regent's Park. Inside the house is far from spacious ; but it might count as being superior, rather than inferior, to any of the three family dwellings in which I had previously been domiciled. My mother and sisters here continued to be near Margaret, Philip, and Eliza Polidori. These three, after the death of their parents, had broken up the common home in Park Village East, and had severally taken lodgings in the same neighbourhood ; they no longer lived together, owing to Eliza's taste for untrammelled independence. My two aunts were naturally often in our house ; not often my uncle, whose weak-mindedness assumed a more confirmed tincture of eccentricity, leading to a very solitary mode of life. He died in 1864. Margaret Polidori was invited by us to give up her lodgings, and to tenant two rooms in our house. This she did, without becoming, in the full sense, a member of our own household ; and here she died in February 1867.

When my father reached London the hand of death was upon him, but for some few days nothing occurred to deepen seriously the anxiety which his condition had excited for months and years past. It was on the 16th April, Easter Sunday, that the final phase of his illness began, and Mr. Stewart, a medical man whom we employed on all ordinary occasions, was called in. On the 22nd Dr. Hare, a physician of reputation who had also advised us for several years past, was summoned as well. The particulars which I append are condensed from memoranda kept at the time by my mother and some others of the family.

I.—I

"Dr. Hare confirmed Mr. Stewart's opinion. Told me my husband is suffering from an eruption of the nature of carbuncle ; and that he considers him in a highly dangerous state, on account of the accompanying debility and diabetes.—24th April. My husband so anxious to get up that I dressed him, and led him in to breakfast. On entering the room, he said, ' *Quanto ho anelato questo momento !*'[1] Observed he supposed William was gone. On hearing the contrary, expressed his delight. Took his breakfast without assistance. Sat afterwards apparently reading, but began to droop exceedingly, and, while I was supporting his head, an alarming change took place in his countenance. Mr. Stewart advised that he should go to bed directly. Dr. Hare said he was suffering much from fever, and ended by giving me very little hope of his recovery. He passed the night in great weakness, almost total extinction of voice ; but perfect consciousness, which was evinced by his opening his eyes, and answering as well as he could to everything we said, recognizing each separately.—25th. In the afternoon he became worse, and was clearly sinking ; restless at intervals, but generally quiet, breathing with tolerable ease. So he continued all night. His eyes looked affection, and he was conscious to our call, answering to the prayers I read from an Italian translation of the Liturgy.—26th. He died without one struggle at half-past five p.m. I, his four children, my three sisters, and his cousin Teodorico Pietrocola-Rossetti, were present at the moment.—27th. The certificate stated the cause of death to be "old age, marasmus."—May 3rd. To Highgate Cemetery, where the service was beautifully performed, and my dear

[1] How I have been longing for this moment !

husband was buried in a very deep grave contiguous to
that of Mr. Ford Madox Brown's wife. I, all his
children, Teodorico, my three sisters, and my brother
Philip, accompanied him to the grave.—[Maria remembers the following]. On 23rd April he said to me
[Mrs. Rossetti] ' *Com' è che Pepe è stato meco in letto ?* '[1]
Also, ' *Dov' è mia madre ?* '[2] I said, ' Don't you remember
she died long ago in Italy ? ' He replied, ' *È stata
meco.*'[3] In the night from 24th to 25th, William being
present, I said, ' *Lo conoscete ? È Guglielmo.*'[4] He
replied, ' *Lo veggo, lo sento, mi stà scritto nel cuore.*'[5]
More than once, when Maria said to him, ' *Dove
sentite dolore?*' he replied, ' *Dove non lo sento ?*'[6] He
seemed to understand the prayers I read the first two
times ; the third is doubtful.—[William remembers also
the following]. At one moment he said, ' *Che consolazione
aver tutti i figli intorno a me ! E non poter vederli !*'[7]
His last emphatic words, in a loud voice, about eight in
the evening of Tuesday the 25th, after some hours of
almost loss of speech, were, ' *Ah Dio, ajutami Tu !*'[8] At
nine a.m. on the 26th, as William kissed him on the
cheek, he kissed William twice. This was the last very
distinct sign of consciousness towards him.—[The follow-

1 " How is it that Pepe was with me in bed ? " This was General
Guglielmo Pepe, much beloved and admired by my father, and still (I
think) living in April 1854. He had been the hero of the Neapolitan
Revolution in 1820, and of the defence of Venice in 1848-9.

2 Where is my mother ?   3 She was here with me.

4 Do you know him ? It is William.

5 I see him, I hear him, he is written in my heart.

6 " Where do you feel pain?" " Where do I *not* feel it ? "

7 What a consolation to have all my children around me ! And not
to be able to see them !

8 " Ah God, help me Thou." The words have been introduced into
the inscription on Gabriele Rossetti's tombstone.

ing is Christina's] : Mr. Cayley called twice at the very last, and waited, but did not see my father, much endearing himself to us."

This last observation relates to the Mr. Charles Bagot Cayley whom I have mentioned on page 36 as a pupil of my father for Italian, and afterwards a translator of Dante.

Having more than once, in other writings, recorded some estimate of my father's character, I will not here appraise it, further than to say that, of all the men whom I have closely known, he was the one in whom the emotion of patriotism was most manifestly strong ; strong as a sense of duty, and strong as a personal sentiment. Filippo Pistrucci was on much the same level as Gabriele Rossetti. I have never known a British subject to whom patriotism seemed so definitely to form the permanent platform of life ; but it may be said, and said with justice, that Rossetti and Pistrucci were exiles, and that therefore the idea of their native country was necessarily more specialized to their minds and feelings than can be the case with a man who continues to live undisturbed in the land of his birth.

Rossetti had made a will leaving everything to his wife. Everything amounted to hardly anything ; there was a little household furniture, along with some few books. There was also the copyright in his own works. No proceeds have ever been forthcoming from them, but it seems within the bounds of possibility that something might yet be realized at some future time. Indeed, as I write (July 1903), Professor Ciampoli, the Librarian of the Biblioteca Vittorio Emanuele in Rome, has, as he informs me, come to terms with a publisher for the production of Rossetti's complete Poetical Works, to be followed probably by his Prose Works. Any proceeds accruing to the Professor are to go towards carrying out the long-pending project of a monument to Rossetti in Vasto ; and there might even, it is suggested, be a monument in Rome as well.   One of the works which Rossetti left to his widow was the *Mistero dell' Amor Platonico*, of which numerous copies came into her hands. She had always regretted the writing of this book, as being dangerous to the religion which she professed and earnestly believed in ; and after a while she burned the entire stock.   When I heard of this long afterwards, I was sorry ; but she had acted within her rights and according to her own sense of duty, and there was no more to be said.   That act is the only one ever performed by my mother having some colouring of bigotry, for, though religious, she was in no way fanatical, nor even prejudiced

And so Gabriele Rossetti, one of the poets of the earlier stages of the Italian reawakening, lies at peace in the land of his exile.   Towards 1871 we were rather urgently pressed to allow his remains to be transported to Italy for ceremonial reinterment ; but, with the exception of my brother, we were all decidedly opposed to any such procedure, and the scheme had to be dropped.   The same grave now contains the bodies of his daughter-in-law Elizabeth Eleanor Rossetti, my brother's wife, 1862 ; Frances Mary Lavinia Rossetti, his widow, 1866 ; and Christina Georgina Rossetti, his daughter, 1895. Close by, in the grave of Elizabeth Brown (the maternal grandmother), lies my infant son Michael Ford Madox Rossetti, 1883.   Some of the Polidoris also are buried in Highgate Cemetery, but in other graves.

X

SOME SHAPING OF MIND
AND CHARACTER

THIS may be the best point at which to introduce a
few observations—going back however to a much
earlier date in my narrative.

A certain enlargement of mind should come natural
to the juniors in a family wherein the seniors show
marked differences in religious or general opinion; if
there is a difference of nationality as well, the effect
will be all the greater. These influences told upon me.
Under such conditions a boy is saved from imagining
that the last word has been said upon some highly
important subjects, and that the only course for him to
adopt is to follow in line with his great-grandfather.

In the Rossetti and also in the Polidori family these
differences of opinion prevailed.

Gaetano Polidori was nominally a Roman Catholic;
and, as his general temperament disposed him to stability
in all things, and thus to conservatism, he evinced no
sort of wish that Roman Catholics or Christians should
either abjure or belittle their religion. At the same
time he had himself—so far as I saw—no dogmatic form
of faith at all : his tone of mind on such subjects
assimilated more to what one finds in Latin authors—
a Cicero or a Horace. He never went to any place of
worship ; not at least in my time, though I gather that,

for mere conformity's sake, he did so at a much earlier date. According to a compact made prior to his marriage, his sons were all brought up as Roman Catholics, his daughters as Protestants in the English Church. Of his sons, the only one who had an intellectual tendency, Dr. John Polidori (the travelling physician of Lord Byron in 1816), was dead some years before my birth ; he was, I suppose, sceptical rather than irreligious. Philip, as being weak-minded, did not count. Henry, a man of ordinarily fair capacity, but rather limited in range, was a very strict Roman Catholic, and such he continued up to his death in 1885. I think he made at times some endeavours (not of a surreptitious kind) to convert my sisters to the Roman Church ; with me he never did so, but I have occasionally attended a Catholic chapel in his company. Mrs. Polidori was a religious woman according to the then standard of the Church of England, long anterior to any Oxford movement or Puseyism or ritualism ; all her daughters were equally religious, constant and zealous church-goers. There were four of them—Margaret, my mother Frances, Charlotte, and Eliza. My mother was the only married one, and stood obviously foremost in point of mental faculty. Her religious belief was solid, her religious feeling warm ; yet her tone was not exactly that of a devotee, but quiet and unobtrusive, and her faith was chiefly evinced as a perpetual rule of conduct.

Gabriele Rossetti resembled Polidori, in so far as he was both a nominal Roman Catholic and an abstainer from all public acts of worship ; but he felt and thought a deal more about religious matters than I could ever perceive my grandfather to do. He had a great rever-

ence and fixed regard for the fundamentals of the
Christian religion, or (to reduce the thing to its simplest
terms) for the gospel utterances of Jesus Christ ; but
besides being a vehement opponent of all papal and
sacerdotal pretensions, he dissented altogether (so I
apprehend) from Catholic or ecclesiastical dogmas, and
from the supernatural or legendary elements in the
Christian tradition. He wrote ponderous volumes to
prove that Dante, Petrarch, and other great writers,
were in reality anti-Christians ; and I consider that, in
all the years while he was thus writing, or until I was
well advancing into manhood, he mainly agreed in the
opinions which he thus attributed to these famous men.
I allow that passages might be cited from most of his
writings, and especially from those pertaining to the
closing years of his life, which tell in the contrary direction ; these passages are partly prudential or self-protec-
tive, and partly the outcome of a frame of mind less
vigorous and alert than that of his prime. Let me
repeat however that, while I do not regard my father as,
even towards the close of his life, within the pale of
dogmatic orthodoxy, I am fully conscious of the vener-
ation with which he always contemplated the person and
the mission of Jesus. He thought Christianity—such
as it was announced by its founder—to be the essence of
true religion.

Surrounded as I thus was from infancy by persons
entertaining divergent forms of faith or of speculative
opinion, it stands to reason that I soon came face to face
with the problem—What is that I myself believe in ?
Do I agree, or most nearly agree, with my mother or
with my father ? with my uncle the Roman Catholic or
with my aunt the Protestant ? (The idea of being an

"Anglican," and in that sense a Catholic, did not exist in the early years of which I am speaking—or at all events had not permeated our household.) I rapidly found that I agreed most nearly with my father or my grandfather. My bringing up had, indeed, been wholly religious—my mother taking me, with the rest of the children, to churches of the English establishment, and instructing me out of the Bible, Prayer Book, Church Catechism, and the like. Neither did my father interfere with this—he never presented his own opinions to me in any concrete form, nor even advised me to ponder before adopting or professing any particular conviction. I was however quite aware that there was "a great gulf fixed" between his ideas on these subjects and those of the doctrinal Christians in the family. I can remember too that on one exceptional occasion he made a vigorous *sortie*, commenting upon the scriptural narrative of Abraham ordered by Jehovah to sacrifice Isaac, and saying that he himself, under the like conditions, would have responded, *Tu non sei Dio, sei il diavolo!*[1] Nothing was neglected which might have made religion persuasive to me ; it was presented in a clear, unambiguous form, impressed upon me but not "forced down my throat" ; and it came recommended by the tender kindness and bright example of my mother—not to speak of my sisters, whose feelings and habits always pointed to religion as the needle to the pole. Moreover, there was not any rooted antipathy on my own part to religious practices ; I took no particular pleasure in going to church or saying my prayers, but was also not seriously reluctant. But all would not do. Either my mind is naturally sceptical, and difficult to convince of one side

---

[1] Thou art not God, thou art the devil !

of any truth to the total exclusion of the other ; or else the balance of reflection (such as I was capable of) went definitely down in a certain direction. I can hardly have been fourteen years of age when the Christian faith, as a scheme of mysteries and miracles—and with this any and every form of faith involving a supernatural mythology—became inoperative upon my mind ; and so it has always remained. I am not weak enough to plume myself upon this fact, which simply depends upon the constitution (be it a good or a bad one) of my mind ; there is no reason why a " free-thinker " should be a potent thinker, or a devotee a weaker vessel. A fact it is, and, being a fact, it has claimed a place in these reminiscences.

The term " Agnostic " was not invented in those years. As soon as it got invented, I found it to be the clearest and the simplest definition of my mental position in relation to the supernatural—a position which amounts to this ; that a number of things are affirmed by many people concerning matters beyond their observation, and beyond mine ; and that, as I know nothing about those things, and am not conscious that anything can be known about them, I likewise *profess* to know nothing. The affirmations *may* be true, but I do not know nor particularly surmise them to be so.

It appears to me natural that an Agnostic should be more or less a necessitarian or fatalist ; such is the case with me. The one thing that seems pretty clear to an Agnostic as regards the constituent parts of the universe is that they are a series of effects arising from causes. The theologian may say: " Yes, causes going up to a First Cause, namely, God. Then why will not you, the Agnostic, openly entertain and avow your belief in the First Cause?" But this will not quite do for the Agnostic. He replies : " I postulate a cause for every effect ; therefore I must postulate a cause for your professed First Cause. You say (and this appears to be an inevitable deduction) that there was not any cause for the First Cause. And I rejoin, if there was not any cause for the First Cause, then I will stick to the ultimate cause that I can with any clearness trace, namely, the universe as cognizable by the senses and the intellect; and I acknowledge (it is the very essence of my agnosticism) that I don't know whether there was or was not a further cause beyond that ultimate-traced cause. There may have been ; but I, unfortunate and limited creature, know not of it." A convinced belief in causes and effects appears to me to be practically a belief in necessity. As Philip James Bailey says in his dedicatory sonnet to *Festus*, "Nature means necessity"—a very terse aphorism, and, I conceive, as true as it is terse. When I was a boy of fourteen I first read, and read with rapture, the poems of Shelley, including *Queen Mab*. Rather later on I read the Notes to *Queen Mab*. I acknowledge that these Notes are not the acme of sound philosophical speculation ; but some things in them appeared to me then, and still appear, cogent enough. Here are a few sentences (I do not give anything like the full context). " He who asserts the doctrine of Necessity means that, contemplating the events which compose the moral and material universe, he beholds only an immense and uninterrupted chain of causes and effects, no one of which could occupy any other place than it does occupy, or act in any other way than it does act. Motive is, to voluntary action in the human mind, what cause is to effect in the material universe. The

word liberty, as applied to mind, is analogous to the word
chance as applied to matter : they spring from an
ignorance of the certainty of the conjunction of antecedents and consequents. The advocates of free-will
assert that the will has the power of refusing to be
determined by the strongest motive. But the strongest
motive is that which, overcoming all others, ultimately
prevails. This assertion therefore amounts to a denial
of the will being ultimately determined by that motive
which does determine it, which is absurd." Shelley also
quotes a passage from the once much-perused French
book by Baron von Holbach, *Le Système de la Nature.*
"Dans un tourbillon de poussière qu'élève un vent
impétueux, quelque confus qu'il paraisse à nos yeux, il n'y
a pas un seul molécule de poussière qui soit placé au
hasard ; qui n'ait sa cause suffisante pour occuper le lieu
où elle se trouve, et qui n'agisse rigoureusement de la
manière dont elle doit agir. Dans les convulsions
terribles qui agitent quelquefois les sociétés politiques, et
qui produisent souvent le renversement d'un empire, il
n'y a pas une seule action, une seule parole, une seule
pensée, une seule volonté, une seule passion, dans les
agens qui concourent à la révolution comme destructeurs
ou comme victimes, qui ne soit nécessaire, qui n'agisse
comme elle doit agir, qui n'opère infailliblement les effets
qu'elle doit opérer, suivant la place qu'occupent ces
agens dans ce tourbillon moral. Cela paraîtrait evident
pour une intelligence qui serait en état de saisir et
d'apprécier toutes les actions et réactions des esprits et
des corps de ceux qui contribuent à cette révolution."
These words, written shortly before the great French
Revolution, read like an ominous forecast.

The motto of the ducal family of Bedford, written

over Covent Garden Market, " *Che sarà sarà*,"[1] was familiar to my eye in boyhood : it has been present to my mind, as a far-reaching and regulative truth, all my life.

From my father, and also, though in a very minor degree, from my mother, I received in boyhood a certain bias in relation to political or national problems; and here again this same bias continues to be mine to the present day. My father was an earnest advocate of free nationalities, free institutions, independence of thought. He had suffered in the cause of constitutional liberty, and he longed, and indeed worked, for the emancipation of Italy from Austrian and dynastic thraldom. With these conceptions I sympathized, but my sympathies remained in a somewhat passive stage until the advent of the great year of European revolution, 1848, when I was eighteen years of age. I then found unmistakably that I sided, without any reserve, with the principle of liberty and (if need be) revolution, and entirely against the schemes and devices for keeping nations in leading-strings, or treading their minds and their instincts into the dust. Much about the same time I read Lamartine's *Histoire des Girondins*, which made the period and the ideas of the French Revolution of supreme and unique interest to me. I perceived (among other things) that in calling Robespierre a sanguinary monster one has by no means spoken the last word possible about him, and that even Carlyle's term " Sea-green Incorruptible " leaves some of his

---

[1] "That which will be will be." In the Covent Garden inscription the word "sarà" is left without its requisite accent. My father used to laugh at this, truly saying that the word, thus unaccented, means simply "Sarah."

qualities undefined.   My father, though not without an
abstract liking for republics, was practically in favour
of constitutional monarchy; I went at once to the length
of republicanism.   In England the notion of a republic
is simply a theory having no application to facts.   Such
let it remain, and let me meanwhile abide by my
republican preferences.

It has often been propounded, and surely with a considerable element of truth, that a man whose opinions
do not change from youth to age is something very like
a fool, for his opinions in youth must have been highly
immature, and similarly and more blameably immature
must they be in his advanced age.

> How young art thou in this old age of time,
> How green is this grey world !

So wrote Shelley, who continued "green."   If I am a
fool according to the above definition, I must take my
fate as it comes ; for true it is that my opinions, in the
matters which I have been discussing and in some others,
have not altered, and have even undergone modification
in only a slight degree.

To return from these more general considerations
to a few details affecting my bringing-up in matters of
religion.   The first church to which I was taken was
Trinity Church, Marylebone Road, where the rector,
Dr. Penfold, was an impressive reader of the Biblical
lessons.   He figures in my memory as an overbearing
old gentleman, who once bullied my mother on some
flimsy pretext about pew-rent.   His sermons have left
no trace on my recollection ; they may have pertained
to the "cut-and-dry" order, not serviceable to a child,
nor possibly to any one.   When I was some ten years of
age we went more habitually to St. Katharine's Chapel,

Regent's Park; here the Rev. Mr. Appleyard was a telling preacher, and I used to enjoy the vigorous singing of the Te Deum, with a large and rich-tinted stained-glass window for background. I can recall hearing the clergyman read out that chapter of the Book of Kings which relates how King Jehu treacherously convened and slaughtered the worshipers of Baal, and obtained the express commendation of Jehovah for the act—and thinking to myself: "Surely that was rather a 'fishy transaction' to be thus commended; is this what our religion consists of?" It may well be that my mother, like myself, thought this (and also the "Sacrifice of Abraham") a strange exhibition of the nature and attributes of the Deity; but her faith was of that simple and thorough kind which assumes, without finessing, the absolute and divine truth of everything to be found in the Old and New Testaments. She was not however the slave of every irrational dogma propounded by old women in or out of cassocks; and I have heard her say, "I will never believe that Socrates is condemned to eternal torment." Finally we all attended regularly at Christ Church, Albany Street; my mother liked to join company with her sisters Margaret and Eliza Polidori (also Charlotte when occasionally along with them), and these sisters went to Christ Church, which was hard by their residence in Park Village East. The incu. ent of Christ Church was the Rev. Mr. Dodsworth. Soon after we began attending there, the high Anglican—or, as people then termed it, the Puseyite—movement progressed vigorously, and affected the services in Christ Church, and the religious tone and practices of my mother and my aunts, and in a more marked degree of my two sisters. Mr. Dodsworth and

three or more of his curates joined the Church of
Rome ; the Rev. Mr. Burrows (afterwards Canon
Burrows of Rochester) succeeded as incumbent. For
Mr. Burrows I always entertained a sincere respect—
fully believing him to be devout-minded, earnest, sensible, and assiduous in parish work. About the time
however when his ministrations began, my disposition
to be a member of any congregation whatever had
dwindled down to a minimum. At what date I ceased
church attendance (save in some very rare instances, to
please my mother) is uncertain to me : it may have
been in 1847, if not 1846. I was never confirmed,
neither was Gabriel.

I must have cost my excellent religious mother many
a pang in those years, and in after years as well : a painful reflection, but where is the remedy ? She herself
preferred honest and open disbelief to hypocritical conformity. I have never had an itch for forcing my
opinions upon the attention of persons who did not
like them—least of all upon the attention of my mother ;
but on the other hand I have not been minded to dis-
guise or palter with them when circumstances prompted
their avowal. Thus there was neither concealment nor
obtrusion of my secession from the faith of my maternal kindred. On their part there was sorrow, and I am
sure perpetual prayer for my conversion ; but they did
not make matters worse by urgencies or arguments,
which would have been certain to prove equally un-
availing and exasperating. My sisters, who were
devotees in a more express though not a more genuine
sense than my mother, likewise abstained from harass-
ing me on those topics : a truce—it might be called
an armed truce—subsisted on all sides. It was never

broken, and seldom even trenched upon. Obviously I was not the first member of the family to cause these anxieties to my mother; her father and her husband, and Gabriel along with myself, had all been a trial to her on the like grounds. As to Gabriel, I may say that he, as being the senior, had probably preceded me a little in the path of heterodoxy. In most things he took the lead of me; but I do not perceive that he specially influenced me in this matter; and on the whole, both in boyish and in adult years, he was, if not more strictly a Christian believer, less definitely alien from the faith than myself. His fine intellect dwelt little in the region of argument, controversy, or the weighing of evidence; it was swayed by feelings, and not by demonstrations or counter-demonstrations. A thing either impressed and convinced him, or else it formed no part of his inner experiences.

Religionists or semi-religionists are fond of enlarging on the tortures of doubt, the spiritual conflicts which assail the sceptic, the sense of utter bereavement and disinheritance with which he bids adieu to the radiant realm of faith, and sinks into the gloomy wastes and caverns of disbelief. I am perhaps a thick-skinned person; at any rate—and I say it in the interest of truth—these grievous distresses did not befall me, either when my thoughts began to waver on matters of early-instilled faith, or when wavering was over and I knew my own mind. I have found it quite possible to get on in peace without traditional convictions—not (I hope) without some ideals proportionate to the constitution and the limitations of my character, mental and personal.

XI

SOME ARTISTIC ACQUAINTANCES

I HAVE already set down something about the matter of artistic and literary acquaintances in connexion with the Præraphaelite Brotherhood and with my beginnings in literature. But there were several persons besides with whom I became acquainted and in some cases intimate, and of these I will now give some account. The narrative is here carried up to some such date as 1855, but without my professing any strict accuracy in this respect. I begin with the artists; as they will occupy a good deal of space, I reserve the literary men for the ensuing section.

William Bell Scott was by profession a painter, and before we knew him he had settled in Newcastle-on-Tyne as master of the so-called Government School of Design, this being the earlier phase of the Department of Science and Art. As a painter, Scott had excellent powers of invention in the line of historic or romantic subject-matter, but he was not a good executant; on the contrary, truly a bad one—faulty (though far from wholly ignorant) in drawing, poor and sometimes tawdry in colour, and noticeably deficient in texture and surface-work. If any one wishes to test the correctness of these remarks, let him go to the National British Gallery and look at Scott's small picture of *The Eve of the Deluge*. My brother and I were, for some years before 1847, fairly familiar with Scott's work as an artist, and we did not entertain any exaggerated opinion of its merits ; it was chiefly as a poet that he interested us. Moreover, he was brother to a painter of much superior mark—David Scott—some of whose ideal and historical inventions were well known to us and sincerely admired. He died in 1849 without our ever having met him. William Bell Scott made the personal acquaintance of the Rossetti family—female as well as male—towards the end of 1847, and (as previously stated) he stood high in the regard of all of us. In 1850 I took a short holiday in Edinburgh, having heard the praises of that ancient capital vigorously sounded by Mr. Lowes Dickinson. I found that he had not exaggerated the scenic and picturesque attractions of "Auld Reekie." My love being then all for the olden and semi-uncouth, and not for the modern and sightly, I lodged—defying some material inconveniences—in the Lawn Market, one of those groups of giant many-storied buildings of which Edinburgh now numbers (I should say) hardly one for a score or two that existed in 1850 ; indeed, being in Edinburgh once again in 1903, I hardly observed a single specimen of them. I was invited by Scott to spend some days in his house in returning from Edinburgh. This I did, and found myself in very much the sort of intellectual atmosphere which I best relished, the talk being of art, poetry, and speculative outlooks in religion and policy ; the former from the sceptical point of view, the latter from the democratic. Scott was essentially a " thinking " man ; he had a good deal of knowledge on several subjects, with the Caledonian's love for abstract cogitation, and he imparted his thoughts freely and in an interesting way. In his company one was never at a loss for some topic of conversation. Learned in the ordinary matters of school tuition he certainly was not. I was once horrified to find that he had inscribed, upon the back of a chair presented to him by his friend Miss Boyd of Penkill, the words " Alice Boyd ad Gulielmus Scott"; and it required some persuasion to convince him that this would never do. In September 1850 he was just thirty-nine years of age, and I twenty-one; but he treated me with frank goodwill, much as if we had been equals in years. He was not at that time by any means well off, but he made me thoroughly at home.

We had not hitherto known distinctly whether Scott was a married man or a bachelor. I found him to be married. Mrs. Scott was a sprightly little woman, constantly talking in a pattering sort of way; whatever turned up, her tongue turned up. Her fathom-line for intellectual matters was not perhaps deep, but it was always prompt; more especially she had a knack at pirouetting round religious subjects, and she tried her luck in every doctrinal camp, from secularism to Roman Catholicism. At last she seemed to think herself well based in Anglicanism of the ritual type. In character she had her whimsies, but was essentially very estimable, a steady friend and always willing to oblige. We prized her in the long run much better than we had done at first sight. Her mother, Mrs. Norquoy, widow of a seafaring man, was along with her—a rather formal but affable dame of the old school, whose prosaic utterances and outlook upon life formed an amusing interlude to those of " Duns Scotus," as we sometimes called him, more generally " Scotus." There was moreover a large spaniel—described by Dante Gabriel in one of his family letters as "a strenuous dog from whom also I suffer much."

Between 1850 and 1862 I often passed with the Scotts, at their invitation, the whole or part of my annual vacation. During this interval they moved to another house in Newcastle, and progressed not a little in the evidences of worldly comfort. The open friendliness of their reception and demeanour never failed. After the latter date they abandoned Newcastle and settled in London.

While still domiciled in Newcastle, the Scotts used very generally to spend in London some few weeks in the year, and they introduced us to Dr. John Epps, the homœopathist, and his wife, who had been the school intimate of Mrs. Scott. This couple lived next door to the British Museum in an agreeable, roomy house. Dr. Epps, then not much turned of forty, was a bald-headed man, more than moderately deaf, with a very fresh complexion, and a face beaming with kind-humoured goodwill. I never consulted him professionally, and don't well know what his medical qualifications may have been ; in conversation he always adhered to the homœopathic theory. He had a habit of kissing every female visitor who entered his rooms ; one need not doubt that this was pleasing to himself. To my sisters it seemed decidedly odd ; but that form of the *agape* appeared to be a settled and imprescriptible institution in the house, so they submitted without fussing over it. For Mrs. Epps they had a very warm feeling, as being one of the most amiable and ingenuous-natured women they ever met. This I always regarded as a welcome symptom that my sisters, though zealous churchwomen, were not bigots, for Mrs. Epps was a dissenter, and entirely alien from anything tending to sacerdotalism. The Epps couple were childless, but the daughters of Dr. James Napoleon (brother of John) Epps were constantly to be met in their house—one of them is now Lady Alma-Tadema. I saw a little also of other off-shoots of this stock, including Mr. James Epps, of cocoa celebrity.

The name of Johannes Ronge is perhaps familiar to few persons at the present date; it was once of European fame. Ronge, a native of Silesia, was a Catholic priest who towards 1849, getting disgusted with some ecclesiastical impostures regarding a renowned relic, "the Holy Coat of Treves," went about denouncing this chicanery, and for a while was talked of as almost a new Luther. He was excommunicated and disfrocked, or possibly he abjured Catholicism of his own accord. He came to England, having in his company Mrs. Ronge, a German lady, who (as it turned out on inquiry) had left or been divorced by her original husband, and had joined lots with the iconoclastic reformer. Mr. and Mrs. Ronge were at one time in Newcastle; and Mrs. Scott, with her passion for side-lights upon the faith, would not be contented without making their acquaintance. Through this channel I also, when the Ronges were rehoused in London, saw a little of them. Ronge, who was then still under middle age, was a broad-built man, well-featured rather than otherwise, with small eyes, and a dark, somewhat impassive countenance. He seemed to me to be a rationalist, more than anything to be definitely called a Christian. I cannot profess to have taken kindly to him. Mrs. Ronge, Bertha, who had with her a nice little daughter by her first marriage, pleased me much better ; a cheery, comely woman, not perhaps markedly intellectual, but interested in matters of the mind. She died some few years after I had first met her, and Ronge himself was not long-lived.

Another person whom I knew through Scott was Signora (Enrica) Filopanti, a graceful and estimable Italian lady, who maintained herself in England for a few years by teaching. She was married to a revolutionary and rather irrational Italian named Barile. He chose to call himself Filopanti, and to serve the cause of humanity in the aggregate, not including his wife, who was thus left to shift for herself. A short poem by Christina, entitled *Enrica*, 1865, relates to this lady, who is still living in Italy. There was moreover Mr. James Leathart, a lead merchant of Newcastle, who had taken to picture-buying at first in a small way and without much principle of selection. Scott influenced him towards the Præraphaelite School ; and he gradually formed a very excellent collection, purchasing, among others, several of my brother's pictures. In the course of years his judgment in art became more than commonly sound, his eye for colour especially being good. Mr. Leathart was a kind-hearted, hospitable, agreeable man ; his fortunes prospered, and he removed into a large sightly house, Bracken Dene, Gateshead. He married a lady much younger than himself, attractive in all respects ; they had a large family, one of whom married into the family of Mr. Rae, also a distinguished picture collector. Mr. Leathart died at a fairly advanced age in 1895, and his widow not long afterwards. His pictures were exhibited in London in 1896, securing a good deal of attention, and were ultimately sold.

I wrote by request a preface to the catalogue of them, and an article in *The Art Journal*.

Of Ford Madox Brown I have not as yet said so much as his importance in my family history demands. He was just twenty-seven years old when my brother first knew him in the spring of 1848. He was of middling stature, with a thoughtful, resolved, and well-moulded face ; as to actual good looks he improved as he got older, and was at his best towards the age of forty, and as an oldish man was impressively patriarchal. What struck us at first more than his personal aspect was his slow, deliberate, uniform voice, slow but in no way hesitating, nor wanting in copiousness of discourse. He was then a young widower, having at a very early age married his cousin Elizabeth Bromley, who had died of consumption in 1846. She left a daughter, Emma Lucy (always called Lucy), who became my wife in 1874. Brown had a small income from wharf property, just sufficient to keep him going. Although a painter of some real mark in and before 1848, his professional work brought him in as yet scarcely anything, and he kept on at painting with a well-developed sense of being very scantily appreciated. When I first knew him he had a studio in Clipstone Street, Portland Place. He afterwards moved into Newman Street ; and it was, I think, at his house-warming there, in January 1850, that I first met my future wife, a quiet candid-looking little girl, aged less than seven, modestly self-possessed.

After a not long period of widowerhood Brown married again, his second wife being Emma Hill, daughter of a deceased farmer, and without educational advantages. She was extremely young when he first met her, and got her to sit to him for the heads of some of his pictured personages ; the earliest was perhaps the Princess of Wales (wife of the Black Prince) in his very large painting of *Chaucer reading the Legend of Custance at the Court of Edward the Third*. She had a pink complexion, regular features, and a fine abundance of beautiful yellow hair, the tint of harvest corn. Most of Brown's female heads up to a late date in his life, Cordelia, Juliet, Mary Chaworth, were from his wife ; to whom, spite of some domestic vexations, he continued firmly and fondly attached. She died in October 1890. In her character there was a considerable fund of complaisant amiability ; of any countervailing blemishes I will here say nothing. She had two children, besides a boy who died in infancy. The first was Catherine (constantly called Cathy), who has good executive faculty as a painter, and some aptitude for music and singing, and who in 1872 married Dr. Franz Hueffer, a German musical scholar and (in a minor degree) composer ; he became musical critic of *The Times*. The second child was Oliver Madox. Of this singularly gifted youth, born in 1855 and deceased in 1874, I shall have to speak in the sequel.

Brown had several connexions of whom I saw a little from time to time ; of most of them, very little. Sir Richard Madox Bromley, who became Governor of Greenwich Hospital, brother of his first wife. Mrs. (Helen) Bromley, widow of another brother, a truly worthy Scotch lady, hearty and amiable, who kept a school at Gravesend, where she conducted the early education of Lucy Brown. Her daughter Elizabeth, who married an Anglo-Indian (Eurasian) Government official, Mr. Samuel Cooper ; him I met a good deal at one time, and I valued him sincerely. There were others, but I need not specify them here.

To the following artists I became known at an early period, mostly owing to their being familiars of Madox Brown : William Cave Thomas, Charles Lucy, Lowes Dickinson with his brother Robert, John Cross, Mark Anthony, Thomas Seddon with his family, also the surgeon John Marshall. I will say something about each of them.

Mr. Thomas is still, I trust, alive as I write ; he must be very old, being the senior of Brown, who was born in April 1821. Mr. Thomas studied art in Germany, under the famous Cornelius. He became a learned and severe draughtsman, and won a prize or two in the Westminster Hall competitions (towards 1845) for decorating the Houses of Parliament. He produced also various easel-pictures ; but his style was not much conformable to British tastes, and after a while it became apparent that he would not achieve that measure of distinction to which his beginning had pointed. He is a man of theory as well as practice, and has published some writings on abstract questions of art doctrine. In Germany he would long ago have found his proper level and recognition in some professorship of art. His standard of life and thought has always seemed to me a high one, insufficiently recompensed here.

Mr. Charles Lucy was another of the Westminster Hall painters and prizemen ; certainly much less solidly grounded than Mr. Cave Thomas, but more adapted for meeting the likings of the British public. At least two of his pictures, *Cromwell at the Death-bed of his Daughter Mrs. Claypole* and *Nelson in the Cabin of the Victory*, were in their day highly popular as engravings. He was a short man, of very ordinary appearance and address, more like a country estate-agent than an artist. He was married, friendly and accommodating in disposition. Madox Brown, when I first knew him, was on very intimate terms with Mr. and Mrs. Lucy; but after a while he seemed to have dropped them entirely, owing (if I am not mistaken) to their taking less kindly than he would have wished to the second Mrs. Brown. On any point of this sort, and indeed of some other sorts as well, Brown was tenacious and even peppery, and any one who wanted to stand well in his regards needed to walk circumspectly.

Of Mr. Lowes Dickinson the portrait-painter I have already made some slight mention; he, like Mr. Thomas, is one of the few survivors of those times. I have never known Mr. Dickinson to fail in the character of an attached steady friend, always glad to do one a good turn. He belongs to the family of old-established print-sellers and photographic agents in New Bond Street. His brother Robert was in my earlier time at the head of this firm; of him likewise I saw something, but much less than of Lowes. Towards 1849 they promoted the formation of a drawing-class in Maddox Street, Regent Street, and I joined it for some little while. My brother thought rather well of my drawings from the life: I was always conscious however of their being stiff and ungenial, and never deceived myself into thinking that I possessed an artistic aptitude worth developing. This was not the only drawing-class that I joined; there was one, for instance, set going by Thomas Seddon. I worked with moderate diligence and a result less than moderate, and finally, still youthful, I dropped the experiment.

John Cross had had his art training abroad, principally I think in Paris. Very little was known of him in England when he produced, in the Westminster Hall competition of 1847, his oil picture of *The Death-bed of Richard Cœur de Lion*. This work, now in the Parliament House, at once made him famous, and people expected him to take a very leading position as a painter. No such sequel ensued, for his later works were less observable, and obtained little or no hold upon the public. Cross was a married man with a large family ; he had always been in a very struggling condition, and so he continued up to his death, towards 1861. He must have been forty years old or nearly as much when I first knew him. He had a well-cut visage, but with rather glassy and ineffective light eyes. His voice and delivery also were far from forcible. This did not matter so much, for he was taciturn, and neither made nor tried to make any mark in conversation. He seemed to be a man of very solid character, sincere, modest, and retiring. After his death a subscription was got up to make some provision for his family. Sculptors came forward as readily as painters, the distinguished sculptor Mr. Foley being particularly active. We had the satisfaction of getting a moderately good sum together, and Mrs. Cross obtained a post as matron in some suitable institution.

Mark Anthony the landscape painter was an old friend of Madox Brown. His powerful paintings, rich in colour and impasto, were objects of my earnest admiration even before the Præraphaelite Brotherhood had been formed, and on becoming an art-critic I had frequent opportunity of seeing and lauding his exhibited works. I may have rated them rather too high, in comparison with some other examples of landscape art; but the works which Anthony produced, between some such dates as 1847 and 1857, were certainly very remarkable, and stood out saliently from the throng. He became anxious to graft something of Præraphaelitism upon the style which came natural to him and in which he excelled. This did not really improve his work, and later on he seldom produced paintings wholly worthy of his prime. I did not, I presume, meet Mr. Anthony until after I had written and he had seen some review article praising his work in terms which, if not excited, were assuredly fervent. After that, I was often in his house (a small residence in Monmouth Road, Bays-water), and for four or five years he counted as one of my leading friends. He was among the earlier practi-tioners of photography, and was very successful in catching fleeting expressions of glee or gloom—as in especial with his three pretty little girls. He took two or three photographic likenesses of my brother and myself. Those of my brother would now be of no small interest, as showing his appearance at a youthful age of which few records remain; the photographic prints however are in a woefully faded condition. Anthony was a tall, well-built man, of an agreeable physiognomy not far from handsome, courteous and fair-spoken. I knew besides his wife, and have seen his mother, a very fine old lady of imposing presence. His domestic life was not so correct as it should have been; a case came into court, and it was held that this, along with any other causes, furnished the Royal Academicians with a handle for refusing him—what his pictorial merits mani-festly claimed—election into their ranks. This soured him and injured his prospects; but he continued actively at work, tenanting a well-known studio at Hampstead. I saw him occasionally in his later years, which came to a close towards 1885. One of these days people may again pay more attention to Anthony's works than they have done for several years past. He far excelled a number of landscape painters of a popular but "shoppy" and essentially unimportant class.

Thomas Seddon was one of a rather large family, the children of a furniture-maker in Gray's Inn Road : I knew all or nearly all the members of this household. In my time the father stood high in his vocation ; but he had (as I understood) been at one period much more flourishing and affluent, and had been damaged by fulfilling large orders from the Prince Regent (George IV), who would not or could not pay the bill, and Parliament refused to pay it for him. When I first met him, Thomas Seddon was in his father's business ; but he had long had an inclination and an aptitude for the pictorial profession, and to this he finally betook himself when approaching the age of thirty. He travelled to Egypt and Jerusalem, where he was joined by Mr. Holman Hunt ; came home and married, and then returned to Egypt. He had scarcely fixed in Cairo when dysentery attacked him, and he died in November 1856, at the early age of thirty-five. Various friends, among whom Holman Hunt and Madox Brown were conspicuous, promoted a subscription for purchasing his principal picture and presenting it to the National Gallery. This work is *Jerusalem from the Valley of Jehoshaphat*, now to be seen in the National British Gallery at Millbank. A more conscientiously presented portrait of the scene could not be found, and it is a well-executed painting to boot. I hardly know whether, in the present days of photography, fine art of this kind is greatly needed. It was still needed then; and at a rather earlier date, when no one painted on so punctilious a principle, it was still more requisite. Ruskin was the treasurer for the subscription, and myself the secretary. This undertaking gave me a good deal of employment. I remember having looked right through the *Court Guide*, name by name, so as not to miss thinking of any persons who might be addressed with presumable advantage. Thomas Seddon was a good-looking man, a general favourite with all sorts of people. He had very high spirits, with a keen eye for the funny side of things, and would laugh consumedly over the diverting anecdotes which he told in abundance. Here is one. His mother had recently engaged a young female servant, whose richly curved proportions soon excited some amount of observation in the family. Mrs. Seddon, whose standard of decorum was of the highest, took the matter up. " Susan," said she, " I am sorry to interfere upon any such point, but you must not mind my speaking about the size of your bustle; it would really be better if you would wear a smaller one." "Why, ma'am," replied the reddening damsel, " I don't wear one at all." With all his jocularity, Thomas Seddon was a serious-thinking man, increasingly subject to strong religious impressions. This fact is very clearly brought out in a memoir of him by his brother which was published not long after his death. The statements here made to this effect are beyond a doubt authentic; but I have always thought the other side of the shield might have been shown more distinctly, thereby producing a truer likeness of the genial and much-deplored Thomas Seddon. Of all his London friends, I was the last to see him; for I happened to encounter him in the island of Jersey in 1856 as he was preparing to proceed to the East.

His younger brother John P. Seddon—the architect who was concerned in restoring Llandaff cathedral and Great Yarmouth parish-church, in building the range of bungalows at Birchington-on-Sea, etc.—has also been, and still remains, among my well-prized friends. It was he who handsomely placed one of these bungalows at the disposal of Dante Rossetti in his last illness, soon terminating in death. The ladies of the Seddon family were at all times on the most cordial terms with those of the Madox Brown household: there was perhaps no one for whom my wife had a sincerer respect and regard than Mrs. Seddon, who attained a good old age. One of the daughters, Emily, married Mr. Henry Virtue Tebbs, well known in the legal world and as a collector of many objects of art.

At the drawing-class previously referred to, with which the Seddons were connected, I met three or four persons whom I continued to know at later dates— George Price Boyce, John R. Clayton, and John Leighton. To Mr. Boyce I shall recur further on. Mr. Clayton was of promise as a painter in the ordinary way; but at an early age he entered a firm for stained glass, Clayton and Bell. Mr. Leighton, known under the fancy name Luke Limner, is connected with a bookbinding and decorative firm of high repute. During several recent years he took some part in public life, standing as a candidate for Parliament, and for the London County Council and other bodies.

I now come to the last person with whom I have to deal as being known to me through the Brown connexion

—John Marshall. With this very distinguished surgeon, who became President of the Royal College of
Surgeons and Professor of Anatomy to the Royal
Academy, and who attained other high professional
honours, Brown, before I met him myself, was well
acquainted. Brown had a sharp eye for a good doctor,
being grandson to a celebrated medical reformer, Dr.
John Brown, of Edinburgh and afterwards of London,
much decried and highly famed as the founder of the
so-called "Brunonian system of medicine." He generally consulted Mr. Marshall as his family doctor, and
he induced my brother to do the like—and from 1865
or thereabouts my brother was very much in Marshall's
hands, and so continued till the premature close of his
life in 1882. Mr. Marshall (who became Dr. Marshall
towards the end of his useful career) was a strongly
built man of middle height, with a fine crop of straight
grey hair in his more advanced years. His features
were not particularly noticeable, except the eyes—very
dark and bright, with an air of observant vigilance
which I have hardly seen equalled. Madox Brown got
him to sit for the profile head of the jester in his large
picture of Chaucer : this head resembles him fairly
enough, but can hardly be pronounced a likeness. Mr.
Marshall took an intelligent interest in matters of fine
art ; as evinced by his seeking the professorship at the
Royal Academy, and by his important book *Anatomy for
Artists*. One of his sons showed, as a mere boy, a
singular turn for landscape painting, by which Dante
Rossetti was greatly impressed.

Next I proceed to a large group of artists whom I
knew more or less independently of any introductions.
I came naturally into contact with them, owing to their

being known to my brother and hence to me, or through some other casual circumstances. They are Alexander Munro, Arthur Hughes, Walter Howell Deverell, John Hancock, Bernhard Smith, Charles Allston Collins, George Price Boyce, his sister, her husband Henry Tanworth Wells, William Burges, John Leech, Kenny Meadows, Edward Lear, Robert B. Martineau, and Henry Wallis.

Alexander Munro the sculptor was an Inverness man, the son (as I heard) of a shoemaker; having shown some early propensity to art, he came under the notice of the ducal family of Sutherland, who promoted his fortunes and enabled him to mix in very distinguished society. His art was elegant and graceful; it suited the requirements of a fashionable circle. I will not say that it fully met the higher demands of sculptural art, whether in point of majesty or of strong and varied character; but it had its appropriate place, and occupied this for a while. Munro was a good-looking young man, with fairly regular features and Celtic blue eyes. His manner was refined as well as open-hearted. He was warmly and firmly attached to my brother, and from the first entertained a high idea of what it was in him to do. My brother returned in full measure the steadiness of his friendship, and deplored the early breakdown of the sculptor's health, which compelled him to reside abroad, and brought him to the grave after some years of suffering. While in London, Munro occupied a large studio in the Pimlico quarter, and saw plenty of company there—artistic, literary, and miscellaneous. I have frequently been in that studio of an evening when some thirty to fifty men may have been present. Munro's sister—a pleasing young woman who was afterwards governess in the house of Lord Mount-Temple—did the honours of the establishment, so far as they fell (but this was only little) within the female domain. Later on Munro married, and he left a family, well worthy, I believe, of their excellent parent.

Mr. Arthur Hughes, who is still living and very young for his years, was, when I first knew him, an Academy student just starting as an exhibiting painter. His face, giving evidence of his Welsh parentage, was singularly bright and taking—dark, abundant hair, vivid eyes, good features, and ruddy cheeks which earned him among his fellow-students the nickname of "Cherry." If I had to pick out, from amid my once-numerous acquaintances of the male sex, the sweetest and most ingenuous nature of all, the least carking and querulous, and the freest from "envy, hatred and malice, and all uncharitableness," I should probably find myself bound to select Mr. Hughes. In Thackeray's novel *The Newcomes* there is a character—a young and unassuming artist, happy in the sentiment and exercise of his art, and untroubled by most other things—who goes chiefly by the name of J. J. This character might have been moulded upon that of Arthur Hughes. As a painter, he was one of those who most sympathized with the ideas which guided the Præraphaelite Brotherhood, and his style conformed pretty faithfully (not servilely) to theirs; if the organization had been kept up a little longer, and if new members had ever been admitted (a point which encountered some difference of opinion), Mr. Hughes would doubtless have been invited to join. He has produced many charming pictures—of a kind which, without being didactic, appeals intimately to the feelings ; yet, as they had (like himself) no "pushing" quality either in subject or in execution, they never brought him into a position of great prominence, and he has reached the twilight of life without receiving the full measure of his due.   But, in the region of art as of worship,

They also serve who only stand and wait.

Such men produce good work, and in the long run it is recognized as good.   Mr. Hughes married early and had a numerous family ; he is the uncle of another very able painter slightly known to me, Mr. Edward Hughes.

Walter Howell Deverell, a special associate of my brother, was familiar also with Holman Hunt and with others in our circle.   He was nominated for the P.R.B. in the later days of that league, and might be considered semi-elected, but not absolutely enrolled when the P.R.B. drifted aside, and, along with it, the question of election.   Deverell was one of the handsomest young men I have known ; belonging to a type not properly to be termed feminine, but which might rather be dubbed "troubadourish."   He was a son of the secretary to the then "School of Design" at Somerset House, and had very good talents for art, with a decided bent towards dramatic subject-matter—indeed, he was not without a certain inclination for the acting profession.   The father was a man of culture, and the son had received the usual advantages of education.   In his very brief life full artistic attainment was not to be expected ; of artistic ability he gave ample promise and explicit evidence.   His principal picture (it belonged at one time to William Bell Scott) was from Shakespear's *Twelfth Night :* the scene where the Duke Orsino, with the disguised Viola and the Jester, has minstrels to entertain him. Here Orsino is painted from Deverell himself, but without doing him full justice, Viola from Miss Siddal,[1] and the Jester from Dante Rossetti. Deverell's head appears in two other pictures known to me, the *Claudio and Isabella* of Holman Hunt and the *Chaucer* of Madox Brown. In this latter work he is the youthful page or squire who is seated in the foreground in enamoured converse with a lady ; this is the likeness of Deverell which (though not truer than any other in features) gives the best idea of his general look. Deverell, as I have said elsewhere, was the first artist who noted Miss Siddal, my brother's future wife, as having a face suited to be painted from. In his character there was much manliness mixed with warmth and facility. He was not of the "business-like" order ; but untoward family conditions threw much responsibility upon him towards the end of his life, and he met it with fortitude and spirit. He died of Bright's disease in February 1854, aged only twenty-six. After losing sight of Deverell's relatives for several years, I came in contact, in 1898, with his brother Wickham Deverell, and with this gentleman's wife and family. Some steps were then taken, with my co-operation, for the purpose of bringing out something to serve as a brief record of Walter Deverell's career, but as yet this project remains unrealized. The requisite materials are now in the hands of my friend Mr. Charles Fairfax Murray, owner of a rich collection of paintings and works of art.

John Hancock the sculptor must have been known to

---

[1] I may as well say that this name is spelled "Siddall" in the family, but my brother had a habit of writing "Siddal," and I follow his lead.

my brother at a very early date—probably as far back as 1847. He was related to the old-established family engaged in the business of silversmiths and jewellers; and he made an early success with a bas-relief, *Christ's Entry into Jerusalem*, which won a prize offered by the Art Union, and was engraved. His success after this was not often considerable; and, owing partly to unfortunate circumstances into which it is not my affair to enter, he gradually sank out of observation, and he died in middle age. One of his youthful works was a medallion-head of my brother—to me a very interesting likeness, though it does not much indicate the look of Dante Rossetti in his maturer years : it remains in my possession. Hancock was an ungainly little man, wizened, with a long thin nose and squeaky voice; at times he occupied the same sculptural studio with Thomas Woolner. Some one—it must have been Dante Gabriel— put him down as a co-proprietor in *The Germ ;* but any practical work in that enterprise was not in Hancock's line, and he did not respond to the call.

At other times Woolner's co-tenant was Bernhard Smith, who was in all physical respects the direct opposite of Hancock : an extremely fine young man, well turned of six feet and broad to correspond, with a healthy, hearty English look and manner, and a clear, resonant voice. Not to like him at first sight would have been impossible, and he " wore well " besides. I scarcely know now what he had done as a sculptor— certainly not anything conspicuous; occasionally he produced a small picture; but I do not think that in either art he had any remarkable faculty. Finding little opening in the æsthetic realm, he made up his mind to emigrate, and in 1852 he accompanied Woolner to Australia. There he became a police magistrate—relinquishing, I suppose, all idea of continuing as an artist ; and many years ago he died. It has sometimes been said that Bernhard Smith was a member of the P.R.B., and indeed it is a fact that Dante Rossetti, in inscribing a book to him when he was once about to leave London, added these initials to his name. This however was one of the rather arbitrary acts in which my brother indulged himself now and again ; for in truth Smith never was a P.R.B. ; he was not elected, nor even put up for election ; and it might be added that he had not done anything fairly entitling him to rank as a colleague of Millais and Holman Hunt.

Charles Allston Collins came much nearer than Bernhard Smith to occupying this position. He was a son of William Collins, R.A., the painter of domestic life, coast scenery, etc.—whose works, after some length of time in which they were little sought after, have again of late years commanded high prices, somewhat higher perhaps than they merit. I met Charles Collins tolerably often towards 1851 ; his brother Wilkie Collins the novelist much seldomer—indeed, I can barely profess to have known him. Millais was very intimate with Charles, and was enormously admired by him ; and advocated his election into the P.R.B. after Collins had exhibited two or three pictures in which the principles of the new school (as to the detailed and exact painting of objects, etc.) were most fully exemplified. I question whether any other member of the Brotherhood seconded Millais very warmly ; certainly Woolner was in opposition. Collins considered that he ought to have been elected, and, not having been so, he was nettled, and disposed to hold aloof. Not many years afterwards he dropped the painting profession, married a daughter of Charles Dickens, and took to light literature ; he died when on the confines of middle age. Collins was one of those artists who, along with very sufficient executive powers, seem to have little of the artistic nature : so at least it struck me, and so perhaps, as he relinquished the career, it struck himself. There was an impression abroad that the Præraphaelite Brothers and their allies were inclined to " Puseyism " or " the Oxford Movement." As to the actual P.R.B.'s this was not correct : some of them were religiously (without being Puseyitically) inclined, some others were quite in the contrary direction. The only ally of the Brotherhood as to whom I perceived the statement to be well founded was Charles Collins ; he took an obvious interest in religious matters, and his interest went steadily in that High Church direction. This formed a bond of sympathy between him and my sister Maria, who at one time (say towards 1855) saw a good deal of Collins along with his widowed mother. The nearest approach to a " preference " that I knew her at any time to entertain was bestowed upon Collins. To myself he was agreeable enough, but I never felt strongly drawn towards him. He was a spare young man, with a rather high nose and reddish hair ; his physiognomy—entirely different from that of his brother Wilkie—did not suggest the painter, but rather the professional man.

George Price Boyce, the son of a leading pawnbroker, was perhaps first encountered by me at the drawing-school got up by Thomas Seddon ; but my subsequent familiar acquaintance with him depended not on any such casual circumstance, but on the fact that he was among the earlier purchasers of water-colours and other

works by my brother, and always on very friendly terms
with him. He began life as a student of architecture,
but soon showed a more decided bent towards landscape
painting ; and it may truly be said that his water-colour
works in this line are, for delicate observation and well-
harmonized diligence of execution, not easily to be surpassed. Boyce was a well-grown young man, of agreeable person and address ; he had fair private means,
apart from his professional earnings. He was very un-
lucky in the way of accidents, breaking a leg more than
once, etc.: however, these mishaps did not greatly affect
him in the long run, and he attained a good old age.
Rather late in life he married a prepossessing French
lady. Boyce had a taste for collecting objects of fine
and decorative art, and had very sound judgment in the
choice of them ; whenever one went to see him there
was something fresh to look at. For several years he
lived in Buckingham Street, Strand, facing the river ;
then in the chambers in Chatham Place, Blackfriars,
which my brother vacated in 1862; finally in Chelsea,
close to the rectory-house. Intercourse with Boyce was
always, in my experience, pleasant and easy : he was not
readily ruffled, but had somewhat precise and punctilious habits, characteristic of an art-collecting bachelor.
Strange to say, this punctiliousness did not extend to
the drawing up of a will. At his death he was found
to be intestate, and I fancy that his property of various
kinds went away in directions he had not forecast. His
mind was not strong in the closing years of his life :
possibly this accounts for his intestacy.

Boyce's vocation for art, though not of extensive
scope, was highly genuine; it was, I judge, exceeded by
that of his sister Joanna. This young lady, in her very

brief life, produced and exhibited a few pictures ; one was named *Elgiva*, hung in the Royal Academy in 1855, and was pronounced by Madox Brown, in his diary, to be " the best head in the rooms." Miss Boyce had a picturesque face, with a noticeable air of concentration and resolve; she was probably conscious of power, but (so far as I saw) was quite free from self-applause— looking upon what she had done as a mere imperfect earnest of what she might aim at doing. She married the portrait-painter Mr. Henry Tanworth Wells, for many years an R.A., deceased in 1903. She gave birth to a child, and soon afterwards died ; her age can, I suppose, hardly have exceeded twenty-eight. All the artists whom I best knew and valued deplored her death as a real loss to art ; they had looked upon her as the leading hope for painting in the hands of a woman. My brother was invited by the bereaved husband to make a drawing of her as she lay in death ; he did so ; and a photograph from the drawing is still among the things which I prize. Mr. Wells, at the date of his wedding, was a miniature-painter, this being the branch of art which he had first taken up, and in which he earned a distinguished place; there was a miniature of his, of more than ordinary size, showing his bride and himself on their wedding-trip. Just about that date the advances of photography reduced miniature-painting almost to its last gasp (though it has fairly revived of late years); so Mr. Wells applied himself to oil-painting instead. He was among the earliest of my artistic acquaintances : I knew him certainly before the forma- tion of the P.R.B., and possibly as far back as 1846.

William Burges, the learned and accomplished archi- tect who undertook vast works of detail for the Marquis

of Bute in renovating Cardiff Castle, and who is remembered by other edifices as well, had been a school-
fellow of mine in the sixth class at King's College.
There however I knew little of him, except that he had
a chubby face like a cherub on a tombstone, and was
excessively short-sighted. I re-encountered him in the
rooms of Boyce, with whom he was familiar. I found
him to take a lively pleasure in his art, and especially in
any aspects of it which combined advanced gothicism of
style with quaint tricks of fantasy. To foist something
like a joke into a cornice, a tracery, or an effigy, was his
delight; in fact I have hardly known any one who, in
his work as well as his talk, was so frankly boyish and
skittish. He seemed to be a happy man, but happy in
a rather small way, just as his jokes were small—unvexed
at any rate by the gnawing cares of this nether world.
I re-met him in 1860 on the Continent, as I was returning
from Florence with Mr. (afterwards Judge) Vernon
Lushington ; and we three travelled together for a day
or two, pausing at Avignon, and so on to Paris.

To John Leech I was introduced by Millais, not long
after Millais had himself been introduced by Leech to
the excitements and joys of hunting. Leech was a man
universally liked (I found in after years that he had been
a special favourite with Edward John Trelawny, of
Byronic fame) : I liked him well, but did not see enough
of him to fan the flamelet of liking into much of a glow.
On one occasion I dined at his house in Brunswick
Square, where Percival Keene, a well-known humoristic
writer of that day, was my *commensal*. Leech was a well-
grown and rather handsome man : the drawing of his
head by Millais, in the National Portrait Gallery, gives
a good idea of his features and expression. It has more

than once been said that he was hunted into his grave
by organ-grinders; and I believe this is only too near
the truth, although the excessive nervous susceptibility
which such a fate bespeaks was not uppermost in his
general demeanour.   Two other illustrators of *Punch*
were slightly known to me later on—Charles Keene
(very slightly) and George du Maurier. Another
woodcut-designer whom I saw once or twice was Kenny
Meadows, whose *Illustrated Shakespear* had been a delight
of my boyhood.   He was an elderly man when I knew
him, living seemingly in a very quiet sort of way, with
two daughters.   I believe that he could be amply convivial upon occasion, but this did not come under my
own notice.   He was an old friend of Bell Scott; my
introduction to him however came through a different
medium, that of James Hannay.

Edward Lear, besides being a universal benefactor
as author of *The Book of Nonsense* (dear to Dante
Rossetti), was a very agreeable and efficient landscape
designer who had been rather far afield in his quest
of the picturesque — Albania, Calabria, Syria, etc.
He was moreover an entertaining and judicious writer
of travelling adventure, as evidenced in his book *A
Landscape-painter in Calabria*.   There is in this volume
a deal of genuine Italian character-sketching : Christina
was very fond of it.   I met Lear in 1852 in company
with Holman Hunt, and passed a week or so in their
society.   They were at Fairlight, near Hastings ; Hunt
painting his admirable sheep-picture *Our English Coasts*,
and Lear, who had resolved to put himself under severe
discipline as a quasi-Præraphaelite executant, producing
one of his larger oil-paintings, *The Quarries of Syracuse*.
This was quite a new start on his part, as hitherto he had

aimed chiefly at telling composition and facile handling.
Lear was a rather tall man, spectacled, with a rounded
nose and ordinary features. He was a sprightly, easy,
unpretentious talker, having knocked about in the world
more than sufficiently to acquire aplomb and suppress
affectation, and being accustomed to move in "good
society." At Fairlight we had vile spring weather
of recurring rain varied with sea mists ; and Lear was
much given to declaiming against the English climate,
which, as he said (and I more than once noticed it to be
true), even if tolerably fine before and after his sojourns
in his native land, was constantly detestable during those
intervals. Another object of his denunciation—but this
was in a later year—was the oriental camel, in his view an
unmannerly and unmanageable beast, affording material
for little save human exasperation. His verdict on the
"ship of the desert" anticipated that which has been
versified in Rudyard Kipling's stanzas on *The Oont*.
Lear, in his later years, settled in San Remo. His sight
had never been strong, and he became blind. At the
beginning of 1887 I was at San Remo with my wife
and two children, and I noticed the Villa Tennyson,
at which Lear resided. I blameably neglected to call at
once ; and then an earthquake (much talked of all over
Europe) occurred, and my family decamped from the
place, and I along with them. Thus, to my permanent
regret, I failed to see good old Lear in his darkened
retirement. He lies buried in the San Remo cemetery.

Robert B. Martineau began studying for the pictorial
profession at a rather later age than most persons ; he
had done, I presume, little or nothing until he sought
out Holman Hunt, and asked to be allowed to work
under his general oversight. It was in Hunt's studio

that I first met him—perhaps early in 1852. Here he painted a subject from Dickens's *Old Curiosity Shop*—*The Writing Lesson* of Christopher Nubbles supervised by Little Nell. For a first painting it was more than promising. Martineau's best work is now in the National British Gallery — *The Last Day in the Old Home*—and is certainly a remarkable success as regards lighting and general realization, with some true points of expression. Martineau was a short - lived man, dying at the age of forty-three. He did not look delicate, but was of masculine build, with a full-coloured visage. He was a very sensible person, not given to much talk, and with a mind rather steady-going than lively, highly trusty and well-principled, and worthy of the utmost regard. He had much taste and some natural gift for music.

With Henry Wallis, the painter of the very admirable picture of *The Death of Chatterton* (now likewise in the National British Gallery and clearly one of the best products of the Præraphaelite movement), I was acquainted somewhat later than with most of the preceding. I say the less of him, in that he is still alive. I have found him a very agreeable companion, of solid character and open mind. He was also of some special interest to me as having known Thomas Love Peacock, the friend of Shelley ; he once gave me two hairs from Shelley's head, which, to my shame, seem to have disappeared. On one occasion I sat to him for a head in one of his pictures—I forget which. Needless to say that Mr. Wallis has for many years past been a leading authority on oriental and other ceramics.

The reader may have observed that almost all the persons I have named in this section were young—not

far from my own age at the time when I met them ;
most of them a few years older, two or three younger
by a year or so. With the elder generation of artists
I made little, if any, acquaintance. I recollect by sight
Benjamin Robert Haydon, Solomon Hart, David Cox,
Sir Charles Lock Eastlake (who knew my father pretty
well), Daniel Maclise, Charles Robert Leslie, Alfred
Elmore ; am not conscious of having ever seen the
greatest British painter of my time—Turner. With
Edward Matthew Ward, Samuel Palmer, F. O. Finch,
William Henry Hunt, Edward Armitage, Richard
Ansdell, J. W. Oakes, Augustus Leopold Egg, and
Frederick and Walter Goodall, I have at times ex-
changed a few words, but I can scarcely regard myself as
having known them.

There is one other family which I must here mention,
and with which I was extremely intimate from 1849
onwards—the Tupper family. John Lucas Tupper had
been a student of sculpture in the Royal Academy,
where he became familiar with Holman Hunt and
Stephens. He adopted sculpture as his profession, and
for some years he practised it on and off ; but when
first I knew of him he had got shunted aside into the
position of anatomical draughtsman to Guy's Hospital
—a position for which, by a decided scientific combined
with his artistic turn, he was handsomely qualified. He
was then a meagre young man, hardly up to middle
height, with a pale visage, abundant dark hair, vivid
dark eyes, and very mobile eyebrows ; his play of
feature in talking was unusual. He was not handsome ;
but got wonderfully improved and not a little picturesque by growing, as he was approaching middle
age, a very copious beard. John Tupper seemed quite

as zealous as any of the P.R.B.'s in the cause of their two leading principles—the need for serious inventive thought in works of art, and for close and detailed study of nature in their carrying out. He had written a fair quantity of verse ; certain specimens published in *The Germ* and elsewhere are very good. Although he had some of the qualifications which go to making an able artist, it may be questioned whether Tupper, even under favourable outside conditions, would have achieved original work of rounded completeness ; perhaps the scientific bent of his mind trammelled him. He produced little beyond a bas-relief (very commendable in its way) of two men playing at chess, and the statue of Linnæus in the Oxford University Museum—a highly naturalistic treatment of a naturalist. A life-sized medallion-portrait of myself, which he presented to me in a friendly spirit, is also a successful work. Tupper never got fairly into the groove of remunerative employment in sculpture ; he gave up the effort towards 1867 and became a drawing-master in Rugby School, where his methods were highly intelligent and thorough, and produced excellent results. His health however was undermined ; he had a terrible catarrhal and spasmodic attack while travelling with me in Italy in 1869 ; and in 1879 he died, much regretted by many, and most by those who knew him best. He was an eminently conscientious and upright man, of varied and very considerable talents.

The father of John Tupper was a printer in the City of London, residing in South Lambeth. I was very frequently in that house, and knew all the family well. The printing firm, in which two sons, George and Alexander, were included, undertook the printing of

The Germ; and this, had there been nothing else, brought me into continual contact with one or other member of the household. The father was a steady-going man of business, and a well-informed one ; the two sons just mentioned (whom we of *The Germ* had to thank for bringing out at their own risk the last two numbers of that magazine) were men of principle, scrupulous in all their business transactions. Along with Mrs. Tupper and her two daughters (both of whom married many years ago), there was in the house a sister of the former, Miss Isaacs, blind, but still kindly and helpful in family matters. The house was a roomy one with a large garden, wherein I have taken many a pleasant stroll and interchanged an abundance of friendly chat.

Of these members of the Tupper family—four of them are still surviving—I have lost sight for some years ; but I have of late seen a good deal of the widow of John Tupper, with his son and daughter. The son (a Rugby and Oxford man) is now in India, a rising young official, expert at languages, and at other matters as well. The widow, a very vivacious little lady, whose energetic exertions for years past in Germany and else-where have kept things going up when they had but too good a chance of going down, lives at present in Hamp-stead with her daughter. The latter has received an excellent musical training and is an accomplished violinist, which audiences will probably find out one day.

In 1896 I was invited to see whether I could secure a publisher for a selection of John Tupper's poems. I did so, and the volume was issued by Messrs. Longmans in the following year. It is, I am confident, of such calibre as to give my old friend his modest but adequate station among those Englishmen who knew how to write poetry towards the middle of the nineteenth century.

XII

SOME LITERARY ACQUAINTANCES

I CAN hardly now say how or when it was that Dante
Gabriel, and through him myself, first met James
Hannay. As Hannay was a Scot, a Dumfries-shire
man, it seems likely that one of my brother's Scottish
friends, either Munro or Calder Campbell (and more
probably the former), brought them together. This
may have been quite or very nearly as early as the
formation of the Præraphaelite Brotherhood. At all
events, in 1849 and for some years afterwards we two
were exceedingly intimate with Hannay, and tolerably
conversant with his "set." This set was greatly unlike
that into which my associations as a P.R.B. had ushered
me. The P.R.B.'s were all high-thinking young men,
assuredly not exempt from several of the infirmities of
human nature, but bent upon working up to a true
ideal in art, and marked by habits generally abstemious
rather than otherwise. To deny themselves the good
things of this life when forthcoming was not their
notion, but, having next to no money to spend, they
stuck to necessities and eschewed superfluities. Dante
Gabriel, it is to be acknowledged, was by nature of an
unthrifty turn ; but, hard compulsion being now upon
him, he only trifled with shillings when he would have
dearly liked to disperse bank-notes. The Hannay set

were equally impecunious, but not equally abstemious. They also may have laid out little money, having laid in still less ; but they breathed the atmosphere of "devil-may-care," and were minded to jollify as best they could.

James Hannay, who had received a good education and retained throughout life a strong gusto for "Ciceronian and Horatian Latin" etc., began in the Royal Navy. Some trivial escapade brought him to a court-martial which decided against him ; but this decision was, on some technical ground, reversed by the Admiralty, so that no slur rested upon him. Being out of the Navy, he betook himself to literature ; and literature appeared to be his more natural sphere of the two, though he never seemed to lose his interest in matters of the sea, and might, I dare say, under favouring circumstances, have made an excellent officer. His first publication was a collection of slight naval tales and jocularities named *Biscuits and Grog*. This had come out soon before I knew him. It was followed by *Singleton Fontenoy*, a three-volume naval novel ; and there was another three-volume novel, *Eustace Conyers*, soon afterwards. These were books of much brilliancy and *esprit;* possibly they are still remembered, and, even if they have shared the mortal fate of all novels save the very fewest, they rightfully count as good work. Hannay saw something of Carlyle, and also of Thackeray, for whom he wrote the notes on the series of *The English Humourists*. Afterwards he took to journalism rather than regular literature, becoming for various years the editor of *The Edinburgh Courant*. This entailed his removal to the Scottish capital, and from that time I saw him but seldom. He was a witty and very telling speaker, often taking a part in debating societies and the like, and being a formidable antagonist who generally tackled others far better than they tackled him. His aspect corresponded very well to his tone of mind : alert-looking, with a winning smile and tolerably regular features, and thick dark hair ; he was plump, with an increasing tendency to fatness. When I first knew him, he might be regarded as a sort of Radical ; this however was only superficial, as his real liking was for " blood " and pedigree, and their ally, heraldry ; the latter usurped his mind to a rather provoking degree, and, to some hearers, damaged the tone of his always copious and sparkling conversation. While still youthful, Hannay married a beautiful and most estimable lady, Miss Margaret Thompson. Their marriage was, I apprehend, in most respects a happy one. She died scarcely past thirty, and he remarried with a cousin. Then he was appointed British Consul in Barcelona by one of our Conservative Governments —this being the party to which in all his later years he adhered. There he died in 1873, aged not quite forty-six. He expired suddenly, and was found dead in his chair.

I have known several men of exalted genius, such as a " clever " man is not to be compared with ; but among the clever I could hardly cite one superior to Hannay, who was besides a most bright-humoured, friendly, and even affectionate companion. In my circle, the man whom Hannay particularly cherished was Dante Rossetti ; to him he dedicated an agreeable edition of Edgar Poe's poems. He had two serious defects : a propensity to drink, which may at first have gone little beyond convivial good-fellowship, but which gradually deepened and darkened, and a quarrelsome habit which gained him several enemies, and perhaps at last left him but few friends. I did not myself find him quarrelsome, and I think the bad habit may have grown upon him rather through a faculty of saying sharp and amusing things, and the "joy of battle" natural to an intellectual gladiator, than from any real taint of spite or ill-nature—of which in my own observation he seemed incapable. Throughout my experience his habits of life were careless and Bohemian, but I never found him other than honourable.

A strange character whom I knew in connexion with Hannay was William North; possibly I met him first in company with Woolner, but he must have been an inheritance from Hannay. North was quite young when I encountered him—not more perhaps than twenty-three; but he was already the author of a novel, *Anti-Coningsby*, which had made some noise. He produced two other novels fully as odd: *The City of the Jugglers* and *The Impostor*. He wrote a little in comic papers and other serials, and was constantly trying and failing to start a magazine. One he did start, of a rapidly consumptive tendency, *North's Magazine*. He also published a strange book named *The Infinite Republic;* it was of the speculative-philosophic kind, prompted (I take it) by Edgar Poe's *Eureka*, and North seemed to regard it as a quintessence of the finest thought of the oncoming age. I have read it; but avow myself incompetent to say whether it is partial sense or unmodified nonsense. Hannay (or was it I?) entitled it "The Infinite Pub" and the "Infinite Demirep." North was the son of a gentleman in good circumstances, but his eccentricities had alienated his father, and he

had to shift for himself. His shifts were numerous—
assuredly more numerous than his shirts. He shifted
lodgings among other things ; and how he managed to
keep a roof above his head was often a mystery to me.
There was one occasion, long laughed over among us,
when North entered a new furnished lodging, and a
large posse of his chums gathered to his house-warming.
Grog was going freely as a *sine quâ non* ; but tumblers
or other civilized drinking-vessels were dismally deficient, and some of us (I think I was one) had to be
accommodated with the chimney ornaments. North was
a republican in politics (but *The Infinite Republic* was not
concerned with that matter) ; religious opinions he had
none, but only anti-religious. To be tied down to
church ceremonies was of course not in his line ; and
when he quitted London for the United States—which
he did at some such date as 1853—he left behind him
two women who had some claim upon him. To one of
these he was seriously and even passionately attached ;
she figures in his verses as Blondine, while the other is
" the dark-souled Brunetta." In New York, as I have
some reason to judge, North made a not inconsiderable
impression by his tales and other writings, and indeed
he was clearly a " clever fellow," who might even be
credited with a spark of genius. But, in America as in
England, money refused to be forthcoming ; so North,
after various struggles, determined to struggle no more,
and he committed suicide. The date would be 1855 or
thereabouts. Spite of his harum-scarum methods of life,
he had the habits and feelings of a gentleman, and held
his head high ; in his conversation there was more of
intellectual excitement than incitement, but there was
somewhat of both. William North was a pale, rather

fleshy young man, with bright eyes, a slightly high clear voice, and very pallid straight hair of a yellowish tinge.

Another man in the Hannay connexion of whom I saw much at one time was Mr. (now Dr.) Benjamin Horatio Paul, a scientific chemist; he made a good professional position, and he was till quite recently the editor of the *Pharmaceutical Journal*. He had studied in a German University. Mr. Paul was an agreeable companion, well informed on a variety of subjects, and not addicted to "fads." Towards 1852 he contracted with a publisher to bring out a translation of the *Memoirs and Correspondence of Mallet du Pan*, an interesting work relating to the French Revolution from the royalist point of view. He invited me to co-operate with him in the translation, and a third of the printed book may probably be my work; my mother and sisters also aided in a minor proportion. In 1854 I took a walking-tour with Mr. Paul in Devonshire and Cornwall. We crossed Dartmoor on foot, and got along (but not always on foot) to the Land's End. I recollect that, when we were nearing Tavistock or some such place, we had fixed upon the Union Hotel as our bourne. We met a countrified sort of man, and asked him the way to "the Union." Our appearance, it would seem, did not inspire confidence in our solvency; we had taken our coats off, and of course were carrying knapsacks. The man pointed to a big building faintly visible in the distance, and informed us that that was the Union. We wended our way towards it, and then found it to be the Union Workhouse. We did not make it our abiding-place. Workhouse or no workhouse, we had a fine tramp of the whole expedition. Early in 1903 I had the satisfaction of receiving a visit from this old intimate —a robust, vigorous man of his age.

Other habitués of Hannay who came within my ken were Mr. Henry Sutherland Edwards, the musical expert and critic, whom I always found polite and eminently good-humoured; Edmund Yates, who after several years made a great success as Editor of *The World*, and not with that alone; Austin, who co-operated with Mr. Ralph in writing *Lives of the Poets Laureate ;* Sidney (a son of Laman) Blanchard, who went to India to assume the editorship of a leading newspaper; and Bridgeman, a jocular writer of those days—a parody which he wrote of Patmore's poem of *The River* tickled us not a little. There was also Mr. T. E. Kebbel, a thinking man and accomplished political writer on the Conservative side. George Augustus Sala was well known to Hannay. I question whether I ever met him in Hannay's company; but later on I saw him a few times at my brother's house. His talents were obvious enough, but he did not attract me in any marked degree. I also encountered Albert Smith once or twice, but this was not in the Hannay circle.

Mr. James Lennox Hannay, who became for many years a police magistrate in London, was a cousin of our James Hannay. As a young man, he had an uncommonly picturesque face, and he sat to Holman Hunt for the head of Valentine in the justly admired picture from the *Two Gentlemen of Verona*. A friend of his, Mr. Aspinall—a young lawyer who emigrated to Australia —was the Proteus in the same picture.

John Ferguson McLennan, the author of the celebrated book *Primitive Marriage* published in 1865, was familiar with James Hannay; but my acquaintance with him came, I think, rather through Alexander Munro, who belonged to the same part of Scotland. McLennan, who had been a Cambridge student of high promise, was on excellent terms with me. In 1854 he got me to accompany him for a few days to Cambridge, and introduced me to two or three men of mark in the University; also to Alexander Macmillan, then a rising young publisher in the town, who afterwards (amid his very extensive transactions) brought out various books for my sister Christina and two for myself. McLennan, when I first knew him, was studying for the Bar: his after-career was in Scotland, as an advocate. He was a rather "gawky" young man, with a tall throat and prominent features the reverse of regular. He was then of the unorthodox turn in matters of faith and speculation; how far this may have persisted later on I know not. His mind was rapid in its processes and full of acuteness; his speech had discernment and point. He was among the men whose society I should have best liked to cultivate; but his removal to Scotland interfered, and after that I only saw him two or three times. Few readers of *Primitive Marriage* may perhaps be aware that McLennan printed at an early date some *Poems on the Præraphaelite Principle;* also, in the name of "Iconoclast," a pamphlet on *Scottish Art and Artists* in 1860, in which Alexander Smith, the "spasmodic" poet, was his *collaborateur.* It raised a considerable fluster.

In my eighth section I have mentioned Mrs. Mary Howitt and her daughter Anna Mary as having first been met by me at the house of Serjeant Cox. Later on I was not infrequently at their residence at Highgate Rise, where I knew William Howitt as well. I found Mrs. Howitt a conversable and very sensible woman, having the housewifely along with the literary tone. All the members of this family had a great belief in dreams, premonitions, and the like ; they did not draw the line at ghosts, and this may have ushered in the extreme addiction which Miss Howitt eventually developed for spiritualism, and for spirit rappings, writing, and drawings. She was of an enthusiastic, impulsive nature, more than duly fanciful. If only the spirits had let her alone, she would have drawn and painted very much better than she ever did under their inspiration. In Mrs. Howitt's turn of mind and conversation I never noticed anything to account for her having, at a very advanced period of life, joined the Roman Catholic Church ; unless indeed her propensity to the marvellous may have led her on to the miraculous, and hence to the great authority for miracles. William Howitt was rather positive in speech and demeanour ; however, he had sufficient of the *suaviter in modo* to admit of my getting on with him easily enough. Henry Virtue Tebbs, of whom I saw a good deal at times, lived in the same neighbourhood when first I knew him.

Through the Howitts I became acquainted with Miss Barbara Leigh Smith, afterwards Mrs. Bodichon, a lady of handsome fortune for whom I entertained and have always preserved the most cordial regard. She was indeed one of the most excellent women I have ever known : lavish in beneficence, untiring in her exertions for the advancement of her sex. She was a great promoter, perhaps the foundress, of Girton College. She had fine abilities in various ways—among others, for landscape painting ; which she might have carried further than she did, but for a feeling (not ill-grounded) that, after bringing her work up to a certain level of execution, she injured rather than improved it by any attempt at higher finish. Mrs. Bodichon was a lady of ample but not very graceful form, with a fine animated face, brilliant complexion, and superb profusion of flame-golden hair (Miss Howitt once painted her as Boadicea). Her manner was replete with energy and heartiness : no woman could be freer from those small femininities which make for affectation. To be frank, straightforward, unprejudiced, generous-minded, was a passport to her esteem ; there was none other. Her London house was No. 5 Blandford Square, near Marylebone Road ; she owned also an estate in Sussex—Scalands, near Robertsbridge. Her husband was Dr. Bodichon, a French army physician whom she met in Algeria. I saw hardly anything of him, but understand him to have been a man of some mark, not free from eccentricity : he might be encountered walking about without a hat and *with* a jackal, enacting the part of a semi-domestic dog. He (like Miss Howitt) took very much to spiritualism after a certain date. Mrs. Bodichon was sceptical about more things than one—spiritualism was one of them. Dr. Bodichon, who predeceased her by various years, lived separately from her towards the end. I know nothing in detail of the motive ; but presume that it was mainly because it suited Mrs. Bodichon, and did not suit the Doctor, to be domiciled in England. She was sister to the distinguished Arctic explorer Mr. Leigh Smith. There were two other sisters whom I saw occasionally—Mrs. Ludlow (married to a General in the Army) and Miss Anne (or Nannie) Leigh Smith. This latter lady, after an interval of something like forty-five years or more, I re-met in Rome in 1902, and had some pleasant talk with her. An intimate friend of Mrs. Bodichon before her marriage, known to me in those early days, was Miss Bessie Rayner Parkes, who had a certain reputation as a poetess; daughter of the medical gentleman who founded the "Parkes Museum." She became Madame Belloc, and was converted to Roman Catholicism; chiefly (as I was informed) because, when living abroad, she came to be deeply impressed by the immense agencies for spiritual and moral and material advance which the Catholic Church wields and ever has wielded over the world.

Charles Bagot Cayley, the translator of Dante, has been slightly mentioned here before. Of all men I have known, he was the most typical example of the scholarly and studious nature, inobservant of the ways of the world, and indifferent to them. He was intelligent in various directions; but his interest was almost exclusively concentrated upon books, and more especially linguistics. His faculty for languages was remarkable: several he knew, and others he could master as soon as he applied himself to them. He has left translations from Æschylus, Homer, Dante, Petrarch, and the Hebrew Psalms; he supervised a translation of the New Testament into the Iroquois language. Besides his translations, he wrote a little in verse and in prose, and in a certain sense he wrote well; but nothing that he produced belonged to the "readable" order. This remark might be extended to his translations, all or most—not to that of the *Divina Commedia*; this is in the rhymed ternary metre of its original, and I question whether, considering the great difficulty of the attempt, it has ever been excelled, or even equalled. Cayley, who was of strictly English blood though born in Russia, was in youth decidedly good-looking, with a very large cerebral development, dark hair and eyes, ruddy cheeks, and fairly regular features—which, with the advance of age, became rather pinched. He smiled much, in a furtive sort of way, as if there were some joke which he alone appreciated in full, but into some inkling of which he was willing to induct a less percep- tive bystander. To laugh was not his style. Cayley's costume was always shabby and out of date, yet with a kind of prim decorum in it too. His manner was absent-minded in the extreme. If anything was said to him, he would often pause so long before replying that one was inclined to "give it up," but at last the answer came in a tone between hurry and confusion, and with an articulation far from easy to follow. In truth one viewed his advent with some apprehension, only too conscious that some degree of embarrassment was sure to ensue. He was however, in manner no less than spirit, a thoroughly refined gentleman, even markedly polite. In my circle he was almost the only man who deferred to social propriety so far as to pay, with toler- able regularity, morning calls to ladies. I have known many men who had a larger share of the active virtues than Cayley, but none who seemed freer from aught that savoured of the wrongful or the mean—none who lived the intellectual life with so little obstruction from "the world, the flesh, and the devil."

Cayley had some small income of his own. By literature he never made anything to be called even partially a maintenance. In youth he was an official in the Patent Office in Chancery Lane ; then, in an evil hour and under solicitation from some acquaintance of a speculative turn, he embarked a large part of his capital in a scheme for setting up advertisement-boards at railway stations. This was in some such remote year as 1855. The scheme at that time proved an utter failure, but, as every railway traveller knows to the grievance of his eye and taste, the plan revived, and has attained the most formidable proportions. After thus losing his money, Cayley had to rub on as he could ; fortunately he belonged to a family in moderately good circumstances. His mother and sisters lived at Blackheath ; his brother was the celebrated Cambridge mathematician, Professor Arthur Cayley. The latter was rather the elder of the two ; he had been the incessant prize-winner at King's College, London, when I was in the school, and he appeared to me (from the little I saw of him) to be almost as regardless of externals as his brother. Before my mind's eye is a hat of his that was a sight to see—or *not* to see. In the house of Mrs. Cayley I met —but only once—another great mathematician, Professor Sylvester, who soon afterwards obtained an American appointment.

Charles Cayley's noticeable face has been well recorded in a picture by Ford Madox Brown—that of *Crabtree watching the Transit of Venus*, in the important series in Manchester Town Hall. Oliver Madox Brown utilized him in a different way in his uncompleted novel *The Dwale-bluth :* the scholarly, wool-gathering clergyman Oliver Serpleton is in several respects limned from Cayley. The book was published in 1876, after its author's death. Whether Cayley read it and recognized the "take-off" of himself is unknown to me ; it may well be that he did so.

I will here insert a small domestic anecdote ; bachelors are not expected to tolerate it. My youngest daughter Mary attained the age of two in April 1883. In her presence, but without her exhibiting any interest in the transaction, I had been reciting to her elder brother more than once the letter-names in the Greek alphabet. One day, which cannot have been later than the autumn of 1883 (for he died in December of that year), Cayley paid us a call. Mary had heard some of us say that he was a good Greek scholar; so she marched up to him, and with vigorous articulation and no preliminaries she declaimed, "Alpha beta gamma delta epsilon eta theta iota kappa lambda mu." She did not attempt the other letters. Cayley received this performance with amused surprise. Mary was afterwards reminded that she had missed " zeta "; but it turned out that she had done this advisedly, fancying that " zeta " was much the same thing as " zitty " (the nursery misrepresentation for " little "), and she therefore rejected it as " silly." This may perhaps have been the very last occasion on which I had a talk with my good friend Cayley.

It was, I believe, in some way through Cayley that my brother and I became acquainted with the pre-eminent Celtic scholar Dr. Whitley Stokes. We shortly lost sight of him, as he went to India, where he became a Legal Member of Council. I knew him again however in later years; and to know him is to respect and like him. He has, I think, some of the same abstracted, unworldly habit of mind as Cayley, but this in a very minor degree and conjoined with a full measure of insight into affairs. Two brothers—Franklin and Henry Leifchild, the latter a sculptor—were intimate with Cayley, and were known to me both in that connexion and otherwise. Franklin Leifchild had literary ambition, and with a little more good luck than ever attended him he might have made a name.

The last literary acquaintance whom I have to mention at this stage of my career—and one of the most illustrious at any stage—is John Ruskin. In my *Memoir of Dante Rossetti* I have explained that Ruskin first observed and admired (towards February 1853) some works by my brother, and made his personal acquaintance in April 1854, immediately before Mrs. Ruskin, who afterwards became Lady Millais, separated from him. My own first sight of Ruskin was in November 1854, when he delivered some lectures, which I attended, upon matters of art. Ruskin was then nearly thirty-six years of age, of fair stature, exceedingly thin (I have sometimes laid a light grasp on his coat-sleeve, and there seemed to be next to nothing inside it), narrow-shouldered, with a clear, bright complexion, very thick yellow hair, beetling eyebrows (which he inherited from his father), and side-whiskers. His nose was acute and prominent, his eyes blue and limpid, the general expression of his face singularly keen, with an ample allowance of self-confidence, but without that hard and unindulgent air which sometimes accompanies keenness. His mouth was unshapely, having (as I was afterwards informed) been damaged by the bite of a dog in early childhood. He had a sunny smile, however, which went far to atoning for any defect in the mouth. The cheek-bones were prominent, the facial angle receding somewhat below the tip of the nose. As my brother's report of Ruskin's personal appearance had never been eulogistic, I was agreeably impressed by what I saw of his looks, as well as by his voice and manner. There was a perceptibly Scottish tone in his speech, with a slight Northumbrian burr. As a public speaker he was at times most eloquent, and he never failed to be interest-

ing and engaging ; in fact, the extreme interest of his
personality pervaded all that he said, and ensured its
acceptance from, at any rate, that point of view.   I was
by the end of 1854 a most ardent admirer of Ruskin's
writings (unknown to me, as to almost all the P.R.B.'s,
when the Brotherhood was first formed) ; and so I
listened to his utterances as a lecturer with the liveli-
est gratification and respect.   At one of these lectures
I became known to Ruskin, and was shortly invited
to dine with himself and his parents in their house
at Denmark Hill, Camberwell.   The house (is it still
standing ?) was a well-looking detached edifice, white,
with a pillared front, situate in its own spacious garden
grounds.

I recollect Ruskin's father very well—a spare man,
hardly up to middle height, of straightforward, observant aspect, and alert, frank address.   He had a full
crop of bristly grey hair and very bushy dark eyebrows.   He was (as many of my readers will know)
a sherry-merchant who, rising from small beginnings,
had made an ample fortune ; in one instance he brought
to table some old Amontillado sherry which had been
on board the " Victory " when Nelson fell in the battle
of Trafalgar.   I drank the historical liquor with a due
sense of satisfaction, but its flavour was almost gone.
Mrs. Ruskin, the mother, was a lady well advanced
in years, of rather imposing presence ; in her manner
there was a certain reserved decorum mingled with
essential kindliness.   John Ruskin was at this time a
strict Christian believer of the anti-Romanist order ; no
doubt his parents were the same, and I take it that any
wilful intrusion of a contrary opinion would have been
anything but welcome to them.   There was something

touching in the family relation between "John" and his parents. He was necessarily regarded by them as a "shining light" who had done and would continue to do very considerable things in the realm of thought; none the less he was their boy, living *en famille* as the subordinate member of the household. And his own demeanour, so far as I ever witnessed it, was in full conformity with this estimate of the filial relation.

I saw Ruskin pretty frequently between the years 1855 and 1860; chiefly at his own house, sometimes in my brother's studio or elsewhere. After this our meetings were fewer. Ruskin and my brother ceased to see one another in July 1865, though they resumed to a small extent after some interval. I dined with him in December 1866, and again in 1867, and I question whether it was ever my good fortune to speak to him afterwards. He became Slade Professor in Oxford, and then a resident at Brantwood, Coniston, and my chance of encountering him was gone. In 1866 I found his cousin Miss Agnew residing in the house along with his widowed mother, whose sight was failing; the former is now Mrs. Arthur Severn, and of late I have again had the pleasure of meeting her along with her husband, both at Brantwood and in London.

Did I like Ruskin? Most assuredly I did. His manner to me was gentle in the extreme, and almost profusely amiable, with more of "sentiment" in its tone than I had been used to in other circles; there was very little of that in the P.R.B. I did not find him dictatorial or pragmatic; but one element in our relative position was the tacit assumption on both sides that he knew a great deal about matters in which I also was interested, and that my cue was to profit by what he could and would impart to me. Founding upon this assumption, I held an intercourse with Ruskin both easy and alluring. There was no pretence on my part of unqualified acceptance of every word of wisdom that fell from his lips : I gave expression to my own opinions, with deference but also with candour.

The matters which brought me most into contact with Ruskin were as follows. In February 1855, being asked by Mr. William J. Stillman, then a landscape painter and editor of an American art-review named *The Crayon*, to recommend some person as English correspondent to that serial, Ruskin recommended me, and I acted accordingly for a year or two. About the same time there was a short-lived art-review in London entitled *The Artist*, to which I was a contributor ; and, finding there some petulant misstatements as to Ruskin's published opinions on some questions of architectural or other art, I wrote to correct them—an act with which Ruskin expressed himself pleased. He was also pleased (so I was informed) with an article about him which I published in *The Broadway* towards 1869. I had in *The Spectator* reviewed various volumes of his, but without his knowing (so far as I remember) anything about these critiques. As already observed, he was the treasurer, while I was the secretary, for the fund raised to purchase for the National Gallery a picture by Thomas Seddon, deceased in 1856. I was also in 1857 the secretary for an undertaking named the American Exhibition of British Art. The promoters of this scheme—including myself in a subordinate degree— were very desirous of obtaining from Ruskin some expression of adherence or counsel; but this he declined to give, on the ground that he knew nothing of

America. In the autumn of 1857 I took a fancy for studying drawing in the class superintended by Ruskin in the Working Men's College; he taught upon a rather peculiar system, which amounted to regarding the object to be copied as a series of planes varying in their degrees of lighting or shadowing, and drawing it as such without much, or without any, preliminary outlining. I drew under Ruskin's supervision, upon this system, for two or three months; he seemingly considered me a reasonably fair scholar, but far indeed from being among the best; and there were some who produced very remarkable work on the plan in question. In the winter of 1858–9 Ruskin was diligently engaged in the National Gallery in sorting and arranging the vast collection of water-colours and drawings bequeathed by Turner. I volunteered to examine Turner's notebooks, and extract any entries in them, prose or verse, which might appear to be of interest. This was a somewhat tough job, the entries being slovenly and obscure.

One day during this process, 8 February 1859, I was asked by Ruskin to meet him at Long's Hotel in Bond Street, share his dinner there, and go on to the National Gallery. As we were leaving the hotel, he said to me, " To-day I am forty years old : how much time gone, and how much work demanding to be done ! " Mr. Cecil Rhodes (not, I take it, a person of a very Ruskinian attitude of mind) is recorded to have said something of the same kind on his death-bed in 1902.

Besides these matters which brought me into direct personal contact with Ruskin, there were two where he and I may have seemed to outsiders to be a little at odds ; but this was only on the surface. In 1867 he wrote a series of letters to a personage of my acquaintance rather noticeable in his way, Thomas Dixon, a cork-cutter at Sunderland, and the letters were at the time published in some newspaper. In this correspondence, dating soon after the close of the American Civil War, Ruskin expressed hostility to the cause of the Northern States ; Dixon in reply, rather unnecessarily, cited me as among those who entertained and had published contrary opinions—and indeed I had throughout felt very strongly on the side of the North, and against the attempt of the South to perpetuate slave-holding in a separate Republic. Ruskin hereupon responded in terms making light of my claims to attention ; and his response was printed in the newspaper. It may be that what Ruskin here said was perfectly conformable to reason ; of this I am not the best judge. I would rather have been left out of the controversy altogether than brought into it unasked in that form ; Ruskin omitted the passage (with some others) when the letters were reissued in book shape, *Time and Tide by Wear and Tyne*. The second occurrence was the much-talked-of trial of the action Whistler *v.* Ruskin in 1878—an action with the inception of which, as can easily be conceived, I had nothing whatever to do.   I have been and am a hearty admirer, within bounds, of the art of Whistler, in many of its examples ; and, though I had not written anything about the particular picture which Ruskin had seen fit to assail (representing Cremorne Gardens with fireworks), I *had* written something about a different picture which was produced in the course of the trial. Such being the case, I was suddenly and without the least forewarning subpœnaed, just before the trial, to give evidence as a witness on

Whistler's behalf. I of necessity obeyed the subpœna, and expressed in the witness-box my true opinion of more than one of the artist's paintings, including that which Ruskin had vilified, and which indeed I considered very inferior to some others. I was thus compelled to act, willy-nilly, in opposition to Ruskin's interest in the action. I regretted to have been coerced into so delicate, and in some sense so false, a position ; and I wrote to him explaining the exact facts. I may here perhaps as well say that I think Ruskin was substantially wrong in this matter. He had expressed himself in contemptuous and irritating terms regarding work done by an artist already of no slight distinction, and regarding this artist himself. His estimate, so far as one particular picture was concerned, may perhaps have been not very far from the mark : but there is such a thing as courtesy in criticism ; and a critic of so much potency as Ruskin, in the wielding of his pen and in his influence over the public, ought not to have lost sight of that.

The fact is now well known that the mind of this vigorous and subtle thinker, great writer, and most generous and in many respects admirable man, broke down at times ; to blink the fact would be useless. I gather that the year 1860, when he was abroad, was the first year in which he showed something of a morbid habit of mind, or incipient hypochondria. Certainly, when I saw him in my brother's chambers in February 1862, immediately after the death of my sister-in-law Lizzie (Siddal), I found the whole tone of his thought on religious subjects changed, and the ardent devout Protestant figured as a total disbeliever in any form of the Christian or other defined faith. I might add the expression of my opinion that the great ascendency which Thomas Carlyle obtained towards this time over the mind of Ruskin did him more harm than good : Carlyle being one of those strong but extreme men who may brace very robust natures, but who usurp upon the innate function of more delicate organisms. Personally I did not, from first to last, witness any symptom of impaired reason in Ruskin. He always presented the aspect of a man of very sensitive mind and feelings, somewhat strained and overstrained, and a little liable to take a contrary or perverse bias—in the sense that, when there was every fair presumption and anticipation that he would be well pleased and affirmative, he turned out to be punctilious and negative. Thus, for instance, while I was studying at the Working Men's College, my friend John Tupper asked me to see whether Ruskin was willing to look at some moderate-sized work of his in sculpture and to vouchsafe an opinion upon it. I willingly complied. Not so Ruskin, who said that he did not understand sculpture, nor profess to estimate it, never having studied the human form. Another remark of his to me regarding sculptural art may be worth recording : that sculpture dissociated from architecture seemed to him out of its proper sphere, and appealed to him comparatively little. In this bias of his towards non-compliance there was clearly nothing irrational, but it appeared to hint of a certain deviousness of temperament, or even a " bee in the bonnet." I conclude by saying, " All honour and love to one of the most exalted spirits of our time, John Ruskin."

XIII

THEATRICAL AND OTHER DIVERSIONS

BEFORE I take leave here of the earlier period of my youth, I will say a few words about amusements in which I have indulged from time to time. I have already confessed that for the various forms of athletic pastimes—such as cricket or golf or football—I have neither aptitude nor taste ; still less for anything in which the essential zest consists in killing, persecuting, or inconveniencing an animal—hunting, shooting, fishing, and the like. To stick a pin through a butterfly, or voluntarily to crush a worm on an earthen path, or to give a stamp gratis to a daddy-long-legs, appears to me about as pleasing as to set two cocks fighting, or to plunge a banderilla or a sword into a bull in a bull-fight ; and that appears to me not pleasing in the least. Dante Gabriel used to say : " A black-beetle is a moderately agreeable animal ; it is when you squash him that he becomes disagreeable." Also I have mentioned in my *Memoir of Dante Rossetti* some of the amusements, such especially as colouring theatrical prints, which absorbed much of his and my attention in childhood, and to this I shall not recur.

Of childish or boyish pastimes or romps, nothing pleased me better than ninepins and blind-man's buff.

I was likewise fond of cards. The easiest of all games, Beggar my Neighbour, was my favourite, and rather later the game which the Italians call *tre sette*. At this last my brother and I—towards the ages of fifteen and fourteen—have often sat playing for two or three hours at a stretch. We never then staked money, and indeed could not have risked anything much beyond a penny or halfpenny. Whist I have frequently played without any skill or any serious relish. Since I attained the age of thirty-five or so my card-playing has been rare indeed. I have occasionally taken a hand to make up a card party, but I might say that this was never for my own gratification.

Dominoes I enjoyed in boyhood ; drafts, little ; chess, much. This is the only game which I have cared for in fully adult years. I would fain play it well, but as a fact I play it worse than indifferently. A real chess-player would not regard me as a chess-player at all.

It appears to me that there are four "manly exercises" in which all men ought to be fairly expert ; they are swimming, boating, riding, and cycling. With some shame, I acknowledge that I am not proficient in any one of these. Swimming and cycling are unknown to me. Of boating I have done a very little, and of riding still less. Of boxing I did at one time, towards 1857, under the incitement of my cherished intimate Holman Hunt, learn some rudiment ; it pleased me well and was of some benefit to me, but I did not pursue it. A good steady country walk I have always enjoyed ; not that I ever performed anything in this way deserving any sort of mention. I fancy I never greatly exceeded twenty miles in one day.

More than once people have expressed some surprise

to me that, living as I have done so sedentary a life, with little exercise, no athletics, muscular strength below the average, no particular observance of hygiene, few diversions, and a considerable share of close day-by-day occupation (reading and writing the chief things), I should nevertheless have reached an advanced age in a condition of health which, compared to that of many septuagenarians, may be reckoned observably sound. Such however is the fact, and a fact for which I cannot be too thankful. It is true that since 1878 gout became apparent in my constitution, and this has been (not too agreeably) supplemented by sciatica and rheumatism ; but these troubles have not ruled me with that rod of iron which might, at their first development, have been anticipated. The fact that I have always been temperate in diet (abstemious I could not call myself), and more especially temperate of late years as a corrective against gout, may perhaps account for some of my sound health. When a friend tells me that I must have a very strong constitution because, having done no cricket and football and not much open-air exercise, but in their stead a ponderous load of sedentary work, I am fairly healthy at the age of seventy-three and upwards, I am tempted to reply that other men, if they would live a quiet life, without a dour persistency in violent exertion or in distracting amusements, might perhaps at a like age find themselves in at least as good case as mine is. In other words : It is open to argument that an aged man, if healthy, is so in virtue of his having done a deal of vigorous physical exertion, without its being assumed that his constitution is exceptionally sound ; and it is also, on the other hand, open to argument that another such man is healthy in virtue of his having pursued a moderate and quiet course of life, without that vigorous exertion, and also without the assumption of a specially sound constitution.

In mere boyhood I went but very seldom to a theatre; rather less seldom to an opera, as my father (chiefly through knowing the great operatic basso Lablache) received every now and then an order for the opera at Her Majesty's Theatre, and I with others of the family got the advantage of it. I can recall to mind some operatic events which seem now of highly remote date; such as the first (I quite believe it was the very first) London season of the celebrated Giulia Grisi, whom I then saw in *La Gazza Ladra*. I recollect also the renowned tenor Rubini, and of course the unmatched Lablache; clearly before me moreover is the great impression created by the death of Madame Malibran at an early age, but I never heard her voice. All this was some few years before the appearance even of Mario on the operatic stage. I witnessed likewise the return of Madame Sonntag to the boards, after some years of retirement: she sang the part of Zerlina in *Don Giovanni*. As ballet-dancers, I have seen Fanny Elssler (in *The Daughter of the Danube*); Cerito various times; Taglioni perhaps only once. Later on—say between 1850 and 1870, and afterwards too—I heard many of the leading vocalists: to run over their names here might be superfluous. It may be a prejudice arising out of that freshness of juvenile impressions which no subsequent maturity of judgment can wholly rival; but I can hardly divest myself of the notion that Grisi, Lablache, and Mario (Rubini did not so strongly impress me), reached, in the combination of singing and acting, a height to

which none of their successors on the stage of Italian
opera has fully attained; I might however add Madame
Alboni, and also Jenny Lind. Madame Viardot Garcia
I saw possibly only once ; she was then past her prime,
but appeared to me singularly fascinating.

In theatricals again I can remember a remote event—
the first season of Rachel on the London boards; she was
acting Chimène, in Corneille's *Cid*, when I saw her first.
Afterwards I saw her in *Phèdre*, *Adrienne Lecouvreur*, and
one or two other pieces. I should not hesitate to say
that, of all the actresses I have beheld, Rachel was the
greatest; at once the most subtle and the most intense.
I cannot think that Madame Ristori, whom I met once
or twice in private society at Little Holland House,
was, for all her undisputed excellences, truly a rival of
Rachel. I received more unmixed satisfaction from
Madame Favart, whom I once saw in Paris as Dona
Sol in Victor Hugo's *Hernani*, and also in another
piece.

Among male actors I would place highest Tommaso
Salvini, whose Othello I witnessed; next to him possibly
Frédéric Lemaître, the Robert Macaire, César de Bazan,
etc., of the central nineteenth century. As regards
Salvini, an expression which Browning used in conversing with me may be worth recording. He said that
he had seen Salvini act Œdipus, and that it was
absolutely the finest effort of art he had ever beheld;
not only the finest in the art of acting, but in any art
whatsoever, including painting, music, etc. I do not say
that this statement of Browning's was a perfectly reasonable one, but certain it is that he made it to me, and
this in a tone of entire conviction.

As I grew up towards manhood, and for many years

afterwards, I went with some frequency to the theatre ; have not at any time been what is cacophonously termed a "first-nighter." I remember very well the tragedians Macready, Phelps, Mr. and Mrs. Charles Kean, Gustavus Vasa Brook, Charlotte Cushman, Helen Faucit, Miss Glyn (as afore-mentioned), and some others ; not to speak of later men such as Fechter. Of these actors, Macready must certainly have been the best, taken all round ; though the hardness of his visage and his style rather disposed one to lean towards some of his competitors. I hold that Brook as Othello, and Fechter as Hamlet, surpassed Macready in those particular parts. I once saw Mrs. Butler (Fanny Kemble) as Desdemona. She had then returned to the stage for a short while, after an interval of several years ; she was not young, and she *was* fat, and yet she appeared to me a very charming woman and an admirable actress—dignified and gentle. For a touch of positive genius—having a tragic affinity, though he acted in burlesque—I am not sure that, among British actors, I ever saw the equal of Frederick Robson, who figured as Shylock, Medea, etc. The Lyceum and Adelphi Theatres, during the time of the Keeleys, Madame Céleste, Miss Woolgar, and Wright, all most enjoyable, and of Paul Bedford, whom I wholly disliked, were favourite haunts of mine ; also the Princess's, with the Keans and Alfred Wigan—the last a most able and finished performer. I saw at the Lyceum Miss Fairbrother as the dandified Captain of the Forty Thieves, in the burlesque of that name ; just before she quitted the stage, much to the regret of the admirers of her shapely limbs and sweet visage, and was domesticated with the Duke of Cambridge. Naturally I recollect scores of other actors of a now remote period, as well as such contemporaries as Irving, Ellen Terry, etc.; but these I need not pretend to deal with.

As to concerts and other musical performances, my position has been rather an anomalous one. The Rossettis were not a musical family ; they had no gift in that direction (if I except my father to a certain extent), and no craving to be constantly hearing music. All the same, I always took and still take a very vivid delight in the art : a delight as strong as that which I feel for painting or poetry, and, at the moment, still more thrilling perhaps. But, having other occupations which absorbed my time and attention, I have never learned anything about musical art in detail, and have often gone on for long spaces of time without hearing it at all. An ignoramus I am, but not a wholly contented one ; indeed, the reverse of that. Being an ignoramus in music, I will not intrude upon the reader any impressions of mine concerning it ; further than to say that, whatever may be the homage duly payable to Wagner, I could never feel that, because of that homage, one could reasonably slight or ignore some beautiful music of preceding times, including the now much-neglected operatic work of the Italian school.

XIV

DANTE ROSSETTI AND
ELIZABETH SIDDAL

IN my *Memoir of Dante Rossetti* I have spoken at some
length of Miss Siddal; how my brother knew her
towards 1850; was in love with her soon afterwards;
married her in May 1860; and lost her by death in
February 1862. I also, in the spring of 1903, wrote
for *The Burlington Magazine* an article (bearing the
same title as that of my present section) forming a
brief monograph of her life and doings—No. 15 in my
preface. It is not my intention to go over these
matters here again in any detail. A few subsidiary
points may however be mentioned, as bearing upon my
own personal reminiscences.

Miss Siddal sat in the first instance to Walter Deverell
for two or three of the heads in his works; and afterwards she sat not only to Dante Rossetti, but also to
Holman Hunt and Millais. In those days, therefore, I
saw her not unfrequently; for the several P.R.B.'s were
wont to look one another up without stint and without
ceremony, though always (it must be understood) with
some regard to the professional requirements of artists
who could not be lightly disturbed when actually en-
grossed in their art work. Afterwards, when my brother
and Miss Siddal were engaged lovers, and when she was

BY DANTE G. ROSSETTI.

CARICATURE OF MISS SIDDAL AND HIMSELF.

CHATHAM PLACE, c. 1855.

very continually attending in his studio, partly in that relation, and partly also because she had begun drawing and painting on her own account under his direction, I saw her seldomer.   No rational man wants to be No. 3 in that very well-known condition of the facts when "two are company but three are none"; therefore I was careful not to put my brother out of temper, or "Lizzie" out of countenance, when there was every reason for surmising that they would be in *tête à tête*, and extremely well satisfied so to continue.   Notwithstanding these considerations, I did see them together now and again : not exactly often, but also not rarely.

I entertained a very sincere regard for Miss Siddal ; who, apart from her remarkable gifts (truly noteworthy in a person who had grown up to womanhood outside of artistic or literary influences), always appeared to be pure-minded and fine-natured in an eminent degree. Merely to look at her was enough to persuade one of this.   Yet, as I have said in my memoir afore-cited, her inner personality did not float upon the surface of her speech or bearing ; to me it remained, if not strictly enigmatic, still mainly undivulged.

During her brief married life I saw very little of her, and by no means much of my brother.   This was a matter of casualty, dependent upon her constant ill-health, my brother's occupations and also my own, the distance between our residences, and so on.   There was no sort of reluctance on my part, nor I think on hers, that we should meet much oftener than we did.   The opportunities were scanty, and neither of us was addicted to *making* opportunities when they did not naturally present themselves.   There were certainly various persons who saw more than I did, or than my mother and sisters did, of Lizzie when married to my brother : Madox Brown and his family, William Morris and his wife, Edward Burne-Jones and his wife, and Algernon Charles Swinburne ; these chiefly, and there may have been one or two others besides.

Mr. Swinburne penned a noble and touching eulogium of Mrs. Dante Rossetti, which he inserted in a review to meet a temporary purpose, and which I extracted in my memoir of my brother. In connexion with the published memoir he also wrote to me some additional particulars, and he expressed a wish that they might be printed on any suitable occasion. I ought to have printed them when I edited the volume No. 9 as named in my preface ; it then escaped me to do so, and I have ever since regretted the omission. In my article for *The Burlington Magazine* I did extract a sentence or two. I now reproduce Mr. Swinburne's words in full as follows :—

" Except Lady Trevelyan [this was the first wife of Sir Walter Calverley Trevelyan, of Wallington Hall, Northumberland, a lady known to me chiefly through my intimacy with William Bell Scott], I never knew so brilliant and appreciative a woman—so quick to see and so keen to enjoy that rare and delightful fusion of wit, humour, character-painting, and dramatic poetry—poetry subdued to dramatic effect—which is only less wonderful and delightful than the highest works of genius. I used to come and read to her sometimes, when she was well enough, at Chatham Place ; and I shall never forget her delight in Fletcher's magnificent comedy of *The Spanish Curate*. I read her (of course with occasional skips, though there really is not much need for a Bowdler) the superb scenes in which that worthy and his ' old honest sexton' figure ; and I can hear the music of her laughter to this day when, after disclaiming all knowledge or recollection of an imaginary old friend, they suddenly wake up to the freshest and keenest recollection of him on hearing that he has left each of them a handsome legacy. She thought it better than Shakespear ; and, though I could not allow that, I do think it is better than anything except Shakespear's best, and better, from the comico-metrical point of view, by far than anything of his, whose best comedy is always prose. I won't enlarge on the deeper and sadder side of my brotherly affection for her ; but I shall always be sorrowfully glad and proud to remember her regard for me— not undeserved certainly if the warmest admiration and the greatest delight in her company could deserve it. She was a wonderful as well as a most lovable creature. Watts [i.e. Theodore Watts-Dunton] greatly admires her poem [*A Year and a Day*, first published in my *Memoir of Dante Rossetti*], which is as new to me as to him : I need not add that I agree with him. There is the same note of originality in discipleship which distinguishes her work in art—Gabriel's influence and example not more perceptible than her own independence and freshness of inspiration."

Besides that poem *A Year and a Day*, I published— in the Ruskin-Rossetti volume—eight other poems by Lizzie. Seven of them were, I infer, written before her marriage, and one afterwards. I then knew of yet a few more poems, not easy to decipher from her rough drafts. These I left aside at the time, but later on I determined to make the best of them and copy them out. They are six in number, and I give them here. One only, *A Silent Wood*, was inserted in *The Burlington*

Magazine paper. There are in my hands some other slight scraps, scanty in every sense of the term. I consider that, from this time forward, no further verses by my sister-in-law remain of which the publication would be at all manageable. Those which I here reproduce do not bear any title in her own handwriting : I have thought it better to supply titles. I cannot speak to the dates of these compositions. My only criterion would be the handwriting (a matter in which Lizzie was never an adept) ; and, so far as I see, the handwriting of all the verses, with one exception, might belong either to her unmarried or to her wedded days. The exception is the final piece, called *Lord, may I come ?* This is written in a very shaky and straggling way ; I surmise that it must have been done under the influence of laudanum, which she frequently took by medical orders as a palliative against tormenting neuralgia, and probably not long before her death. There is a wail of pang and pathos in it not readily forgettable. Indeed, one of the most noticeable points in her verses generally (I will not say uniformly) is their excessive and seldom-relieved melancholy—a " darkness that can be felt." It is however a melancholy which to some extent merges into a future hope the sense of settled desolation in this world. The verses give more evidence of a certain spiritual faith, pervasive though undefined, than I ever heard in the writer's conversation.

I

EARLY DEATH

Oh grieve not with thy bitter tears
The life that passes fast :
The gates of heaven will open wide,
And take me in at last.

Then sit down meekly at my side,
  And watch my young life flee :
Then solemn peace of holy death
  Come quickly unto thee.

But, true love, seek me in the throng
  Of spirits floating past ;
And I will take thee by the hands,
  And know thee mine at last.

II

HE AND SHE AND ANGELS THREE

Ruthless hands have torn her
  From one that loved her well ;
Angels have upborne her,
  Christ her grief to tell.

She shall stand to listen,
  She shall stand and sing,
Till three winged angels
  Her lover's soul shall bring.

He and she and the angels three
  Before God's face shall stand :
There they shall pray among themselves,
  And sing at His right hand.

III

A SILENT WOOD

O silent wood, I enter thee
With a heart so full of misery—
For all the voices from the trees
And the ferns that cling about my knees.

In thy darkest shadow let me sit
When the grey owls about thee flit :
There I will ask of thee a boon,
That I may not faint or die or swoon.

Gazing through the gloom like one
Whose life and hopes are also done,
Frozen like a thing of stone,
I sit in thy shadow—but not alone.

Can God bring back the day when we two stood
Beneath the clinging trees in that dark wood?

IV

LOVE AND HATE

Ope not thy lips, thou foolish one,
　　Nor turn to me thy face:
The blasts of heaven shall strike me down
　　Ere I will give thee grace.

Take thou thy shadow from my path,
　　Nor turn to me and pray:
The wild, wild winds thy dirge may sing
　　Ere I will bid thee stay.

Lift up thy false brow from the dust,
　　Nor wild thine hands entwine
Among the golden summer-leaves
　　To mock the gay sunshine.

And turn away thy false dark eyes,
　　Nor gaze into my face:
Great love I bore thee; now great hate
　　Sits grimly in its place.

All changes pass me like a dream,
　　I neither sing nor pray;
And thou art like the poisonous tree
　　That stole my life away.

V

THE PASSING OF LOVE

O God, forgive me that I merged
  My life into a dream of love!
Will tears of anguish never wash
  The poison from my blood?

Love kept my heart in a song of joy,
  My pulses quivered to the tune;
The coldest blasts of winter blew
  Upon me like sweet airs in June.

Love floated on the mists of morn,
  And rested on the sunset's rays;
He calmed the thunder of the storm,
  And lighted all my ways.

Love held me joyful through the day,
  And dreaming ever through the night:
No evil thing could come to me,
  My spirit was so light.

Oh Heaven help my foolish heart
  Which heeded not the passing time
That dragged my idol from its place
  And shattered all its shrine!

VI

LORD, MAY I COME?

Life and night are falling from me,
Death [and day] are opening on me.
Wherever my footsteps come and go
Life is a stony way of woe.
  Lord, have I long to go?
Hollow hearts are ever near me,
Soulless eyes have ceased to cheer me:
  Lord, may I come to Thee?

Life and youth and summer weather
To my heart no joy can gather :
Lord, lift me from life's stony way.
Loved eyes, long closed in death, watch o'er me—
Holy Death is waiting for me—
    Lord, may I come to-day ?
My outward life feels sad and still,
Like lilies in a frozen rill.
I am gazing upwards to the sun,
Lord, Lord, remembering my lost one.[1]
    O Lord, remember me !
How is it in the unknown land ?
Do the dead wander hand in hand ?
Do we clasp dead hands, and quiver
With an endless joy for ever ?.
Is the air filled with the sound
Of spirits circling round and round ?
Are there lakes, of endless song,
To rest our tirèd eyes upon ?
Do tall white angels gaze and wend
Along the banks where lilies bend ?
Lord, we know not how this may be ;
Good Lord, we put our faith in Thee—
    O God, remember me.

[1] I do not know of any "lost one," unless the reference is to the still-born infant (1861). I learned however of late years from Mr. James Siddal (brother of Lizzie) that, shortly before her acquaintance with Dante Rossetti, she had been in lengthened and very exhausting attendance on the sick-bed of another much-loved brother, whose illness ended in death. Possibly this is the allusion—as also in the line "Loved eyes" etc.

ELIZABETH E. SIDDAL (ROSSETTI).

FROM A DRAWING BV D. G, ROSSETTI, C. 1855.

XV

FURTHER ACQUAINTANCES
BURNE-JONES, MORRIS, SWINBURNE,
AND OTHERS

MR. HOLMAN HUNT returned towards the beginning of 1856 from his expedition to Jerusalem and the East. He and I at once resumed our old intimacy, shared with two other Præraphaelites, Woolner and Stephens: of Collinson I had wholly lost sight, and of Millais nearly so. In these respects Dante Rossetti was in a position not unlike my own ; but in course of time some differences of his with Hunt, and more especially with Woolner, arose, which shall not concern us here. Hunt was now a painter of great prominence and no little celebrity: society courted him, and there seemed to be no reason why he should hold society at arm's length. Through this state of things I found myself, as a friend of Mr. Hunt, in the way of seeing several new faces. Shortly before the time when he returned to England, Mr. Edward Burne-Jones sought out my brother, and a warm friendship with him soon ensued. This again introduced me into a fresh circle. I must say something about these two new lines of acquaintanceship, and shall begin with the Holman Hunt connexion. Of all these persons I shall speak rather in relation to what they were when I first knew them than with regard to their later developments, though neither will these be entirely left out of count.

On resettling in London, Mr. Holman Hunt resided in a house in Claverton Terrace, in the Bayswater or Tyburnia district: Mr. Robert Martineau (already mentioned) housed with him, and also Mr. Michael F. Halliday. The latter was a clerk in the House of Lords. This post allowed him a large amount of leisure, and, having artistic inclinations, he became a painter—not quite a professional painter, yet something more than an amateur. I will not say that his pictorial art was excellent: it was commendable, and got diffused in one or two popular engravings. Mr. Halliday was an amusing little man to know. He was very short, with a certain tendency to a hump; he had light hair, and a general look that reminded one somewhat of a poodle-dog or silky terrier. He was not at all of the nervous or self-repressing type, and was well versed in the ways of the world, and thoroughly manly in his habits. His disposition was friendly; and, if he took to a person, he adhered to him with much staunchness. In fact, I have hardly known any one to whom the term "a good fellow" might be more properly and fully applied. He died rather suddenly in 1869, in early middle age.

A much-frequented dwelling in those days was Little Holland House, now demolished, standing close to Melbury Road, Kensington. There was (if I mistake not) a sort of joint or several tenancy between Mr. George F. Watts the celebrated painter, and Mr. Thoby Prinsep with his family; the ostensible appearance of things was that the Prinseps were the tenants, while Mr. Watts was accommodated with a studio and its adjuncts. To visitors of artistic taste the highest attraction consisted in Mr. Watts, and the numerous examples of his painting, whether portraiture or other works: one very conspicuous specimen was the spacious canvas representing a Brewer's Drayman and his team, now in the National British Gallery. Aside from this, shoals of people called to see the Prinseps—people fashionable, literary, artistic, political, and what not. Mr. Prinsep was a highly distinguished Indian official: a large, grand-looking man, but so good-natured in tone and manner that one almost lost sight of his stateliness. Mrs. Prinsep was well matched with him: sumptuously handsome, and with cordial and facile ways which set all her guests at their ease. We strolled in and out of rooms, sunned ourselves in the pleasant garden-grounds, and sought companionship at our option. One of Mr. Watts's pictures represented Mrs. Prinsep and her sister Lady (then Mrs.) Dalrymple; a second represented the Countess Somers, another sister, who had been Miss Virginia Pattle. There were two other sisters: Mrs. Cameron, the famous amateur photographer, whose pictorial effects in sun-portraiture remain (so far as I know) still unrivalled, and Mrs. Jackson, married to a physician in the Hampstead neighbourhood—mother of a most beautiful girl, who became Mrs. Duckworth, and afterwards Lady (Leslie) Stephen. The only son of Mr. and Mrs. Prinsep whom I saw regularly in the house was the future painter and R.A., Val Prinsep. When I first met him, he numbered (I think) only fifteen years, but must even then have been well turned of six feet in stature, with prodigious limbs, and a delightful head of hair of the kind which Rudyard

Kipling has taught us to call "fuzzy-wuzzy." The ready good-nature of his parents had descended upon their son, and made him a pre-eminently winsome demi-giant. Lady Somers and Mrs. Jackson I saw only once or twice; Lady Dalrymple and Mrs. Cameron frequently —also Mrs. Cameron's husband, a planter from Ceylon, a venerable-looking gentleman, much older seemingly than his years. Mrs. Cameron was of a very expansive nature, and honoured me with a large share of her good-will. Lady Dalrymple remains associated in my mind with a big scrapbook of blank paper which she pre-sented to my brother (like myself, a not infrequent visitor in Little Holland House), and into which he inserted, along with a few others, a more than copious series of drawings of Miss Siddal—and a series fuller of the charm of beauty and purity could not easily be found. The drawings got gradually dispersed: one of the best remains with me. Five of them were re-produced in *The Burlington Magazine*.

Mr. Watts bore his part amid the stream of visitors to the Prinseps, yet not so as to clog his own pro-fessional occupations. His demeanour was thoughtful and sedate, and it seemed to be universally understood that he was a man to be approached with respect rather than with anything savouring of the "free and easy." He was not a self-praiser—quite the contrary; and appeared to me rather to deprecate than to court the tribute of admiration which was continually and de-servedly paid to his works. For a year or two about this date, impressed by the remarkable quality imparted to Holman Hunt's paintings by high tints of colour and minute finish of detail, he essayed a style of corres-ponding aim—his *Portrait of Mrs. Nassau Senior* was a

salient example of this ; but it soon became apparent
that his own broader and more generalized treatment
was what suited himself best, and he recurred to it—to
the satisfaction, I should say, of all his most intelligent
admirers. I may be pardoned for stating here that, at
a later date, Mr. Watts wished to add to his series of
portraits of distinguished persons that of Christina
Rossetti. He wrote on two occasions expressing this
desire ; but it happened that in both instances (the
second was very near the close of her life) the condition
of Christina's health was such as to preclude her sitting,
and, greatly to my regret, the project remained unac-
complished. She too was regretful ; although her
general feeling in any such matter was one rather of
humility and self-effacement than of pleased acquiescence.

One of the persons whom I met at Little Holland
House was Frederic Leighton, afterwards P.R.A.,
Baronet, and Peer of the Realm. This must have been
in the year following that when he first exhibited in
London his renowned picture (bought by Queen
Victoria) of *The Procession of Cimabue.* Leighton, I
need hardly say, was a brilliantly handsome young man,
with a large store of gifts and graces. He became a
very friendly acquaintance of mine, and I could probably have cultivated this relation into positive friendship, had I laid myself out for so doing. He was a great
admirer of Mrs. Sartoris (the celebrated vocalist Adelaide
Kemble) ; and I remember that later on, having by some
casualty come into possession of a booklet of sketch-
portraits of this lady done by Hayter (of *Book of Beauty*
popularity), I presented it to Leighton, who welcomed
the gift. I saw Mrs. Sartoris herself once or twice in
this same house ; she had been slightly known to my

father on her first arrival in London from Paris. Leighton always presented the appearance of a favourite of fortune, and his great and varied abilities enabled him to sustain the position with *éclat;* the protagonist of the painting profession, the darling of society, the recipient of multiform flatteries. That a man should be entirely unspoiled by such honied attentions was perhaps not possible. I could not however see that he became *much* spoiled, so far as character and his attitude to the world were concerned; his art, I have no doubt, suffered to some extent—losing in virility and actualism, and drugging grace with sleek artificiality. Let us rather recall the finer qualities, and they were indeed many and salient, of his art. Visitors to Leighton House, of the present days and years, may well be tempted to believe that he was not only a choice but almost an unfailing master.

Another *habitué* of Little Holland House was Richard Doyle, constantly called Dicky Doyle, the dainty (though not artistically highly trained) designer of fairy fantasies and queer comicalities, ex-illustrator of *Punch.* I hardly ever entered the house without encountering Doyle. His figure was noticeably erect, his head always high. There was however nothing stiff or starched in his manner ; he seemed ready to meet any advances, to respond to any courtesies, and to be the man of general amiability in the company. He was not, so far as I observed, jocular or definitely sprightly in talk, yet somewhat arch. He impressed me (but it may have been a mistake) as a man who, having suffered some serious disappointment early in life, had now no particular object except to spend the passing hour pleasantly, and make it pleasant for others as well as himself. He was certainly a very general favourite, and his premature death was felt as a loss in a wide circle.

Here also I saw Baron Marochetti the sculptor, a highly prosperous-looking gentleman, of large but not very marked physique, suggesting rather a financing banker than an artist; Sir Henry Taylor, the author of *Philip van Artevelde* (a drama which had had a great fascination years before for my brother and myself), a man of singularly handsome, suave, and dignified aspect, intimate more especially with Mrs. Cameron, who produced some noble photographs of him; Mr. Matthew J. Higgins (prominent under various pseudonyms, such as Jacob Omnium and Paterfamilias), a colossal figure—say almost six foot six—with a complacent face and a vast chin; Mr. Gaisford, a Sussex squire with a rather romantic aspect, owner of a fine library—I re-encountered him at a later date in connexion with Edward John Trelawny; Thackeray's two daughters, and once or twice himself. One day there were several of us in the garden, and somebody proposed that each should write down the titles of a dozen books, such as he would rather keep by him than any others, if compelled to restrict himself to so small a number. I jotted down my list, and, as I was finishing it, Thackeray came to my shoulder, took the pencil from my hand, and added the title *Peerage*—a volume upon which he had laid some stress in his *Book of Snobs* and elsewhere. I was able to assure the great novelist that that was not in any sense one of my books of predilection. The scrap of paper was retained by me, and it now figures as a Thackeray document among the collection of autographs formed by my daughter Helen.

At Little Holland House I witnessed something of

the " first season " of one or two beautiful débutantes. One was Miss Treherne, who not long afterwards became Mrs. Welldon, and who since then has figured in various law-courts. Assuredly she was a lovely young creature, with a captivating look of joyous sweetness and a delightful singing voice. Nothing about her then foreboded that she would live a life of so much turmoil, crossed by so many grievances.

I now proceed to the Burne-Jones connexion, including, as one of its main constituents, the firm of Morris, Marshall, Faulkner, & Co.

My brother made the acquaintance of Mr. Edward Burne Jones (whose original surname of Jones was afterwards modified into Burne-Jones) towards the final week of 1855. The circumstances which brought the two together have often been recounted. Here it will suffice to say that Burne-Jones, son of a carver and gilder, and an Oxford student destined for the Church, conceived a very high idea of the artistic powers of Rossetti, obtained sight of him, produced for his inspection some of his own designs, immature but full of noble promise, and was by him confirmed in the idea of adopting the career of a painter. There is no exaggeration in affirming that the feeling with which Burne-Jones regarded Rossetti, at that time and for years ensuing, was one of passionate homage, stopping a little on the hither side of worship. Soon afterwards came the affair of the decoration of the Union Debating Hall in Oxford with a series of tempera-paintings from the Arthurian legend, now destroyed by the inroads of English climate upon work carried out with very imperfect and hazardous technical processes. Dante Rossetti was at the head of this ill-starred enterprise,

seconded by Burne-Jones, William Morris, Arthur
Hughes, Val Prinsep, J. R. Spencer Stanhope, and
J. Hungerford Pollen, and (so far as a sculptural group
was concerned) by Alexander Munro.   Afterwards,
towards 1861, followed the firm of art-decorators named
Morris, Marshall, Faulkner, & Co.   Mr. Peter Paul
Marshall—an engineer and amateur painter, son-in-law
of John Miller of Liverpool—started the idea of this
firm ; the practical working of it lay mainly with William
Morris, Madox Brown, Burne-Jones, Philip Webb the
architect, and Dante Rossetti ; Mr. Charles Faulkner,
an Oxford mathematician, joined owing to his close
friendship with Morris, and rendered various efficient
services, but he had little to do with the technical
operations.   Mr. Hughes was also, in the first instance,
put down as a member ; seemingly he did not ever act
as such.

Irrespectively of Dante Rossetti, three of the persons
who took part in the Union designs and in the famous
firm—Madox Brown, Burne-Jones, and Morris—have
had their biographers. Three others have died—Munro,
Marshall, and Faulkner.   It would be quite outside the
scope of these Reminiscences of mine to say much as
to the careers even of such pre-eminent personages as
Burne-Jones and Morris ; all that I shall attempt is
to give a few particulars of the men as I saw them.

Burne-Jones was a man of fair stature, with a clear
but pale complexion, deep-set eyes very serious and
candid-looking, a noticeably spacious high forehead, and
yellowish hair, which had thinned before he became
elderly. His manner was very gentle, and utterly alien
from any vaunting self-assertion. He was never in
strong health, yet to call him an invalid might be going

too far. I did not find him much of a talker ; but he made from time to time some very discerning and even weighty observation, and ample evidence of his thoughtful and exalted tone of mind is now on record in the admirable book written by his widow. The general tone of his conversation, as heard by myself, was however curiously boyish ; and he had (in at any rate one instance within my knowledge) a boyish way of becoming fancifully fond of a person, and afterwards loathing him. I will not suggest that in this particular instance Burne-Jones was without justification ; I only mention the case as symptomatic. With this juvenility of temperament and feeling, he was an easily lovable man, of fibre refined and delicate rather than tight-drawn. His nature had the musical ring of glass, not the clangour of iron. I give my view for what it may be worth ; others, who saw him more constantly or later on in life, may be of a different and a better-grounded opinion.

The admirers of Burne-Jones as an artist are numerous and fervent—I am one of them ; the admirers of Dante Rossetti are likewise not few nor lukewarm. I may perhaps be excused for saying a little about the comparative claims of the two artists. The first consideration is that Rossetti preceded Burne-Jones by several years, and initiated a certain aim and tendency in design and painting which ran through various phases, and influenced the course of art through various developments. There is also the consideration that he stood without rival in the fact of being a poet in words no less than in painting. But, to limit myself to the painting art alone, he it was who produced the works which so impressed Burne-Jones as to incite him to follow on in something of the same line of art. Rossetti therefore was the originator of whatever claims to be original in this relation ; and it seems to me that his works are not only the more original in order of precedence, but also in their own essential quality ; in Rossetti the *personal factor* counts for more than it does in Burne-Jones. "I was one of those whose little is their own" is a sentence once jotted down by Rossetti ; and I deem it a correct one as defining his own position, and his claim to be borne in remembrance. It seems to be true that in painting (and, for that matter, in poetry as well) he does not resemble any predecessor. He does not resemble the masters of the old Italian school, nor those of the old Flemish school (to whom he paid much attention at the opening of his own career), nor the German or French Neo-Catholics, nor the great Venetians, nor the Florentine or Roman masters of the central period—nor of course such later giants as Velasquez or Rubens or Rembrandt, nor any painter of the British school. Rossetti therefore struck out a line for himself ; Burne-Jones followed to some extent in the same line, but he added much of his own not to be found in Rossetti. Of his own, much ; and from olden art not a little. His romantic treatment of classicism derives partly from Mantegna and Botticelli ; his Christian art has affinities with Carpaccio, the Bellini, etc., and, notably in the cast of draperies, even with art so remote as that of Byzantine times. At one period, after he had been in Italy, he took special delight in Raphael, though I question whether any marked symptom of this appears in his own work : "Nothing," he then said to me, "is so lovely in my eyes as a maiden by Raphael." His schemes of work, the dimensions of his canvases, were large out of all comparison with

Rossetti's ; his drawing, after he had come into the full mastery of his powers, was better ; his preliminary studies were far more elaborate and complete. He treated a much fuller and more varied range of subjects ; for Rossetti, though he had ambitious projects throughout his youth, seldom in mature age carried out any compositions including more than one or two figures. Thus I think that Rossetti was the more original artist, and the more intense within his own limits ; Burne-Jones the more richly and variously productive. Essentially Burne-Jones was an eclectic—although an eclectic with a great and beautiful faculty of his own. He did not take any great pleasure in any art save that of Europe. Towards 1863 James Whistler and my brother, and myself also, became greatly bitten by Japanese art (and I remain so to this day). Not so Burne-Jones. " No, William," he remarked, " Japan and Asia will not do ; for fine art we need the Caucasian mind." Herein he concurred with Ruskin.

In point of the mould and expression of the faces painted, I must be allowed to consider Rossetti by far the higher master. He had ideals and types of the most marked kind, of extreme loveliness, and he threw into them a depth and subtlety of expression which I fail to find anywhere in Burne-Jones. The faces of the latter, indeed, seldom seem to me to be decisively beautiful or touchingly expressive. He rejected the notion that painted faces should indicate shifting emotions. His faces are monotonous. Rossetti too has often been accused of monotony of type. This is at best only partially true, for he depicted from time to time various faces of very marked diversity. What brace of women could be more unlike than Miss Siddal and Mrs. William Morris ? I conceive that the charge, when brought against Burne-Jones, is much more nearly correct.

Other imputations which have constantly been advanced against both these artists are that they are mannerists, and morbid in feeling. It appears to me that Burne-Jones, as being partly an eclectic, is more intrinsically a mannerist than Rossetti, as being an originator ; but Rossetti did in fact carry certain mannerisms of type or form to a more marked excess than one finds in his competitor. As to morbidity, I do not see that Rossetti was ever exactly morbid in his work—he was somewhat peculiar in his individualism, which partook at times of the fantastic and remote. Burne-Jones was more truly morbid ; in this sense—that he, in various instances, diffused an air of languor and quietism over subjects which, to an ordinary mind, are more suggestive of vivacity and ardour. But after all this amounts to little more than saying that, being himself, and with his own range of feeling and ideas, he painted in conformity with these, and not with those of other people. As he *saw* the thing, so he painted it. Some one else would have painted it otherwise.

As colourists both artists are generally allowed to stand high. I shall not discuss their comparative deservings, but will simply observe that Burne-Jones was much the more inclined of the two to try experiments in colour from very diverse starting-points.

I will sum up by saying (and let my reader take it for whatever it is worth)—Rossetti as a painter was essentially personal and originating ; Burne-Jones was essentially a revivalist. Who was the more successful, or we may at once say the better, painter ? Burne-

Jones. Who had the more potent pictorial faculty ? Rossetti. Will the superiority in actual painting, or the superiority in pictorial faculty, count for the most and reach the furthest in the long run ? My belief is that the superiority in pictorial faculty will do so.

This little debate on the æsthetics of Burne-Jones and my brother has led me somewhat away from my immediate theme, which is the circle of friends whom I knew as connected with the former. To this theme I now return, and I come first to William Morris.

I regard Morris as about the most remarkable man all round—the most *uncommon* man — whom I have known. He was artist, poet, romancist, antiquary, linguist, translator, lecturer, craftsman, printer, trader, socialist ; and was besides, as a man to meet and talk to, a most singular personality. Among my intimates he was one of the few who had some little turn for sport : he would go out fishing, boating, and the like. His frame was cast in a large mould, but was by no means tall—not well up to middle height. His face was on the whole very handsome, though it looked as if some slight additional shade of refinement in one feature or other would have made it yet a good deal handsomer ; the eyes were rather small. The portrait of him by George F. Watts is a decided likeness ; still, I hold that it does Morris less than justice—it does not present him at his best. Dante Rossetti used to say that Morris looked like a knight of the Round Table, and this was not far from the fact. He figures as Sir Lancelot in Rossetti's design for *The Lady of Shalott*, in the illustrated Tennyson. The author of *The Earthly Paradise* was the least paradisal of men, if we regard Paradise as a scene of fruition and serene content : he was turbulent, restless, noisy (with a deep and rather gruff voice), brusque in his movements, addicted to stumbling over doorsteps, breaking down solid-looking chairs the moment he took his seat in them, and doing scores of things inconsistent with the nerves of the nervous. He relished a good glass of wine, and was by no means averse from a savoury dinner, and an ample one. His nickname was Topsy, or Top — for years I seldom heard him called by any other name. This pseudonym had been imposed upon him in Oxford University before my brother or myself knew him. The stories of Morris's oddities and escapades were numerous ; exaggerated sometimes, yet in essence true. At the present day, and to his host of well-warranted admirers, Morris the many-gifted presents an almost heroic aspect, and well that it should be so ; but to his familiars in the days of youth—who none the less most thoroughly appreciated his surprising powers—he was the object of almost constant " chaff." Dante Rossetti might be regarded as a leader in these skirmishings, but he was only *primus inter pares*, and the *pares* were many. If Morris had not been a genuinely " fine fellow," and had not had a rich sense of humour which enabled him to enter into a joke against himself as against any one else, he would never have stood it ; he did stand it, and on occasion gave as good as he got. He was volcanic, and would rage and swear on very small inducement ; but, being very easy-natured too, and knowing that the men of his circle truly delighted in the splendour of his genius, and gave full expression to the value they set upon it whenever opportunity offered, he took the chaff (in a double sense) along with the grain. In the firm of Morris, Marshall, Faulkner, & Co., he was the leading spirit, though not in early days the leading artist; that position belonged to Burne-Jones, Madox Brown, and Dante Rossetti, whom I name here in the order of their productivity of art-work for the association. Webb was also active; but, being by profession an architect, he did not so regularly contribute designs for the purposes of the firm. It may be recollected by many of my readers that Morris appeared first as a poet (*The Defence of Guenevere* etc.), and was admired as such among his intimates before his turn for decorative art had developed to any serious extent, and long prior to his launching out upon any socialistic scheme or propaganda. In the earlier days Morris seemed to me to be alien from all political interests, and it was not on the ground of actual or surmised socialism than anybody bantered him.

Here is a specimen of the sort of raillery indulged in. The anecdote has been in print ere now, and perhaps with more precise accuracy of detail than I can command; I narrate as near as I remember. The incident took place before I knew much—possibly before I knew any-thing—of Morris in person. In 1856 a serial, now of no little celebrity, was brought out, *The Oxford and Cambridge Magazine*; Morris was a leading contributor, in the way of poems, stories of chivalry, etc. When the magazine was on the downward grade, and obviously destined to extinction, he sent in a story called *Golden Wings*, in which a knight and a lady played principal parts. The knight, as one may readily guess, was a champion in the prime of his years; the lady as youth-ful and as beauteous as need be. When the tale was in course of printing, some waggishly disposed person (ostensibly the printer, but I did hear that it was really Charles Faulkner, or possibly even Burne-Jones)

revised the manuscript by interpolating here and there
the word "old"; so that we found, when the magazine
was published, that the *old* knight declared himself as a
passionate suitor of the *old* lady, or perhaps he sliced
a rival in two at a single blow, or whatever else.
Whether the small clientèle of *The Oxford and Cambridge
Magazine* was mystified by Morris's story as printed,
and whether Morris himself gave vent to a variety of
expletives, I leave to be imagined.

Several months after I had written the above, I was
reading Mr. J. W. MacKail's *Life of William Morris*—
a most interesting book, which would make one love the
man if one had not done so before. In Vol. I, p. 303,
I find that Morris, writing to a lady on 26 March
1874, expressed himself as follows, as a tag to a
"growl" against some of the conventions of society :
"Do you know, I have got to go to a wedding next
Tuesday; and it enrages me to think that I lack
courage to say, 'I don't care for either of you, and you
neither of you care for me, and I won't waste a day
out of my precious life in grinning a company-grin at
you two.'" Now "next Tuesday" was 31 March, and
that was the wedding-day of Lucy Brown and myself,
and Morris was bidden, though not to the wedding
itself, still to the extra quiet wedding-breakfast which
succeeded it at Brown's house. So I see that the bride-
groom whom the latter referred to was no other than
myself. That Morris did not care for either of us (he
gave us as wedding-present a *Nuremberg Chronicle* of
1493) cannot now be helped ; he was mistaken in
thinking that I did not, in all reasonable measure, care
for *him*. But indeed I had never seen ground for
supposing that Morris regarded me with anything that

could be called predilection—and I might say the like
of Burne-Jones. It was Madox Brown (not myself,
averse as I am from everything of the sort, and most
prompt to believe in the aversion of others) who be-
spoke Morris and his wife to the wedding-breakfast, at
which, to the best of my recollection, the only other
guests were my mother, Christina, and Dante Gabriel.
Let me say (though it has no connexion with the fore-
going) that I was surprised to find in Mr. MacKail's
book some passages indicating that, while Morris was
acutely sensitive to the charm of Kelmscott Manor-house
and its surroundings, my brother was obtusely blind
to it. The very reverse is shown in his published
Family Letters, especially those of the summer of 1871
and 1873.

Edward Burne-Jones was an important man, William
Morris was an important man; the third whom I have
to name in this sequence, Algernon Charles Swinburne,
was and is quite equally important. He is the one of
whom I saw by far the most, and indeed I was for
several years as intimate and confidential with him as
with any one (save Dante Gabriel); the other two also
I met very frequently in those years. This brilliant
young Oxford man was (as I am told) first introduced to
my brother by Mr. (afterwards Dr.) George Birkbeck
Hill during the period when Rossetti and his pictorial
colleagues were engaged upon the paintings for the
Union Debating-hall. That was probably in 1857,
during which year Swinburne attained the age of twenty.
He looked still younger: at twenty you might have
taken him for seventeen, at twenty-eight for twenty-two,
and so on. My own acquaintance with this glorious
poet began a little later—possibly towards the close of

ALGERNON CHARLES SWINBURNE.

DRAWING BY DANTE G. ROSSETTI, 1860.

1860. His first published volume, the dramas of *Rosamund* and *The Queen Mother*, belongs to 1861. Mr. Swinburne is well known to be a man of very remarkable personality, as well as genius; it would not befit me here to sift minutely the characteristics and the doings of a living and a dear friend. In such a matter as this, Mr. Swinburne is himself a model to the best of us; for, spite of his exceptional impetuosity of nature and of speech, no one has been more rigidly observant of the nicest code of honour in keeping to himself any matters, major or minor, to which he has become privy in the confidence of friendly intercourse. I will here only dwell upon a few of the salient merits of Mr. Swinburne, in his personal character; his poetry stands in need of no testimonial from any one, and surely not from me. Swinburne belongs by birth and nurture to the aristocratic class; and, though he has put forward very advanced democratic and republican views, his temperament and demeanour witness to his origin. In a certain general atmosphere of political and some other ideas he and I sympathized very warmly: in the application of them we often differed. He hated Napoleon the First; upheld the Southern against the Northern States in the American Civil War; sided with the Turks against the Russians in the war of 1878; loathed Gladstone's Home-rule policy; and believed England to be wholly in the right in the Transvaal conflict. In all these respects I belong to the opposite camp. Neither can I fall in with Swinburnian diatribes against Carlyle, Emerson, and Walt Whitman. These divergences of opinion however have never made the smallest breach in our mutual good understanding. Among people whom he likes, no one can be more affectionate, sweet-natured, and confiding, than Algernon Swinburne. His courtesy is extreme, his attachments are steady. Superb as are his own powers, he is most willing to recognize in others any points of superiority, whether to the mass of mankind or even to himself; and, where he recognizes this, he can be not only compliant but I might say deferential. That he can retaliate fiercely, and this upon quondam friends as well as professed foes, is a fact sufficiently notorious; I cannot however recollect a single instance in which he attacked without being first needlessly provoked. To provoke him is a tolerably easy process, and a very imprudent one; for no man living has a more vigorous command of the powers of invective, to which his ingenuity of mind, and consummate mastery of literary resource, lend a lash of the most cutting and immedicable keenness. As a generous praiser of what he considers praiseworthy he stands supreme : it may very fairly be said that in this line he is *too* generous—never that he is parsimonious. His golden words, like the beams of the morning and the evening sun, flush into splendour whatever they fall upon. I have myself been the recipient, in public and oftener in private, of some of this prodigal bounty; and can never read without an emotion between pride and shamefacedness, as well as gratitude, the Dedication which the great poet and writer prefixed to his volume published in 1868, *William Blake, a Critical Essay.* Let me add that another man who knew the high delight of praising, and practised it in many an instance, was my brother; he was indeed less gorgeous in his utterances than Swinburne, but not less warm and emphatic. From both these noble souls how remote was any taint of envy or detraction, any effort to elevate themselves by the under-valuing of others—how natural to both, how inevitable, the response to what they saw to be beautiful and worthy!

As I have no idea of discussing here the merits or the blemishes of Mr. Swinburne's poetry, so especially I leave aside his volume issued in 1866—*Poems and Ballads*—which excited a fury of abuse such as readers of the present day would find some difficulty in crediting. A little incident however occurs to my mind, which exhibits this animus in a form so bizarre and insensate that it is worth recording. In 1868 Mr. Legros exhibited in the Royal Academy an excellent picture of some monks or friars at their repast—called *The Refectory*. There was a tabby cat painted in the picture. In that year was published a pamphlet of Notes on the art of the season. Mr. Swinburne wrote one section of it, and I the other. Swinburne— who is a great lover of cats (a fancy which I share with him), and also (a fancy which I only very faintly share) of serpents—wrote of this painted quadruped as "a splendid cat." The picture was bought—presumably before Swinburne's eulogium had appeared—by a person of some distinction. Many years afterwards, in 1895, I had occasion to look at this painting in the house of the heir of the original purchaser. To my surprise, the cat had disappeared. "Why," said I, "there used to be a cat in that corner of the picture." "Yes," replied the owner, "there was ; but my predecessor, on seeing that Swinburne had found a good word to say for the cat, got her obliterated forthwith." Such was the feeling of the enlightened British world for *Poems and Ballads* and the author thereof.

I add a few words as to the three members of the

Morris firm of whom I have as yet said but little—
Marshall, Faulkner, and Webb. Mr. Peter Paul
Marshall, a Scotchman, was, as I have already mentioned, an engineer by profession, and an amateur
painter by liking. In this latter capacity he showed
much more than average talent, producing several clever
landscapes and an effective little picture of Stephenson
making early experiments leading on to the locomotive
steam-engine. He came into our circle through our
being acquainted with his father-in-law Mr. Miller, who
bought pictures by Madox Brown, Dante Rossetti, and
others. Marshall was a strong, personable-looking
young man, with much heartiness of character and
demeanour. Of Charles Faulkner I saw but little :
when I met him he seemed lively and straightforward.
He had no sort of defined connexion with art-work,
but must plainly have had a marked natural aptitude
for it ; for, when a wood-engraver was wanted for the
frontispiece which Dante Gabriel made for Christina's
Goblin-Market in 1862, Faulkner was somehow pitched
upon, and immediately produced the very spirited woodcut with which we are all familiar. Of the seven
members of the Morris firm, Mr. Philip Webb still
survives, and he alone. I saw enough of him to admire
his talents as an architect and as a designer of animals
etc. for stained glass or other decorative work ; not
much beyond this.

In connexion with the paintings in the Oxford Union
Debating-hall I have made reference to Mr. Spencer
Stanhope and Mr. Hungerford Pollen. Mr. Stanhope
might originally be considered more an amateur than
a professional painter, but he soon made art his vocation
in life, painting in a style very visibly related to that

of Burne-Jones. Whatever the style, he is a man with plenty of ideas of his own, and has invented and composed several very superior works. As a rule, I do not sympathize with the "imitators of Burne-Jones": they seem to me generally to lose their hold upon the soundness and solidity of nature, without attaining to much excellence of art, or even of artifice. Mr. Spencer Stanhope is (so far as I know) by far the most capable painter identified with this movement. He has for many years past been settled in Florence, where, after a long interval, I had the pleasure of once again meeting him in 1898. Mr. Hungerford Pollen, originally a clergyman in the Church of England, became a convert to Roman Catholicism; he did not enter holy orders in the Catholic Church, but married and continued a layman. A more beautiful and attractive lady than Mrs. Pollen, whom I met occasionally in the house of the Prinseps, was hardly to be seen in society. Mr. Pollen engaged in artistic and literary matters. I saw him at times in my brother's house and elsewhere, and entertained the highest respect for his character. I might say the same of Dr. Birkbeck Hill, whom I have named as an Oxford man along with Mr. Swinburne. In youth I met him little or not at all, but towards 1896, when he was editing the *Letters of Dante Rossetti to William Allingham*, I came into frequent and most agreeable contact with this pre-eminent Johnsonian expert and with some members of his cultivated family. Another of them, Professor Leonard Hill, was known to me in 1890, and rendered us, in his surgical capacity, an essential service at a time when a troublesome accident had befallen my youngest daughter.

In 1858 an association was started called the Hogarth

Club ; I belonged to it, along with several of the artists and others whom I have mentioned in these Reminiscences. This Hogarth Club, and afterwards the Burlington Fine-Arts Club, are the only clubs of which I was ever a member ; always living at home *en famille*, I never joined, or tried to join, any of those living and dining clubs which form a supplement—and a very attractive supplement—to the domestic establishment. I hardly remember who first mooted the idea of the Hogarth ; maybe it was Madox Brown, and he certainly put forward the name of "Hogarth"—a painter whom he deeply reverenced as the originator of moral invention and drama in modern art. Dante Gabriel, Burne-Jones, and some others, fell in with the idea with much zest, and we secured one or two rooms for the club in Piccadilly, and afterwards in Waterloo Place. Three principal objects were held in view : (1) the combination of the artists concerned with amateurs and purchasers well affected to their aims in art ; (2) the holding from time to time of exhibitions of works by the club members ; and (3) the rather important point that these exhibitions, being club affairs and therefore not strictly public, would leave the artists free, if so disposed, to send the same works to the Royal Academy or to other exhibiting institutions which exclude productions previously made public. I need not dwell upon the fortunes—which were anything but brilliant—of the Hogarth Club. An exhibition was held—I think only one—and was in some measure well reputed ; but the membership and the subscriptions fell off, any sanguine expectations of good results were disappointed, and the club was dissolved in the spring of 1861. Without repeating the names of such artist-members of the Hogarth Club as I have already referred to on other grounds, I may mention Bodley, Street, and Woodward, the architects; William Shakespear Burton, Eyre Crowe, William Davis, and W. L. Windus (both of Liverpool), Alfred Fripp, Alfred Hunt, Inchbold, and Oakes. Frederic George Stephens was the honorary secretary, Robert B. Martineau the honorary treasurer. As honorary members we had David Cox, Francis Danby, Delacroix, Dyce, William Henry Hunt, J. F. Lewis, and Mulready: Swinburne and Lord Houghton, and no doubt some others of name, were among the non-artistic members. All the artist-members whom I have named will be recognized as men of some mark. Of Woodward, who died in early middle age, I have spoken in my *Memoir of Dante Rossetti;* some others I need not here deal with. I will however say a few words about Street, Burton, Davis, Windus, Alfred Hunt, and Inchbold.

Mr. George Edmund Street, who for some years before his premature death ranked as second to none in the architectural profession, was a man of stalwart physique, with a curt, decisive delivery; in politics a Conservative, and in most things an enemy of " gush," but very earnestly devoted to his own aims in his art, friendly and pleasant to talk to. One felt that he meant what he said, and would do what he undertook. William Morris, who had in early years contemplated becoming an architect, was a pupil in Street's office for some months. I have more than once dined at Street's hospitable table (then in Russell Square) with his first wife, a lady, like himself, easy and most unaffected. His second marriage (with a member of a family, the Hollands, with which my sister Maria was highly intimate) offered every expectation of happiness, but collapsed grievously in a few months with the lady's death. The decease of Street himself, not very long afterwards, came as a surprise and a shock to a large circle; he seemed still only at the meridian of his prosperous career.

As to Mr. Burton, I have seen in print some rather startling particulars of a device, as trivial-seeming as it was wicked, which availed to turn the wheel of fortune dead against him at a moment when his prospects looked abundantly fair. In my early manhood I saw little of him personally; but I have met him and his wife occasionally in later years, and know him to be a painter of high aims, and of attainment insufficiently recognized. One of his recent large pictures was taken, as I saw with much gratification, from the *Blessed Damozel* of Dante Rossetti.

William Davis, William L. Windus, and Alfred W. Hunt were all first known to me in 1857, when I was staying by invitation in the house of Mr. John Miller of Liverpool (the most open-handed of merchants, and the most lovable of Scotchmen and picture-collectors) as a convenient station wherefrom to visit the great Art-treasures Exhibition of that year in Manchester. Davis the landscape-painter was an Irishman, married, and with a large family—something like a dozen children. In my own circle his landscapes, skilfully handled with genuine feeling for nature, were much admired, and he had a small knot of buyers—Mr. Miller was one, and Mr. George Rae of Birkenhead (so well known as an owner of Rossetti and other paintings) another; but a half-empty purse was the lifelong inevitable destiny of Davis, which he bore with as near an approach to cheerful contentment as could be expected. He was an unassuming man, without much schooling (I suppose), but intelligent—a Catholic in creed. In his person there was nothing to attract attention : his features were good rather than otherwise, his complexion high as through constant exposure in the open air. He finally settled in London—probably an imprudent step, as his art never made much way with the public. He died rather suddenly of angina pectoris in 1873 ; and some artists and others (Madox Brown and Rae prominent among them) did their best, partly by collecting together some pictures, to provide for the more immediate necessities. A deserving landscapist of the present time, Mr. Valentine Davis, is a son of the able but not fortunate Irishman—for whose work the day may come yet. And indeed, on looking at the numerous examples of his work now in the possession of Mrs. Rae, one says confidently that come it must.—Mr. Windus is chiefly remembered as the author of a picture, *Burd Helen*, exhibited in the Royal Academy in 1856, showing the " Præraphaelite " influence ; my brother admired it much, and vigorously summoned Ruskin to give (which he did) some prominence to it in his critical pamphlet of that year. There was also a pathetic picture, *Too Late*, which reappeared in the Glasgow International Exhibition of 1901, and made a suitable impression on the visitors. When still at an early stage of his artistic career, Mr. Windus—for a private reason which did him honour, but which it is no business of mine to detail—withdrew from active professional work ; and thus the tale of his achievements is very different from what it might naturally have been.—Mr. Alfred Hunt was an Oxford man, and I think that he (like Burne-Jones and Morris) was originally destined for the

Church. He took to landscape-painting in a spirit choicely compounded of enthusiasm and pertinacity; and I, with multitudes of others, have often had occasion to admire the highly refined, elaborate, and truthful products of his skill. Mr. Hunt was a thin, keen-looking man, with prominent teeth; he left a widow and a daughter, both of them of established repute as novelists.

Hunt made a very good position as a painter, chiefly in water-colour, and an income (I presume) fairly to correspond; yet he was a disappointed man. Why? Because the Royal Academicians did not favour his contributions in oil-colour, and did not elect him into their body. This is one of the curses of the habit, to which the British mind is too prone, of looking on fine art mainly as a profession: if a man does not obtain "the honours (so called) of the profession," he thinks himself ill-used. Perhaps, in so thinking, he is perfectly correct; but it is a weakness to go further and make himself unhappy over the matter. The real point of attainment is to do justice to his art, and to himself as an artist. The honours of the profession are (apart from advantageous contingencies in money-making) mere gauds, which the true artist might very well be content to leave to be scrambled for by his inferiors. There was some depth of sense, as well as some strain of perversity, in Dante Rossetti's resolve to exhibit nothing, and let the honours of the profession take care of themselves. Burne-Jones showed the same decisive temper of mind in more instances than one; none the less, he became a Baronet in virtue of his art.

John William Inchbold is the last man on my present list. A few years after the Præraphaelite movement had begun he came forward as a landscape-painter in strict conformity to the guiding principles of that movement. His works were observed with much satisfaction by sympathizers; a very good specimen is in the National British Gallery. But the fate of being an unsuccessful man overtook him, like some others: I mean the fate of being, not only unsuccessful in a direct sense, but harassed by ill-success into losing or frittering away his finer powers in the art. After some years he advanced no further, but retrograded all too visibly. He was a nervous, impressionable man, with a ruddy complexion, and a rather blunt address, in which a certain uneasy modesty contended with a certain still uneasier self-value. He was not the sort of person to "get on" with prosperous people, nor to conciliate such as had to struggle as hard as himself. He was however highly conscientious and right-meaning, and those who knew him best were the readiest to see him from the friendliest point of view, and to regret when his life, with its numerous troubles, came to an end, towards 1890, at a not very advanced age.

Along with Burne-Jones and Morris, and in a minor degree with Swinburne, I have naturally had some acquaintance with their families. To say much on this topic would be an impertinence, and I shall limit myself to a very few brief indications.

A lady more agreeable to know than Lady Burne-Jones would not be easy to find—one more frank, cordial, spirited, and clever. She was one of five sisters, Misses Macdonald, four of whom have taken a somewhat conspicuous place in society. One is Lady Poynter, the wife of the President of the Royal Academy; a second, Mrs. Lockwood Kipling, mother of Rudyard Kipling, and authoress of some well-accepted verse ; a third, Mrs. Baldwin, who has published some novels ; one of her books I have read, a noticeable little volume of ghostly or supernatural tales, named *The Shadow on the Blind*, etc. Lady Burne-Jones's daughter is married to Mr. MacKail, the biographer of Morris. Of Sir Philip Burne-Jones, a painter of no little individuality who has managed to steer clear of the very obvious but fatal temptation to imitate his illustrious father, I have not seen anything personally since the days of his early childhood.

As for Mrs. Morris, any one who wants to form an idea of the splendid and strictly exceptional beauty of this lady in her prime should look at one or two of the numerous heads painted from her by Dante Rossetti. People have an idea that portraits done by him, and still more the ideal heads, are absurdly exaggerated, and quite unlike the originals. This is a mistake. In both classes of work many of the heads are true likenesses, which I may say emphatically of most of those painted or drawn from Mrs. Morris. Assuredly my brother, when he painted from the life, was disposed to bring out the nobler qualities of both feature and expression, and to lay no stress upon slight or casual blemishes ; and what artist, with an eye for beauty and majesty, would not do the same, and would not be inferior to himself if he did it not ? But this is a very different thing from *falsifying* a likeness, or descending to the flatteries of the conventional portrait-painter ; and I will say in the most explicit terms that many of the heads painted by Dante Gabriel from sitters as well known to myself as to him are, in a full sense, close and complete likenesses. The Morrises had two daughters, the younger being

Mrs. WILLIAM MORRIS.

BY DANTE G. ROSSETTI, 1861,

the May Morris so well known in artistic and liberal-minded circles. Her beauty in childhood was most marked, and my brother then took her as a model more than once—not always portraying her as being a child. The sister of Mrs. Morris, Miss Burdon, was also known to me ; she bore a leading part in artistic needle-work for the Morris firm.

With the Swinburne family my acquaintance was truly scanty, yet highly agreeable so far as it went. In 1867 I was invited to their residence, Holmwood near Henley, and stayed there a couple of snowy winter days. The family, as I saw it, consisted of Admiral and Lady Jane Swinburne and three daughters. Only one of these persons, a daughter, is now living. It seemed a most united and consentaneous family group, of that easy and self-possessed simplicity which goes with high breeding. Algernon Swinburne himself, the great poet noised abroad (and just then roundly objurgated as well) throughout the length and breadth of the land, showed at home to the utmost advantage. I regret not having pursued this family acquaintance further.

XVI

THE BROWNINGS, LANDOR, TENNYSON

TOWARDS 1845, or even 1844, the poems of Miss Elizabeth Barrett Barrett first caught the attention of my brother and myself. We revelled in them with profuse delight. Our perceptions of poetry were not then of the totally uncritical order, and we found some things which we thought faulty, both in excess and in defect; but in the main our pleasure was unalloyed. *The Drama of Exile, The Rhyme of the Duchess May, The Lost Bower, Lady Geraldine's Courtship, A Vision of Poets,* and numerous other pieces, held us spellbound. In the course of two or three years we must have read some of these more than half-a-hundred times over; and either of us (but more especially Dante Gabriel, who was much the better at verbal memory) could repeat them with great exactness.

The turn of Robert Browning came a little later on, probably before the close of 1847. We read first some of the series published under the collective title *Bells and Pomegranates: Pippa Passes, The Blot on the Scutcheon, The Flight of the Duchess,* etc. Then ensued *Paracelsus,* then *Sordello.* We found more deep and wellnigh unmixed satisfaction in Browning than in any other living British poet—Tennyson, Miss Barrett, Philip

Bailey, Sir Henry Taylor; perhaps more than in Victor Hugo. If we had then been asked to define the reason for our preference we might have said that we felt Browning to exceed all the others in the dramatic, romantic, and picturesque qualities. As I see the matter now, however, this might not be a very accurate definition ; and probably what genuinely impressed us, to ourselves half consciously, was his strength and variety of mind, and his sense of *couleur locale* : a sense which indeed he often leaves in abeyance through long stretches of works such as *Paracelsus* and *Sordello*, but which turns up every now and then with electric effect. We got hold of Horne's *New Spirit of the Age*, principally for the purpose of finding out any particulars about Browning and his performances. My brother, by readings, recitations, and preachments, imposed Browning, as a sort of dogmatic standard, upon the P.R.B., meeting the readiest response from Woolner and Stephens, and (it may be in a rather minor degree) from Holman Hunt; Millais, so far as I can remember, was too busy with his own affairs to do much reading, whether of Browning or of any one—he was however a devotee of Keats. Another extreme Browningian was John Tupper. Madox Brown proved mainly recalcitrant ; to Dante Gabriel's rather scornful indignation, he continued to uphold Longfellow as the first of living poets, next to Tennyson. Patmore, Allingham, Hannay, and Bell Scott were men who had their own opinions of poetry already formed, and to these they adhered— Allingham being the one most fully sensitive to the great claims of Browning. In the summer of 1850 (a fact which has appeared in print ere now) my brother wrote at a venture to Browning, then in Venice, asking whether he was not the author of *Pauline*; for this anonymously published poem had been noticed by Dante Rossetti in the library of the British Museum, and admired and copied out by him, and he recognized one or two lines re-used by Browning elsewhere, as well as a general conformity of thought and manner. A response came in the affirmative. I had previously begun in *The Germ* a review of *Christmas Eve and Easter Day*, but this remained uncompleted owing to the expiry of the magazine. My brother's first actual sight of Browning appears to have been in 1852. Allingham, who knew something of the latter, then called upon him in London, and Rossetti was privileged to accompany him.

I could not now fix the time when I myself first saw the object of my unbounded homage, the author of *Bells and Pomegranates*, and above all of *Sordello*. It may have been before the close of 1853. The appearance of Browning is very well known to many persons now living, either as a matter of reminiscence or from photographic and other portraits, and I need not attempt a description. He was (as my brother informed me after first meeting him) of rather low stature, but so well-knit and justly proportioned that he hardly counted as a short man. When I made his acquaintance he had a very abundant crop of finely flowing dark hair, with perhaps the first few threads of grey; hair went also round his face and under the chin, but not in the shape of a beard. I consider that my brother's water-colour portrait of Browning gives one of the truest extant likenesses of him: the features correct, and one of the predominant expressions of his whole countenance well caught. This interesting work is now in the possession of Mr. Charles Fairfax Murray. The poet's conversation was of the readiest and most undisguised. It took in all sorts of subjects, whether serious or slight, and showed an equal range of knowledge, observation, and penetration. If light had to be thrown upon some matter of the intellect, it was at once forthcoming ; an anecdote or a jest came pat, and there it was. Both by the tone of his talk and by his personal manner Browning set you very much at your ease. To be conscious of your inferiority was, save for the fewest, at once right and inevitable ; but he did nothing towards screwing the consciousness into you. He seemed to be always simply and straightforwardly himself : brilliant and many-sided, not by any direct endeavour, but because this pertained to him. At all points he was vivid and alert—the turn of his head, his footfall on the floor. If he yawned (which he did occasionally), it looked less like a symptom than a dismissal of ennui. To say that Browning was eloquent in talk would—so far as my experience extends—be going too far ; he was also not rhetorical nor long-winded in exposition ; but his talk included most of the good qualities short of eloquence—especially masculine acumen and versatile promptitude. It was essentially what it needed to be— conversation, not lecturing. The time flew fast in his company. He spoke but little about himself and his poetry, but gave information freely when asked for.

I saw Browning in London, during the continuance of his married life, some half-dozen to a dozen times ; his sojourns here were of course not numerous—he was more generally on the Continent, chiefly in Florence. The most memorable meeting was on 27 September 1855, at the temporary residence of the Brownings,

13 Dorset Street, Marylebone Road, when Tennyson read *Maud* aloud, and Browning read *Fra Lippo Lippi*; of this incident I gave some account in my *Memoir of Dante Rossetti*. The poet honoured me by writing from Italy, to ask me to select an engraver for the photograph of his wife required as frontispiece to a new edition of *Aurora Leigh*, and to supervise the engraving work as it proceeded. I applied to Mr. Barlow, who produced the engraving. Wholly satisfactory as an agreeable and dignified likeness it was not considered by either Browning or myself; but the poet made the best of any imperfections—rather than the worst, as some other sympathizers were disposed to do—and in due course the portrait appeared in the book.

In the early autumn of 1860 I for the first time went to Italy, in the company (and very pleasant company it was) of Mr. Vernon Lushington, then a young barrister, afterwards Secretary to the Admiralty, and finally a county-court judge. Our chief bourne was Florence. Here I had expected to find and see something of the Brownings; but it proved that they were away from Florence for a while, in *villeggiatura* at Marciano near Siena. Browning wrote to me asking us not to leave Italy without looking them up at Marciano; we took good care to comply. We found Mr. and Mrs. Browning, with their son, in an agreeable villa, not a showy one, some few miles from Siena; they received us with abundant cordiality. It happened that the boy had that day had a sunstroke, which might possibly have turned out a somewhat grave affair. Mrs. Browning, the tenderest of mothers, was consequently rather anxious, and she withdrew at times to the sick room; the illness was however already taking a turn for the better, and by the following morning it was practically overcome. The boy, whom I had previously seen in London, had a face very noticeable for bright intelligence, though the features were not delicately chiselled ; his long silky abundant curls (a maternal heritage) gave him almost the look of a girl. At a very early age, seven or eight, he often wrote verses which, childish as they were, seemed of singular promise ; Browning showed some to my brother and myself.

Before our proceeding to Marciano, Browning had met Mr. Lushington and myself at the railway station of Siena. He ushered us into the library containing the celebrated frescoes, by Pinturicchio, of the Acts of Pope Pius II, Æneas Sylvius Piccolomini. I recollect that he pointed out to me in one of these frescoes an object in the sky which he regarded as an interesting point in the invention of the subject, a soul or angel ascending to heaven ; I scanned it, and could not discover that it was anything else than an ordinary bird, but I did not venture to contest the great poet's more ideal interpretation. He told us to visit, which we did, the local museum of paintings, chiefly of the Sienese school, saying that that school, though not competing with the Florentine, was well worthy of attention. I can still hear the gusto with which he pronounced the name of " Beccafumi."

In the villa at Marciano the Brownings were close to another villa tenanted by Mr. William W. Story, the American sculptor, with his wife and family. Along with the Story family, just at this time, was the aged poet Walter Savage Landor, then in his eighty-sixth year. Browning however, who had generously undertaken to look after him, was more closely concerned with

him than Story. The former had promised us that
we should see something of Landor, who accordingly
stepped over to pass that evening with his English
friends; Mr. Story was also there. Landor was a tall, large
man, of robust build ; his person and countenance were
somewhat less stately and imposing than I had expected.
He had grown a full, fluffy white beard, making his look
all the more venerable ; he was partially deaf, but talked
with freedom and energy—I regret to have forgotten
what his topics may have been. Probably they dealt
more with politics bearing upon the question of Italian
nationality and unity than with anything else ; for those
were the days when, following the Franco-Sardinian war
against Austria in 1859, and the cession of Lombardy
by Austria to Sardinia, the national movement had
spread all over Tuscany, Romagna, etc., and the
approaches towards Italian unity were hastening on,
with not any assistance, but rather pertinacious opposition, from Napoleon III. This potentate was one of
the not innumerous objects of Landor's hearty detesta-
tion ; he was so likewise of mine, although, at the time
when he came forward as the champion of Italy against
Austria, one had been anxious to trust him if possible.
Mrs. Browning was, in this respect, entirely opposed to
Landor : she believed most devoutly in Napoleon III,
and looked upon him as the one man able and personally willing to introduce a great and glorious change
into European politics. She said on that evening that
Napoleon's seemingly anti-Italian moves (he had just
been sending, if I am not mistaken, some men-of-war
to the Tuscan coast, to control the Tuscan aspirations
for amalgamating with the Sardinian State) were only
made "for a strategic motive"—a phrase which Mr.

Story repeated to me on the following morning with some sarcasm. Robert Browning, to the best of my observation, assumed at that time an attitude somewhat midway between his wife's and that of Landor. He did not particularly believe in *l'homme du deux décembre*, and he reprobated the acts whereby he had attained imperial power ; but still he was willing to wait for the evolution of events before wholly condemning his character and line of policy. Another point of divergence between Mr. and Mrs. Browning was that of "Spiritualism." Mrs. Browning was a partial if not a complete convert to its theory and practice ; while Browning—not without having looked into the matter with some pains— repudiated it with no little scorn. I saw once or twice some slight symptom of approaching antagonism if Mrs. Browning in talking came to the outskirts of the "spiritual" theme. I have even been told that Browning could express himself with some harshness to his wife when this subject was mooted ; but for my own part I disbelieve anything of the kind. From what I saw, I should have difficulty in crediting that the mutual and beautiful affection of the illustrious pair was ever overclouded in any such way, even when the ultimate object on the husband's part was one of goodwill, to dispel delusions or guard against imposition.

It may have been on this same evening, but I surmise rather on some subsequent occasion, that Browning mentioned to me one of the incidents which had convinced him that so-called mediums are constantly impostors. A personage of some celebrity in Florence, known to all sorts of British and American visitors and to Italian residents as well, was Mr. Seymour Kirkup, an English painter who had settled there in

1824: he was made a Barone of the Italian Kingdom, in recognition partly of his conspicuous achievement, the uncovering from whitewash, towards 1840, of the portrait of Dante by Giotto in the chapel of the Podestà, in the Florentine Bargello. About that date he became a correspondent of my father, whose theories of Dantesque interpretation he ardently adopted ; I in 1860 called on him in his apartments on the Ponte Vecchio, and made his acquaintance, leading after a while to a rather active interchange of correspondence. Kirkup had a housekeeper (the mother of his daughter) named Regina ; she became noted as a medium, demonstration succeeded demonstration in Kirkup's house, and he was firmly persuaded of the genuineness of the proceedings, and of his being brought into relation with various disembodied spirits—one of them being that of Dante. On one occasion Browning and others, along with Kirkup, were present when Regina fell (as it seemed) into a clairvoyant trance, and some signs and wonders ensued. Then the company, headed by Kirkup, moved into a different room, Regina rising and moving with every appearance of being still in the tranced condition. But as soon as Kirkup had passed the door and was out of sight, Browning with some others being still present, Regina's trance came to a pause, and she moved about like any ordinary woman until she had rejoined Kirkup, when she forthwith became once more entranced and once more oracular.[1]

---

[1] This is what Browning told me, as near as I recollect it after a long interval of years. There may be some minor inaccuracy in my report of his statement, but not in the main features of it. The account given by Professor Dowden, in his book *Robert Browning*, p. 160, differs in detail.

I will add here (though with only partial relevancy to my context) that I have myself seen something of table turning and rapping, the use of the ouija, and the like, both with professional mediums and in private company. I have seen it, and I don't know what to infer about the phenomena, still less whether "spirits" have anything to do with them. I must however in candour say this much—that I think movements and rappings do really take place without any intended or conscious action of the bystanders to produce them.

In the course of that evening in the Marciano Villa Mr. Vernon Lushington, with whom our host had no previous acquaintance, happened to speak of the pleasure he took in the music of Ferdinand Hiller. "Ah now," said Browning in his prompt, sudden way, "I understand who you are. When I find a man who shares with me in a liking for Hiller's music, I can see into him at once ; he ceases to be a stranger."

Some circumstances made it more convenient that I should pass the night in the villa of the Storys rather than of the Brownings, and I was very kindly welcomed by the American family. Mr. Story, who had lately earned a great reputation in London by his statue of *Cleopatra*, and who became known as well by more than one volume of verse in which the influence of Browning was apparent, had an ample fund of pointed and attractive conversation ; his personal appearance was not remarkable. On the following morning I found Landor downstairs seated at the table with his writing materials. He wore a large, loose cap, around which various flies were weaving their disquieting dance. Landor's aspect was mildly composed; but, when some one made a passing observation about the flies, he responded with an

I.—R

utterance in which one could easily recognize the original of Dickens's "Mr. Boythorn." "Yes," said the author of the *Hellenics* and the *Imaginary Conversations* in a tone of resolved conviction, "I have considered the matter, and I find that, of the many vile nuisances existing on the face of the earth, flies are the most strictly intolerable." I petitioned the aged poet for any little scrap of his handwriting. He presented me with some verses, to which he added his signature : they have, if I am not mistaken, been printed in one of his latest volumes. At the moment of writing I am not wholly certain what has become of the manuscript ; my impression is that I handed it over to the most eminent of Landorians, Mr. Swinburne.

Both Browning and Story told Mr. Lushington and me that, in leaving the neighbourhood of Siena for Pisa, we must not omit to visit the small town of San Gemignano, containing (as they said) a remarkable series of frescoes by Benozzo Gozzoli, and conspicuous as the only Tuscan town which, after the advent of the Medici dynasty, had retained its full complement of defensive towers. We followed this advice; and thus terminated our brief visit to the Brownings in Italy. I never saw either of them again in that country: Mrs. Browning indeed died in the following year.

I must have found myself in the company of this noble poetess some half-dozen times in all. She was truly *petite* in form, with the smallest of human hands. I consider that the chalk head of her by Field Talfourd, done in 1859 and now in the National Portrait Gallery, is an extremely true likeness—so much so that those who know it hardly need any further description of her face. I find however one fault in the portrait. The

lacrymose look of it can barely be pronounced over-
charged; for Mrs. Browning was of that excessive
sensibility (and her face showed as much) which seemed
to tremble towards tears at any moment—though I never
saw her actually shed them, unless perhaps on the
occasion next to be mentioned. But the fault is that,
along with this true lacrymose look, Mr. Talfourd gives
(to use an undignified term) something of a " snivelling "
look; and this did not belong to our Queen of Helicon.
The spacious rounded brow, the very dark and liquid
eyes, the profusion of dark satiny curls over which
advancing years seemed to claim no control, are all
rightly rendered; also the less attractive forms of the
nose and mouth. Mrs. Browning's face, as I knew it,
was not beautiful, nor yet pretty: for a student of
expression it was fascinating, corresponding with delicate
exactness to the tone of her poems. I can imagine that
in childhood and early girlhood she was an exquisite
fairy-like creature. Her voice was not strong, and was
intermittent rather than flowing in delivery; I never
heard her read poetry, whether her own or that of others.
Neither (so far as memory serves me) did I ever hear
her indicate that she had any knowledge of Christina
Rossetti's poetry. My sister did not publish any
volume until 1862, the year following Mrs. Browning's
death; but she had printed some few compositions to
which my brother was more than likely to call the
attention of Robert Browning. I once saw the manuscript of *Aurora Leigh*. As usual with Mrs. Browning,
the handwriting was most delicate, but crossed and re-
crossed by cancellings and re-writings to a surprising
degree.

There was one rather remarkable scene in which Mrs.

Browning bore a part, in my presence. It was in her house in London, not less perhaps than a couple of years after the Tennyson incident of 1855. Miss Jessie Meriton White, the lady who is now known as Madame Mario, widow of a Garibaldian patriot, was a most ardent Mazzinian and revolutionist, animated by a fierce hatred of Napoleon III, and capable of any act of self-sacrifice for her cause. She passed the evening with the Brownings, and announced that she was about to start for the Continent: what to do I know not now, and perhaps did not very clearly understand then, but it was to be something which might well involve her and others in imminent peril. Mrs. Browning was deeply moved with the dread of some catastrophe, and implored Miss White with passionate earnestness to regulate her enthusiasm, and even to forego her projected expedition altogether. But Miss White was not less fervent than her hostess: she quitted the house, and had soon quitted England as well. I have met this true heroine more than once—mostly in the company of Madame Bodichon. Her florid complexion, flamboyant hair, and incisive speech, made her a noticeable figure, even apart from her uncompromising tone of opinion and her many acts of courageous devotion.

After Robert Browning had re-settled in London I saw him every now and then. At times I called on him while he was living in Warwick Crescent, and found at home either himself or his excellent sister Sarianna, who died at a great age in 1903. At other times he was in my house (in Albany Street or Endsleigh Gardens). Or again I was invited to look at one or other of the pictures painted by his son towards 1878. He also attended the unveiling of the bust and fountain monu-

MRS. BROWNING.

THE LAST PHOTOGRAPH TAKEN OF HER, 1861.
COPY SENT BY ROBERT BROWNING TO W. M. ROSSETTI.

ment to Dante Rossetti, close to the house which the
latter had for many years occupied in Cheyne Walk,
Chelsea. In all these instances he was as amiable, open,
and conversible, as could be. The last time seems to
have been soon after the publication of *Ferishtah's Fancies,*
when he joined a few other friends at an afternoon in
our house : on this occasion Browning and Madox
Brown had a little amicable conversation. But there
had been another occasion a year or so earlier, when
Brown, who fancied that the poet had in some way
slighted or ignored him (probably a mere surmise), and
whose spirit of sturdy independence bowed to no one
however eminent, made me keenly uncomfortable by
starting off in a marked manner as soon as Browning
entered the room ; and he resisted, with a doggedness
which can hardly but have been apparent to Browning,
the polite advances which the latter made to induce him
to stay awhile. Far worse, and a greater obstacle to my
freedom of intercourse with Browning, was the un-
reasonable prejudice which my brother conceived against
him in and after the year 1872 : I have spoken of it in
my *Memoir of Dante Rossetti,* and shall not recur to the
details, equally odd, painful, and vexatious. My firm
conviction is that Browning never wrote or did anything
hostile to my brother ; and he more than once expressed
to me a wish to meet him again, until at last it must
have become obvious to him that there was some im-
pediment or other for which he could not account. So
far as I know or believe, Browning entertained a high
opinion of Rossetti's poems—those published in 1870
and at other dates. I find however, in the book by
Miss Harriett Jay named *Robert Buchanan,* a reference
made by Mr. Buchanan himself to an adverse opinion,

on grounds of morals or decorum, attributed to Tennyson; with the addition, "Browning in private talks had been equally emphatic." As to Browning, I must leave my readers to judge for themselves; as to Tennyson, I make some remarks further on.

Though I saw Browning occasionally up to nearly the close of his life (1889), I never met him in those circles of fashionable or high social distinction to which, as some will have it, he became more than duly addicted in all his later years. The reason of this is plain : I was not myself an *habitué* in such circles, nor indeed did I ever aspire to mix in them, nor did I cultivate the opportunities which offered themselves to me, at sparse intervals, to take a first step, and then a second and third, towards attaining such a result. I have always been contented with that class of society to which, by birth and training, I belong ; though not insensitive to the charm of another and more leisured class, when I happen to come on its outskirts. Thus I cannot say, from my own observation, what may have been Browning's demeanour in that which we call " high society." It has been alleged that he became not only a constant frequenter, but something like a parasite, of such society. I do not believe it ; he appeared to me, from first to last, to be thoroughly natural, straightforward, at ease with himself and others, alive to all kinds and shades of merit ; adequately conscious too, without insistency or parade, of his own superiority, which he can hardly have regarded as admitting of any sort of subserviency to the claims of any other people on any different grounds. That Browning, knowing himself and remembering his wife, should have figured towards the last so much as " a man of society," may be a little surprising to many, myself included. But he may have seen good reasons for such a course, and I discredit bad or mean reasons. One thing we should remember—that he was a great observer of men and women ; and he may have liked to study, in his advanced age, manhood and womanhood in a sphere of life to which his earlier years had not, or had only partially, introduced him. In youth he was a comparatively neglected poet ; in age he was a poet to whom high and low alike paid unstinted homage.

Soon after Browning's death I was invited by the Editor of *The Magazine of Art*, Mr. Spielmann, to write some account of the portraits of the poet. I did so, and paid my humble tribute to a glorious memory and a cherished and indulgent friend. This is not the only instance in which Mr. Spielmann has done me a good turn in literary matters, always in the most obliging manner.

Of Tennyson I saw less than of Browning; on the few occasions when I was privileged to meet him, he treated me with much cordiality, and with what I might be excused for construing as some degree of predilection. Possibly my good friend Thomas Woolner, who was much with the poet from time to time, had given him an advantageous idea of me. In my eighth section I have mentioned the first instance in which I encountered Tennyson, at Coventry Patmore's house; and I must apparently have seen him once or twice in Woolner's company before 1856, when, being for a few days in the Isle of Wight, I called at Faringford, his house near Freshwater, but learned that he and his family were then in Wales. In July 1858 Tennyson stayed at Little Holland House with the Prinsep family ; he sat to Mr. Watts for a portrait, and was inevitably " the observed of all observers." One day my brother and I were there, conversing (like numerous others) with the poet; some of us were asked to stay on to dinner. I noticed that Mrs. Prinsep gave a distinct invitation to my brother for this purpose, I being close by him, but was not quite clear whether she had or had not included myself. Tennyson observed, "I shall see you again at dinner." "Well," I replied, "I am not certain that I was asked." "Oh yes," rejoined he, "I am satisfied you were asked; better stay." And stay I did. But, on sitting down to table, I perceived with some dismay that Mrs. Cameron, who had been present all the afternoon, and who reappeared in the evening, was not at dinner; and compunctious visitings beset me to the effect that after all I had not been asked, and must be looked upon as *de trop*, and that Mrs. Cameron must good-naturedly have foregone her place at the board so that I might not be put to open shame. What can one do under such circumstances? One thing that can be done is to put a good face on it, and resolve to pass a pleasant evening. I was equal to this emergeney, and *did* pass a very pleasant evening.

On leaving London that year, Tennyson went off to Norway. In August he was re-settled at Faringford. As it happened, I also (but not owing to any direct motive of visiting Tennyson) was then in the island, staying within half a mile of his house; I lodged in the Coastguard Station, Freshwater Gate, a rather primitive little erection, and spent the daytime with friends close by. Tennyson, being aware (I forget how) of my presence in the Isle of Wight, and somehow supposing that my locality was Alum Bay, walked thither, about six times the requisite distance, to look me up. I then called upon him at Faringford, and passed the whole afternoon and evening there, and was introduced to his wife, with their two handsome boys. Tennyson gave me the sort of welcome I best appreciate—simple and kindly, without any effusiveness. He expressed himself with the same sort of manly openness, the same expectation that whatever he said would at once be understood for what it meant, as if I had been an old friend familiar with all his ways. Effusiveness, it is well known, was not much in his line, though I can easily believe that his manner, in his family and with some close intimates, was tenderly affectionate in no common degree ; his ordinary address was direct, curt, and rather bluff, as if he did not care to conciliate, but only to be taken for the man he was. It seemed as much as to say—" You may make what you can of me; but in point of fact I am Alfred Tennyson." It is also well known that a grander-looking man, in stature and in mould of form and feature, could not well be found ; his hands were noticeably large but finely shaped, his gait (within my experience) rather shambling.

Tennyson took me out in and beyond his grounds for a little walk before dinner. He called my attention to the stately magnolia growing in front of the house, and said it was reputed (which I could readily believe) to be the largest in England. He regarded the close of winter and the early spring as offering the finest aspect for his part of the Isle of Wight. He spoke somewhat of the trouble he suffered from inquisitive tourists and the like, and of the indifference which people displayed to his rights as lord of the manor ; they thought nothing of bagging his hares and rabbits, which they would not venture to do if he were any one else. Some

trifling incident led him to refer to the extreme short-
ness of his sight—a fact which may appear rather
surprising to readers of his poems, with their countless
evidences of minute and solicitous observation of natural
phenomena. I said, "But I suppose you can perceive
the general tints and look of objects in the distance—as
for instance over there?" "Yes certainly," he replied ;
" it would be hard indeed if I couldn't see that."

In the house Tennyson made two remarks about
Shakespear[1] which have always remained in my mind.
He spoke of the greatness of quality in Shakespear's
sonnets ; adding that in early youth he had even been
wont to maintain that they surpassed his dramas, "but
of course I have long given up that exaggerated notion."
He said also that there was one sentence of Shakespear's
which, though not exactly of the pathetic order, always
affected him with peculiar poignancy, and moistened his
eyes, and he recited it on the spot. It is in the speech
addressed, in *As You Like It*, by the suddenly enamoured Rosalind to Orlando after his wrestling-match—

> " Sir, you have wrestled well, and overthrown
> More than your enemies."

An observation which he made as to the prolonged
march of sentences in Milton's blank verse, and his
own exceptional vocal power in the reading of them, has
been recorded by me elsewhere.

I dined with Mr. and Mrs. Tennyson ; and, as we
left the dining-room for a little talk in the drawing-
room, he entrusted to my hands a bottle of fine old
port brought up from the cellar, saying " You will mind

---

[1] I find some reference to this matter in the *Memoir of Tennyson* by
his son. As the same matter is a personal reminiscence of my own, I
leave it here.

not to shake it." A good glass of old port was one of the lifelong joys of the author of *Will Waterproof's Lyrical Monologue*, as that poem bears witness. I believe I did not shake the bottle; but, as I deposited it on the drawing-room table, I reflected with some nervousness that, in the brief transit from room to room, I had been so occupied in thinking about my host and hostess that I had really not applied my mind with much intentness to his bottle or his admonition.

At a later hour the poet took me up into his working room or sanctum, where he rapidly settled down to a pipe ; and I most willingly did the same, for not he himself was more partial to tobacco than I already was, and have since then increasingly continued. The room contained a rack for disused or half-used pipes, half a dozen or more. He talked of many things. His recent Norwegian jaunt, in which, as he said, he had for the first time appreciated the full power of water in scenery, waterfalls and torrents. He had found the travelling somewhat laborious, and had been struck with the number of smooth-faced beardless men whom he encountered, and their consequent youthfulness of appearance—a driver or postillion of forty looked more like twenty-two. He spoke with deepest tenderness of his wife, who in those days presented the look of an invalid, mostly reclined on a couch or settee : " No one knows or could imagine what that woman is like—the sweetness, depth, and refinement, of her mind and character." He fell foul (but this may possibly have been at a different interview) of the whole critical world, as having failed to discover that the poem of *Maud* is utterly new in structure, being the mere verbal expression of a series of mental states. He spoke of the

Idylls of the King, and of his intention that the whole poem should have an ideal bearing—Arthur amid his Knights corresponding to Conscience regulating the Passions, and so on. Tennyson made moreover some remarks about his father the clergyman, indicating a certain absent-minded or wilful oddity of demeanour— of which (as one might be disposed to say) the poet had himself inherited some traits. In reading the Psalms in church, the reverend gentleman had occasionally to deliver Psalm LXVIII., the 25th verse, which is worded: " The singers go before, the minstrels follow after ; in the midst are the damsels playing with the timbrels." In pronouncing the close of this verse, the clergyman would give a rapid twiddle with his fingers, much as if he were running them over the timbrels, or the keys of a pianoforte. Tennyson illustrated the action with his own hands ; and I can recall the exact intonation with which he reproduced that of his father—rising at the word " damsels," and falling with a negligent cadence to " timbrels."

Tennyson expressed a wish that I should return to the house soon, so as to meet a friend whom he expected, Sir Alexander Grant, of whom he spoke as an elegant Greek scholar. My holiday-time however was very nearly up, and I had to return to the Inland Revenue Office, so I was obliged to forego this gratification.

Few people, I imagine, passed an evening with the Poet Laureate without hearing from him something of his tribulations with strangers or semi-strangers who would persist in writing to him, and thus entailed upon him the very distasteful trouble of sending some sort of answer. His conversation with me ran partly upon this topic. He neither liked to pen the replies, nor liked that the replies should come into the hands of persons unknown to him, who, for aught he could guess, might show them about promiscuously, or make some other use of them which he would regard with antipathy. I remarked that it was pretty well known that some inks are procurable with which one can write in characters perfectly legible in the first instance, but fading away and disappearing after an interval of time. He caught at this idea, and said that he would very gladly be in possession of an ink of that kind, to be used as occasion might suggest. I offered to see about the matter after my return to London. With some compunction I acknowledge that I did not fulfil this undertaking. I had plenty to do on my return, and had no definite idea as to what would be the right place at which to apply for such an ink. The days passed, I heard no more from Tennyson on the subject, and in fine I dropped the project. This was a fault on my part ; but a benefit to some not scanty number of recipients of Tennyson autographs, who, if I had obtained and sent the ink, would assuredly for many years past have been the owners of blank sheets of note-paper.

I liked very much the little that I saw of Mrs. Tennyson on this occasion ; it must have been my only meeting with her. The gentleness and also the polish of her manner were extreme ; but they did not give any impression of what is weak or superficial, rather of a firm underlying solidity of character. The portrait of her by George F. Watts (engraved in the Memoir) must assuredly be a fine likeness, but it represents her at a more advanced age. The medallion-head by Woolner, being the only other likeness that I know, fails to satisfy me. She told me that she, and her husband likewise, enjoyed one of my brother's designs in the "Illustrated Tennyson" as well as, or better than, any other woodcut in the volume. This design is to *The Palace of Art*, King Arthur "watched by weeping queens." I have seen or heard it stated somewhere that he also liked the Rossetti designs of *Sir Galahad* and *The Lady of Shalott*; and that he said (what indeed is true) that he could not discover any connexion between the drawing of St. Cecilia and his verses to which it is appended. I do not remember hearing of any expression of his regarding the *Mariana in the South*, which I regard as fully equal to any other of these Rossetti woodcuts. Recently I have heard it mentioned that Tennyson applied the term "Wardour Street work" to the Rossetti designs generally. This seems to me possible enough; and the term might even be used in a sense not directly derogatory, but as a summary mode of implying an attempt on the artist's part to reproduce the forms and spirit of a remote past—to be "antique," which is inevitably "modern-antique"; and his own *Idylls of the King* show how unlikely one is to avoid the pitfall.

I never heard Tennyson say anything indicating that he took a serious interest in painting or the allied arts; indeed it seems generally understood that he did not. If the subject turned up, he was apt to say a few words about it, and there to leave it. In this respect he was wholly unlike Browning; who (as is well known) took the same kind of keen interest in pictorial or sculptured work or in music that he did in poetry. He was equally ready to talk about all these matters, and he showed a detailed acquaintance with and insight into them all.

After that day in Faringford the instances in which I met Tennyson were few—say two or three. One occurred at the chambers of Mr. Knowles the architect and editor, in June 1870. The poet received me with great benignity. I do not recollect the particulars of his conversation on that occasion, except that he expressed to me admiration of some of the poems of my brother in the volume then recently issued. Some others of them (I forget which) he did not like; and he objected to some of the rhymes, naming "water" and "clear". This was the day when a gentleman named Hewlett gave me certain information about incidents in the early life of Shelley, which led to my writing a paper, published in *The Fortnightly Review*, on Shelley's *Devil's Walk* and his *Declaration of Rights*, and other details in that connexion. My last sight of "Alfred Lord Tennyson" was in the Royal Academy, in some such year as 1888. The exhibition was near its closing-hour when I walked into the Sculpture-room, and noticed Tennyson looking about him in rather a vague and straggling sort of way. Before I could well accost him he was gone. His age was then very advanced, but he was not in essentials greatly different from what I had known him in earlier years.

In the *Memoir of Tennyson* by his son (Vol. II, p. 352) occurs the following passage, being a quotation from a diary which the son kept during his father's very grave illness, rheumatic gout, in the winter which opened the year 1889. "Various prescriptions have reached him from strangers: one, that burnt cork should be placed under his bed; another, that a diet of snails should be tried." It seems then that the use of cork—burnt cork in the first instance, and "virgin cork" (undressed slabs) in the second—was twice recommended for Tennyson; for in February 1890, when he was gravely

ill with influenza, my wife wrote suggesting that virgin
cork should be tried; and tried it was, at a date when
the Laureate was already on the mending hand. My
wife was herself, from 1885 onwards, a great sufferer
from bronchial pneumonia. This affair of the virgin
cork is curious, and I will here give it a place. It was
in the early autumn of 1889 that Christina showed my
wife a printed leaflet, circulated by a clergyman, recom-
mending the use of cork-wood in that disease, and
others of the same class. The wood had simply to be
laid about in a room, especially the bedroom—not
necessarily "under the bed." My wife, though
attaching little credit to this leaflet, consented to try
what would come of the cork tendered by Christina.
She had been passing a succession of very bad nights
with coughing and wheezing. Strange to say, on the
very first occasion that the cork was in the bedroom she
passed an excellent night. The same improvement, the
cork being constantly used, went on for days, weeks,
and months; and all this while, although doctors would
have it that the cork could not be reasonably regarded
as producing any effect whatever, my wife's faith in it
continued steady and on the increase. Her disease
however, notwithstanding the abatement of some of
its symptoms, pursued its course; and it may have
been late in 1891 that the cork, not seeming to prove
of any further avail, was neglected, and ultimately
disused.

My wife and I attended the ceremony of the burial of
Tennyson in Westminster Abbey: a noble and moving
sight, especially at the moment when some of his verses
were sung to music composed by his widow. We had
also admissions for the burial of Browning in the same

building. To my great regret I was prevented from attending ; my wife went with our eldest daughter.

I will give here two anecdotes of Tennyson which, so far as I know, have not yet appeared in print. That they are trivial I at once confess ; they are not however totally uncharacteristic, and one or other of my readers may find them amusing.

My first anecdote comes from Woolner ; he must apparently have got it from Tennyson himself, and at any rate I confide in its accuracy. The poet went off on an Italian trip, imbued, we may be sure, with an ample store of poetic and classical reminiscences, and anxious to see as much as he could within the time at his disposal. He paused at some particular city ; and, his supply of tobacco running low, he inquired at two or three shops for the same kind of tobacco—Bristol bird's-eye was (if I remember right) one of his favourites. To his dismay, no such thing was to be found ; *some* tobacco there was—but not *his* tobacco. What was to be done in this woeful penury of the right sort to smoke ? Tennyson packed up his luggage, abandoned all his Italian interests and desires, and returned to London. He narrated his disappointment to an experienced friend ; and had the further disappointment of being assured that, if only he had known the proper shop to go to, he could readily have obtained the required tobacco.

For my second anecdote the witness was Allingham, to whom the small incident happened. He was at breakfast at the house of the Poet Laureate, who, in a rather feeble moment of facetiousness, asked, " Will you have a hegg ? " " Yes, thank you," replied Allingham ; who had scarcely appropriated the proffered viand when

I.—s

Tennyson added, "I suppose you understood that I was only joking when I said hegg." The idea that petty jeers might be passed upon him owing to any misconception or misrepresentation was galling to the great but susceptible mind of the author of *In Memoriam*.

I will subjoin a third anecdote, told to me by Mr. George Meredith, who laughed at the lady concerned, but of course not at Tennyson, whose part herein was merely passive. Both authors were at the house of a rather fashionable lady, whose sister was presiding at the tea-table. Tennyson, some paces off, expressed a wish for a cup of tea; and the hostess conveyed the message to her sister in the emphatic words, "A cup of tea for the great creature." It is curious that Charles Dickens, speaking of Tennyson, used just the same expression. "What a great creature he is" occurs in a published letter of his to John Forster, dated in 1844.

The *Memoir of Tennyson* by his son is a book which I have seen and heard considerably discussed from differing points of view; some persons holding that it gives a very good account of his life, in the best taste; others, that it produces a weak and washed-out impression, as being overmuch marked by eulogiums and reticences. My own belief is that the book supplies an extremely genuine picture of the great poet up to a certain point, and that whatever is said in his praise is not in the least exaggerated. At the same time I apprehend that, out of deference to his own likings, and out of consideration for survivors (the filial biographer himself included), there is rather too much endeavour to keep out of view those traits, sometimes perhaps rugged but always thoroughly human, which marked Tennyson as a man apart. That he was a poet apart we all know; he was also a man apart. When Dr. Birkbeck Hill was (as already referred to) editing the *Letters of Dante Rossetti to William Allingham*, he had in his hands one letter in which Rossetti spoke of a recent interview of his with Tennyson. He did not here say anything detrimental to Tennyson, whom in truth he greatly admired as a poet, and liked (so far as he saw him) as a man; but he related one or two incidents symptomatic of the more off-hand or unconventional shades of the poet's demeanour. Dr. Hill and Mrs. Allingham agreed in thinking that, before this letter was published, it should be shown to the present Lord Tennyson, for consideration by himself and his mother. The reply came in terms more than sufficiently strong—to the effect (if I remember right) that the publication of such details might "be the death" of Lady Tennyson. Therefore all that part of the letter was excluded from the volume. This incident shows how powerful were the family-feelings in opposition to the publishing of anything which might seem at all to qualify the finer and more dignified traits in the Poet Laureate's character; and one may legitimately infer that the portrait of him presented in his son's Memoir is, while strictly true, somewhat less complete than might be desired in its play of light and shade—the full congruity, which can be the seeming partial incongruity, of warm-blooded life. Perhaps the best potential biographer of Tennyson would have been Mr. Watts-Dunton. He knew the Laureate well, admired him deeply, and knows—none better—what it is right to say and not to say, from all points of view.

XVII

SOME PERSONAL AND GENERAL DETAILS

MY chief object in this section is to speak of various persons with whom I came into contact through one circumstance or another, and whom I have not yet had occasion to mention. But I shall in the first instance clear off, with due reticence as to details, a matter personal to myself, which, if left unnoticed, would leave unexplained the course of my life for a considerable lapse of years.

In the summer of 1851 I was introduced to a lady, not my junior, for whom I soon conceived a genuine affection. In refinement of mind, character, and demeanour, she stood on a level which I have seldom known equalled, never surpassed. That she had some degree of liking for my society and myself was plain enough. I did not for a while attempt to test how far this liking might extend, as the moderate scale of my income and my general position imperatively dictated a prudent reserve. In January 1856 I proposed to this lady, and was accepted. Both her parents were living, and neither of them was frankly in favour of the match; the father however was the only one who definitely opposed. His health began to fail, and, out of filial deference, the lady broke off the express engagement;

but, after an interval of a few months, she elected that it should be renewed. The father died in 1859, the mother, while I was in Italy, in October 1860. In the following month the lady announced to me that, consequent upon her grief for her mother's death, she viewed with dismay the idea of forming any new ties, and she preferred that the engagement should be regarded as at an end. Against myself no sort of complaint was made or suggested. I was unable to consider this second rupture of the engagement entirely reasonable. I submitted to it, and determined to remain a bachelor. And so I did remain for a dozen years and upwards. But it was written in the book of destiny that I should not continue thus for ever.

I now proceed to the ordinary subject-matter of this section, the "people I have known." The great majority of them were met by me before the date which I have last specified, the close of 1860.

Mr. William Bell Scott having, while still settled at Newcastle-on-Tyne, become acquainted with Sir Walter Calverley Trevelyan and his wife, of Wallington Hall, Northumberland, and having undertaken to execute in the entrance-room of the house a series of paintings to illustrate the history and social life of the North of England, I was invited to accompany him to the Hall—soon (as it happened) after I had casually met Lady Trevelyan at a soirée at the London house of Mrs. Loudon, widow of the botanical author. Wallington Hall was then a newly erected or totally renovated building. The paintings by Scott, well chosen in subject, and excellently invented, and in point of execution second to few of his performances, were the chief objects of attraction; there were also a series of decorative paintings of flowers and plants on the pilasters. One of them was done by Ruskin, another by Miss Capel Lofft (who became the second Lady Trevelyan), a third by Mr. Arthur Hughes. Sir Walter Trevelyan, an elderly thin man with a very high nose, was a great leader in the total abstinence and anti-tobacco movements, a recognized adept in some branches of knowledge, especially botany : he ate funguses which no one else would touch, and gave me a dish of them which I remember with a modified degree of pleasure. He had inherited a famous cellar of wines, which he bequeathed to another total abstainer of medical renown, Sir Benjamin Richardson. At his own table a decanter or so of wine was allowed to appear, of ordinary quality ; he of course did not touch it, and his guests would have been in diminished favour if they had indulged in more than a very few glasses. Lady Trevelyan (Pauline Jermyn by birth), much younger than her husband, was a witty and graceful-minded little lady, of cultivated tastes ; she had pur-chased one or more paintings by my brother, the water-colour *Mary in the House of John* being the chief. Wallington Hall was not far from the seat of Sir John Swinburne, grandfather of the poet ; the latter, whom I did not happen to meet at Wallington, entertained and has always preserved a feeling of devoted friendship for Lady Trevelyan, whose name occurs in his observa-tions, extracted in a preceding page, on Lizzie Rossetti.

On another occasion Mr. Scott introduced me to the Marchioness Dowager of Waterford, the renowned beauty (middle-aged when I saw her) and singularly gifted painter ; if she had not been a peeress but a "professional," her ready and animated invention in composition, and her rich fine colouring, would have earned her a name of uncommon distinction. In the schoolhouse near her residence at Ford in Northumberland she had been painting a series of groups—the "Children of the Bible." Scott had been invited to look at and advise upon them, and he obtained leave for me to accompany him. These paintings are not of an elaborate kind, but show the same remarkable faculty as the Marchioness's other works. I learned with pleasure that she was a warm admirer of Christina's poems.

Miss Alice Boyd, the owner of Penkill Castle, Ayrshire, figures prominently in Scott's *Autobiographical Notes*, and has been mentioned by me in the *Memoir of Dante Rossetti*. I was first introduced to her in Scott's house in Newcastle; she died at a fairly advanced age in 1897. I would willingly pay here to her memory the tribute of affectionate friendship and respect which is more than her due; but this has been practically forestalled in my previous book. I was her guest at Penkill Castle for a fortnight or more in 1867. Though not in so high a degree as the Marchioness of Waterford, this lady had a good aptitude for painting : she possessed ideas, feeling, and facility, but not much style in execution. I am afraid that Miss Boyd's closing years must have been seriously embittered by the controversy which arose over the *Autobiographical Notes* of her greatly cherished friend Bell Scott, chiefly in reference to the unhandsome treatment therein accorded to Dante Rossetti. Mr. Swinburne bore an active and a strongly hostile part in this controversy. I myself did very little ; intervening to a small extent, to point out simply that Scott, being provably inaccurate in other matters, ought not to be presumed to be exceptionally accurate in this one, but avoiding any fierce recriminations.

Indeed not even this performance of Scott's had cancelled, or to the present day has availed to cancel, the warm regard in which I had held him for some forty long years.

Another family of which I saw a little through Scott's introduction were the Greenwells of Durham. To this family belonged the poetess Dora Greenwell, who produced some work both refined and of genuine feeling, to which her appearance and manner corresponded. She made acquaintance with Christina, whose poems she prized in the most generous spirit. There were also the Richardsons, a Quaker family in Newcastle, clear-thinking, and active in good works. A lady of this family married the prominent Liberal politician Dr. Spence Watson ; in 1881, when I had to deliver some lectures in Newcastle, they were my hosts, and I conceived a high respect for them both.

In 1856 a gentleman not as yet in any wise known to me, Captain Augustus A. Ruxton, an officer who had retired from the army still youthful, conceived a project of getting up an exhibition of British paintings in America—New York, and if convenient some other cities. He was brother to the author, then recently deceased, of a book which had excited a good deal of attention, named (I think) *Wild Sport in the West*. Captain Ruxton had no sort of connexion with fine art or its professors ; but he felt a liking for pictures, and, having all his time to himself, and a wish to come forward in any way which might ultimately promote his fortunes, he partially matured this American project in his own mind, and then looked out for some one to act as secretary, and to serve as medium of communication with artists. He wished more particularly to secure those of the

Præraphaelite quality. Owing to my recent connexion with the American art-journal *The Crayon*, he fixed upon me ; I had various interviews with him, and I assented to his proposal, with a modicum of salary annexed. Captain Ruxton was a more than commonly good-looking man, of polite and elegant address, and of a rather sanguine temperament. Owing to this scheme, I came into contact with several painters not previously known to me : one was F. O. Finch the water-colourist, who painted small landscapes in a "classic" style, rather conventional and old-fashioned, but decorous—he was chiefly interesting to me on the ground of his having seen something of William Blake in his latest years. Another Blake man whom I met once or twice (but this was at Ruskin's house and had nothing to do with Captain Ruxton) was the fashionable and admired portrait-painter, George Richmond. There was moreover Samuel Palmer the painter of poetic landscape in watercolour, whom I saw once in my brother's studio. When Captain Ruxton's American project had obtained some degree of publicity, it turned out that Mr. Ernest Gambart, then the most prominent and resourceful picture-dealer in London, had also been entertaining a plan of like kind. Some uncertainties ensued ; and finally it was arranged that Gambart should combine his scheme with ours—he being far the stronger in watercolours, while the great majority of the oil-pictures came through our agency. Gambart sent at the same time a collection of French pictures to America for separate exhibition. Ruxton obtained through me an introduction to Madox Brown ; and at one time it was proposed that Brown should accompany the works across the Atlantic, but this came to nothing.

The American Exhibition of British Art, which opened in the autumn of 1857, proved by no means a success; except indeed that the artists in New York, and in their degree the art-lovers and public there as well, showed a great amount of goodwill, and made a reasonably fair show of paying visitors. The like was the case at Philadelphia, Boston, and Washington, to which cities the Ruxton section of the works travelled afterwards. Several sales were effected, including Leighton's *Romeo and Juliet* (the scene where Juliet is supposed to be dead) and a smaller duplicate of Holman Hunt's *Light of the World*; Longfellow purchased another painting. In other respects most things went wrong. The works, in charge of Captain Ruxton and a representative of Gambart's house, arrived in New York just in the thick of one of the most calamitous money-crashes which marked the nineteenth century; the two custodians did not pull well together; people had very few dollars to spend, and not much heart for thronging to places of amusement; a *Venus* by Leighton was huddled out of sight by request, lest the modesty of New Yorkers should be alarmed; at Washington a sudden and violent storm of rain damaged several of the water-colours, including a work by Madox Brown. Besides, the British artists had not after all come forward with adequate zeal. It was the year of the great Art-treasures Exhibition in Manchester, and several men had really nothing to contribute; there was no important oil-picture by Turner, no Millais, no Dante Rossetti— and the American devotees of Ruskin, and sympathizers with Præraphaelitism, had been specially looking out for all these. Ruxton was a loser by his spirited speculation —Gambart, I dare say, not a gainer.

Mr. Stillman, who had been editor of *The Crayon*, exerted himself vigorously in favour of Ruxton's enterprise. He was not as yet personally known to me; but this action of his tended all the more to promote the best relations between him and me when eventually he came to London for a while; which may have been early in 1859. From that time we were fast friends. In temperament, in his attitude towards the inner and the outer things of life, Stillman had more of the man of genius than the man of talent. In actual mental endowment and outcome the reverse was the case. He did not possess genius, but his talents were authentic and versatile, and so was his course of life. His *Autobiography of a Journalist* is in many respects a most interesting book, and should take a prominent place among the capital examples of that class of writing. It gives a true insight into a character and a career, and the mainsprings of both; and, if this is not what we principally want in autobiography, I know not what is. Mr. Stillman—though one may read his book from title-page to finis without learning the fact—was a man of unusually lofty stature, six feet three; in Florence towards 1880 he and his used to pass under the name of "*la famiglia lunga e magra*" (the lengthy thin family, or as one might say in one word, the Lankies). From his second wife "the beautiful Miss Spartali" (daughter of the gentleman who was for many years Consul-General for Greece in London), and his own second daughter Mrs. Middleton, the range of height may extend from five feet nine to six feet one in the tallest daughter; the surviving son, now settled as an architect in America, is I understand a good bit taller than his father. Truly a stately procession through the streets of Florence, where shortish people are the rule.

Captain Ruxton, when I made his acquaintance, was a married man, with three engaging little daughters. Mrs. Ruxton was an uncommonly tall lady, dignified and thoughtful, without any affectations ; she was a skilled performer on that too obsolete instrument the harp. She had been Miss Mary Minto ; and under that name she is mentioned once and again in the published correspondence of Mrs. Browning. She stated to me (but she was necessarily too young to know the fact otherwise than by report) that the christening of Elizabeth Barrett Barrett had been made the occasion for an extraordinarily lavish and opulent display.

I have before spoken of Mr. Vernon Lushington, who was my travelling companion in my first visit to Italy. He had been in 1856 a contributor to *The Oxford and Cambridge Magazine;* towards the same date I met him for the first time at the house of Alexander Munro the sculptor. He had a twin brother Godfrey, now Sir Godfrey Lushington, lately Permanent Under-Secretary in the Home Office; the two brothers were so much alike that I have more than once made a mistake between them. However, it happened that Vernon Lushington, who had been in the Navy in early youth, had by some accident lost a finger : a surreptitious glance at his hand was a useful precaution against such blundering. At Christmastide of one year, I fancy 1859, he asked me to spend two or three days at the family mansion at Ockham in Surrey. Here I made the acquaintance of his father, Dr. Lushington, Judge of the Admiralty Court ; then very advanced in years, but still lively or even brisk in manner, and with a seeming youthfulness of heart which filled him with amiable *bonhomie :* I recollect the almost juvenile gusto with which he listened standing to the singing of "Ye banks and braes of bonnie Doune." As many of my readers will know, he had been, as far back as the year 1816, the counsel who advised Lady Byron in the affair of her separation from the poet ; the one who declared that the allegations made to him were such that, unless a separation were positively insisted upon, he could have nothing further to do with the case.

Towards the year 1858 I was three or four times in the chambers in Gate Street, Lincoln's Inn, occupied by Mr. W. S. W. Vaux, the President of the Numismatic Society—a bulky, rather large man, of the good-natured free-and-easy sort, a fine scholar in his own line. He had serial evenings, partly musical, to which a large number of men congregated—no ladies. The rooms were rather bare ; tobacco, beer, and some other refreshments, were kept going freely ; and the assembly formed a choice specimen of literary, artistic, and theatrical London in a Bohemian mood. I knew several of the frequenters, and picked up with some others here and there. Old chums of mine, of the Hannay set, had been at least equally Bohemian, but on a much minor scale of numbers. Everybody at the Gate Street gatherings could do and say what he liked : the more the merrier, and the merrier the noisier. To be glum was the one thing which would have been out of place.

I was once in a madhouse, Bedlam : luckily my entrance was voluntary, and my departure optional. It was Mr. Ralston of the British Museum Library who asked me whether I would like to go ; and he appointed that we would accompany Mr. John Cordy Jeaffreson for the purpose. This may have been in 1863. We called at the house of Mr. Jeaffreson (author of the *Book about Doctors* etc.) in Doughty Street, Gray's Inn Road, and I was introduced to him and his wife. We three then went round to Bedlam. I had not till now known Mr. Jeaffreson ; our acquaintance was renewed little or not at all until 1873, from which time onwards I saw him, and his wife and daughter, pretty often, and we were on terms of much mutual goodwill. One inmate of the asylum whom I was curious to see was Richard Dadd, a painter of much talent, taking a rather fantastic turn, who was rising towards prominence about the date of 1847, when the seeds of madness developed in him, and in a ghastly moment of frenzy he slew his father. I saw the ill-starred painter ; who was sitting with two or three others in a large airy room, having beside him a mug of beer or some such refreshment. His aspect was in no way impressive or peculiar ; he seemed perfectly composed, but with an under-current of sullenness. He had painted a large picture, which I conjecture is still on the staircase of the asylum, of *The Good Samaritan :* a rational work, showing adequate artistic knowledge of an ordinary kind, but not marked by any of that superior talent which had once been his. We were escorted through various other rooms. One was a large hall containing numerous patients. Here was a woman emitting frequent and dismal shrieks ; another who repeated with piteous emphasis, " What else *could* I expect when I knew that I was born under a curse ? " It was a case of religious mania : she believed herself to be doomed to eternal torment. Such in brief was my experience of " Bethlehem Hospital."

XVIII

CHEYNE WALK
AND ENDSLEIGH GARDENS

MY brother, after his marriage in 1860, had continued to reside, with his wife, at No. 14 Chatham Place, Blackfriars Bridge, extending the range of his apartments. In consequence of her decease in February 1862, he determined to remain there no longer : the place was fertile of painful associations—joys and hopes and griefs of old on which death had set his seal. He removed for a while into chambers in Lincoln's Inn Fields ; then in October 1862 to the house which he continued to occupy up to his death, 16 Cheyne Walk, Chelsea. He had no inclination to be alone ; so in the first instance it was planned that my mother and sisters, along with myself, and also my aged aunt Margaret Polidori who had apartments in our house 166 Albany Street, should all join him in Cheyne Walk ; there was to be yet one other inmate, Mr. Swinburne. This was a scheme not very promising for the comfort in day-by-day humdrum of the female members of the family. It was dropped ; and Dante Rossetti became tenant of the house, with Mr. Swinburne and Mr. George Meredith as sub-tenants (having rooms of their own but dining together with Rossetti) and myself as a third sub-tenant. I paid at first my fair proportion of the rent; but after no long while my brother announced that he had no further occasion for this subsidy, and thenceforth I lived at free quarters in the house. In entering there I did not quit the family dwelling in Albany Street, but settled to be in Cheyne Walk three days in every week—Monday, Tuesday, and Friday, were, I think, the days selected. This arrangement suited me exceedingly well; and few planes of my life are more satisfactory in my reminiscence than that which covers the years from the close of 1862 to the beginning of 1869 or thereabouts. After that, troubles in connexion with my brother's health and spirits became only too prominent; but still there were many elements of cheerfulness at Cheyne Walk up to the middle of 1872. Dante Gabriel's health then broke down in a most disastrous way, and up to the late summer of 1874 he was scarcely in the house at all. I, in his absence, was not unfrequently there up to 31 March 1874, the date of my marriage. Thus, when he resumed residence in Tudor House (as it was called), my partial tenancy of it had wholly ceased; and in afterwards going there—which was sometimes often enough, and at other times seldom—I was merely a visitor, like any other intimate.

That fine old building in Cheyne Walk was beyond all comparison the roomiest and sightliest that I had ever as yet inhabited, nor indeed have I to this day been so handsomely housed elsewhere. I need not describe it at any length; it is still there to speak for itself, and various records of it exist in other books. The rent was extremely moderate, £100 a year: it was not raised until some such date as 1878. Entering the passage, one had on the right hand the sitting-room allotted to Mr. Meredith, and on the left, that of Mr. Swinburne. Both these rooms are of very moderate size : the right-hand one was ordinarily used as the dining-room for us all, but with two or three additional guests the drawing-room was substituted. Facing one on the ground floor was the studio : a well-sized apartment, not lofty, nor so well lighted as was desirable for my brother's painting ; after a while he got a considerable improvement introduced into the lighting. On the first floor was the drawing-room, large and stately ; also a breakfast-room, and my brother's ample bedroom. On a landing half-way up towards the first floor was a high-pitched but rather desolate-looking apartment which served for Rossetti's art-assistant, and at times as a bedroom : in this capacity Mr. Watts-Dunton became very familiar with it. The second floor was occupied by bedrooms, some ten or more : one of them was mine. Then there was the large garden, nearly an acre in extent ; it was not very carefully kept, and to me its haphazard luxuriance was all the more delightful. My brother had a big tent set up on its turf : we dined there occasionally, and lounged in it oftener.

About the only drawback to my daily comfort in this house was the impracticability of settling down to anything like steady work in the evening ; in the day I was of necessity away at Somerset House. My brother's habits of an evening after the late dinner were quite antagonistic to any such work on my part. Friends were very often with us, and much talk went on. If they were not there, he lolled on a sofa, chatting as the humour came, or sometimes dozing. The

I.—T

evenings, when not in the drawing-room, were always spent in the studio. I had not any sitting-room of my own—only the bedroom. In the studio the light was a gas-standard, not well suited to writing. I very frequently had writing-work to do, which I should have wished to attend to in Cheyne Walk no less than in Albany Street. This I had to give up, and I limited myself to reading. I always kept a book on hand, to which I could recur when the opportunity offered. In matters of this sort my brother, though radically good-natured, was not of what one calls an accommodating turn. His own convenience dictated his habits, and persons in his company had to adapt themselves as best they could. In those years he did (it may be said) *nothing* in the evening, beyond talking and lounging as aforesaid. His painting-work was over for the day ; he wrote no more poems since the death of his wife, and the burial of his old poems in her coffin ; he rarely took up the pen for letter-writing, and, if he did so, he dashed off the missive at a rattling pace ; he read no newspapers or periodicals, and was very seldom going carefully through a book. Thus he did not require for himself any of the conveniences of regular quiet occupation. I might have wanted them ; but, sooner than interfere with his habits and propensities, I did without them. We usually sat up late, even if there were no friends with us. I tumbled into bed, and got up moderately early on the following morning, so as to be off to Somerset House—long before my brother rose. In the morning I scarcely ever saw him, and never perhaps had his company at breakfast.

In early youth Dante Rossetti had not had any habit

of buying artistic articles of furniture, or attractive bric-à-brac of any kind; in fact he had no money to spend for such purposes. Unthrifty he always was, but not in youth expensive. In boyhood he bought engravings when he could, and in adolescence books. I, being thrifty enough and with only very moderate means, and living with my family, all of them (though in no way stingy) very economical as a matter of conscience, bought still less than my brother—or practically nothing. After his marriage, and having to furnish some new rooms, Dante attended a little to matters of ornamentation, and it need hardly be said that he did so with the best of taste and an original aptitude. As the time was approaching for removing to Cheyne Walk, he launched out upon purchasing things here and there to a large extent; and this indeed was a clear necessity for his fresh household, as well as a fancy with which he became increasingly urged. He found in Buckingham Street, Strand, an old gentleman named Minister (first unearthed by Allingham) who had a big stock of really capital old-fashioned furniture. He was not a furniture-dealer, and how he came to be thus supplied was a question which rather puzzled my brother; he surmised that Mr. Minister might have been a butler in some family of distinction, and might thus have come gradually into possession of his stock. Anyhow Rossetti regarded him as a " Minister of Grace," and bought a number of things from him. Hence he proceeded to further purchases; and soon the house began to fill with Chinese tables and chairs, Dutch tiles, Flemish and oriental and African curtains and draperies, looking-glasses and mirrors of the seventeenth and eighteenth centuries, a chandelier here and another there, and numerous knick-knacks of whatever kind. He had a particular liking for convex round-shaped mirrors. Many of these things served him for objects to be painted; others were merely for looking at. The " Japanese mania " did not exist at the date when we entered Tudor House. It began in our quarters towards the middle of 1863, and later in that year I wrote for *The Reader* (a weekly review not unlike *The Athenæum*) an article on a certain book of Japanese woodcuts. They are the work of Hokusai, under his later name of Gwakyorogi; but of this fact I had then no knowledge. This may have been nearly the earliest article that appeared in England upon Japanese figure-designs. It was Mr. Whistler who first called my brother's attention to Japanese art : he possessed two or three woodcut books, some coloured prints, or a screen or two. To him, I take it, this new revelation in art had been made in Paris, in the Impressionist circle. I have heard say, and perhaps with accuracy, that Edouard Manet was the " head and front " of Japonnerie, and I know that at an early date in the movement Tissot was a keen collector. Rossetti was equally astonished and delighted with Japanese designs; their enormous energy, their instinct for whatever savours of life and movement, their exquisite superiority to symmetry in decorative form, their magic of touch and impeccability of execution, carried him away. Assuredly he did not suppose that the facial angle of the " eternal feminine " of Japan, as represented (and very untruthfully represented) by her admiring countrymen, is to be accepted as the line of beauty; nor were his previous impressions revised as to how a human leg or arm or torso is constructed. He was still convinced that one's clavicle comes in one particular place, one's biceps muscle in another, one's femur in a third. At Sass's Academy and the Antique School of the Royal Academy he had learned something about a human knee-joint and vertebral column: from that lessoning, and from what he knew (and little it was) of linear perspective, he did not apostatize. Dante bought some of the triple colour-printed designs, and had them framed appropriately, and a few woodcut-books: they are now mine. Upon the colouring of the prints he looked with great satisfaction, as having qualities of force and saliency which no other nation could bring into play with equal effect; he said however that the colouring is somewhat harsh—which is true of a large number of Japanese works, though not of all. I also revelled in Japanese art; and soon, for one print or book that my brother bought, I purchased a half-dozen or more. A continuous band of the colour-prints, lightly framed, was hung round my dining-room after I had removed to Endsleigh Gardens. They made a gorgeous decoration, which was highly commended by Dante Gabriel, Trelawny, and some others. They were not much to the taste of Madox Brown, nor yet of my wife; so, when we removed in 1890 to St. Edmund's Terrace, Regent's Park, they were not replaced in any living-room, but they make a brilliant, and to un-accustomed eyes a rather startling, show in the entrance-passage.

Several of my earlier Japanese items were acquired in London; about an equal number in Paris, where I used to drop in at the shop, in the Rue de Rivoli, of Madame Dessoye—a very pleasant-spoken and well-informed purveyor, with whom I had several amusing chats. I know not what has become of

Madame; ,for years past her shop has disappeared from
the Rue de Rivoli. She told me a little personal
anecdote, over which we both laughed. One of those
half-bred British tourists who make themselves a pest
and a jest among the " benighted foreigners," one who
appears to have considered himself a lady-killer, entered
her shop, and, after looking at various things which she
showed with her usual amenity, he suddenly blurted out
" *Je vous amour*." Madame Dessoye promptly showed
him the door. In London one of the shops I frequented
was that of Farmer & Rogers in Regent Street—a firm
now long dissolved. Here the foreman was Mr.
Lazenby Liberty, who afterwards set up for himself in
the premises, on the opposite side of the street, so well
known to Londoners. In 1877, going to Liberty's, I re-
encountered the proprietor after a good lapse of years,
and he remarked that he regarded me as " the first
pioneer of Japanese art in London." This notion was
not accurate, but it pleased me as coming from a person
so competent on general grounds to form an opinion.

I have more than once produced to artists of superior
faculty and accomplishment Japanese books and prints
which simply astounded them. Mr. Shields and Mr.
Nettleship were two; a third was Mr. Boughton, who however was already sufficiently initiated in this form of art.
I am happy to say too that, when my generation of the
Rossetti family gets extinguished in my own person,
the taste for this wonderful art will continue to survive
in a later generation. All my four children enter into
it with zest; especially the one of the four that has the
most obvious artistic turn, Helen (now Signora Angeli).
The great ambition of this damsel, when she first began
to think a little seriously about learning to draw and

paint, was to study under a Japanese artist. We made
some inquiries after such a personage, but did not
succeed in securing one. As some faint compensation
for this gap in her art-training, she crowded the walls
of her bedroom with the colour-printed landscapes of
Hiroshige and other specimens from the land of the
Mikado.

Was there ever, in real insight and superlative
strength, the grace that comes of strength, a better landscape painter than Hiroshige?[1] Yes, there was Turner.
Who else? Or was there a more stupendous master of
whatever he set his hand to than Hokusai? or one who
understood a tiger—the essence of a tiger, not to insist
upon his skeletal scaffolding and his "anatomy figure"
—better than Ganko? or an inventor of bird and flower
groups, a seer of the life of flower and bird, equal to
Kitao Shigemasa or Sugaku? How pale and petty,
how anæmic and indecisive, do most European things
appear beside such mighty handiwork!

But the knell of Japanese art has sounded for several
years past. A geisha in a "tailor-made costume" from
Paris or London is not exactly one's ideal; nor yet
a successor of Hokusai and Sugaku trying to be
"reasonably correct" or "quite nice" according to
European standards, half understood, half assimilated,
repeated from the teeth outwards, and, from the inner
Japanese man, wholly alien and averse. Over Japanese
art for some while to come one can but trace (I fear)
a mortuary inscription. Possibly there is to be a me-
tempsychosis at some rather remote date. Possibly the

---

[1] I understand that there were three Hiroshiges; the first the best,
but all good, and of closely allied style. In speaking of "Hiroshige," I
do not attempt to distinguish between the three.

contact with European art may at some future time have worked for reform and not for torpor, and the genius which flamed in a Hokusai may reappear "clothed and in right mind" in some Japanese rival of Albert Durer, of Botticelli, or of Tintoret. Meanwhile there has been a singular Japanese inroad into the province of British poetry. I refer to the very remarkable and sometimes startling poems of Yone Noguchi, a young Japanese who has passed several years in the United States, and who, on bringing out in London in 1903 a little brochure of verse, was so good as to forward it to me. I read it with sincere pleasure, and soon afterwards had the gratification of making the author's personal acquaintance. He was next again in America for a while.

We all know that there are enormous defects in the authentic Japanese art; that which all know is known to me also. There are enormous defects in Giotto, Fra Angelico, Van Eyck, Mantegna, and Perugino. An Andrea del Sarto was not "senza errori," though contemporary Florentines chose to call him so. What we really want in fine art is not freedom from error (a thing impossible, and, if possible, not supremely valuable), but inspiration to discern and to exhibit—the intuition and the faculty. We want

"Di Michelangiol la terribil via,"

but we admit, if we are candid, that it whirled him along into some extravagances. Regarded from this point of view, Japanese art has nothing to ask of European attainment or models; it is an integral organism, and some creative spirit has "breathed into its nostrils the breath of life." Chinese art, of a very ancient date, is the reputed original of Japanese art; however this may be, the Chinamen of recent centuries seem quite unable to compete with the Japanese in energy and fire, or in depth of perception. The secret of the excellence of the latter in art seems to be ultimately this—that they were semi-barbarians (if that is the right word), and as such specially autochthonous and exclusive. They have ceased to be so, and are ceasing to be the artists they were; a British illustrated newspaper has given them a torpedo shock, just as a Parisian hatter, a German drillmaster, and a Yankee or Clydeside steamer-builder, have renovated their fashions, their army, and their marine (and very good use, as we now know, they have made of such new lights). As semi-barbarians, they were more instinctive than the artists of other races — more like the foxes, rabbits, and cranes, which they love to depict; in observation and manipulation they had the same advantage over the ultra-civilized that, in the senses of sight and hearing, a savage has over a European. Being thus instinctive, they represent with a portentous suddenness of truth whatsoever is instinctive in nature — the insect, the octopus, the frog, and the fish, the protracted creeping sinuosity of some serpent, sublime as the serpent of eternity, the majesty of the swooping eagle, the fluttering of the sparrow, the jerk of the hen's head, the tall grace of the deer, the crunch of the cat's teeth in the rat; and so the flying foam of the sea, the deluge of rain, the cloudcapped Fujiyama; and so the animal passions of men, the lithe blandishments of women, the volcanic furies of fighters, the frenzies of a heroic adventure. Again, this instinctive quality flashes forth with singular lustre in what we call the grotesque; for a devil, a hobgoblin, a monster, a dragon, or for the gruesome in mere oddity and absurdity, or for spurts of whim and grace in whatsoever unconsidered trifle, no European, of any age or country, could untie the latchet of the Japanese master's shoe. Look at such a performance as *The Temptation of St. Anthony* by Salvator Rosa or by Teniers ; and then turn a page or two of a book by Hokusai, or almost equally well by some designer of name unknown or obscure, far inferior to him.

Lord Leighton was an artist not generally supposed (nor rightly supposable) to be indifferent to grace, suavity, and elegance, as elements in fine art. It may be worth while to listen to an utterance of his at an address which he delivered in 1888 to the Art Congress in Liverpool. He termed the Japanese "a race which possesses the artistic instinct, in certain of its developments, in a greater degree than any other in our time. With them the sense of decorative distribution, and of subtle loveliness of form and colour, is absolutely universal, and expresses itself in every most ordinary appliance of daily life—overflowing indeed into every toy or trifle that may amuse an idle moment. In the movement imparted by them to the figures in their designs there is often much of daintiness and dignity, the outcome of that keen perception of beauty of line in the abstract which we have seen to be dominant in them."

But even a Japanese maniac leaves off at last talking about his particular hobby. Perhaps he next reopens the last Japanese book or the last set of woodcuts bought of Shozo Kato (of New Oxford Street), or perhaps he attends to his proper business. I shall do the latter, and resume what I had to say about my brother, and his furnishings and furbishings in Cheyne Walk.

Dante Rossetti's passion for Japanese articles—chiefly woodcuts, but he did not limit himself to these—was strong; his passion for blue china was stronger and more prolonged. Of this china, some was Japanese, but the more numerous and finer specimens were Chinese. He bought rather largely, and very tastefully; and—unfortunately for himself as well as others—he ferreted about for such things to an extent which availed to send up the market price of them. Mr. Whistler, and no doubt some other amateurs, were eager on the same tack. My brother also acquired a large and very sumptuous Chinese porcelain screen, of varied colouring, which is now a valued possession of Mr. Watts-Dunton. I gave a few details about this matter of blue china in my *Memoir of Dante Rossetti;* and might have given still more, to be in due proportion to the interest which for three or four years he took in this pursuit. The zeal of a collector was upon him; and that zeal is not always "according to knowledge," nor yet according to morals. But it seems that in collecting, as in love and war, everything is fair. I will give a little anecdote : I know it to be true, as the person concerned—not without compunction, and yet with some sort of glee as well—avowed the fact to myself. I have only to add that it has no relation whatever either to my brother or to any one else whom I have named as addicted to collecting.

Y. Z. was fond of collecting engravings, especially those of a certain school and period : for convenience sake we will suppose them to be (though they were not so in reality) French engravings proper to the first half of the eighteenth century. He had got together the various prints—a dozen or so—forming a particular

series, save only that one of the required prints was
lacking. One day he entered an auction-room prior to
a sale, and inspected a portfolio. Here he found the
entire series of those same prints, including the missing
specimen. The insatiable greed of the collector raged
or raved in him at the sight. He actually stole that
missing print, and walked off with it. Y. Z. was a
mature, a moral, a reflective, and a cautious man, and
yet he committed this serious offence and veritable act
of lunacy. He might have been detected, and then his
whole life was wrecked, and his whole collection of engravings a withered leaf in the whirlwind. His means
were amply sufficient for bidding for the lot, and so
securing, at an outlay not worth debate, the particular
print which he wanted, along with the others as dupli-
cates.

Between " pots " and " beasts " a good deal of Dante
Gabriel's time and attention was shared at Cheyne Walk;
" pots " being his generic term for blue china, and
" beasts " for animals that he kept in the garden, or
sometimes in the house. I have spoken of this matter
elsewhere ; and, though it is among my cherished reminiscences, I must cut it short here. There were quad-
rupeds, birds, and reptiles. From contemplating a
Japanese salamander in a tank or a white mouse nursing
her brood, in the studio, and hearing a wood-owl hoot
or a parrot talk in the corridor, you could pass into the
garden, and see a kangaroo skipping, a racoon washing
and swallowing a biscuit, or an armadillo pacing his
rounds—not to speak of a zebu chasing (on one
occasion not unfrequently reported) Dante Gabriel
Rossetti round a tree. The wombat, and after him the
woodchuck or Canadian marmot, were too precious to

be allowed much out of doors : they were my brother's companions day by day, and the wombat would follow at the housemaid's heels when she went upstairs to make the beds. An anecdote is current of the wombat, and I accept it as only somewhat exaggerated—not untrue. My brother had asked, as he pretty often did, several friends to dinner ; he himself never smoked, but for the satisfaction of his guests he had provided a box of superior cigars. The dinner over, he proceeded to produce the box. The box was there, but the cigars were gone : the wombat had made a meal of the entire assortment.

Burne-Jones had a habit of drawing funny fancy sketches of wombats ; delighting as he did in the animal's fat lumpish look and want of " sculpturesque " form. I used to possess (or I think they were in strictness a gift from the artist to Christina) three admirably amusing sketches of his, framed together. There was *The Wombat at Home* with his wife and family ; *The Wombat Abroad*, scurrying with unwonted agility after his nightly provender ; and *The Wombat saved*, himself and his mate walking along a plank into Noah's ark. I fancy there is an impression that, in the artistic circle to which be belonged, Burne-Jones was the discoverer—as he certainly was the most frequent delineator—of the wombat. This however is a mistake. I must claim that proud pre-eminence for Christina and myself. In or about 1858 we two were in the Zoölogical Gardens, and our steps led us towards a certain enclosure hitherto unknown to us, and little scrutinized by most visitors. Christina, who had as good an eye for a " beast " as Dante Gabriel, caught sight of " phascolomys ursinus " a second before myself,

and exclaimed, "Oh look at that delightful object!" I
soon instructed my brother what part of the Zoölogical
Gardens he should go to in order to contemplate the
form and proportions of the wombat; he, I surmise,
afterwards put up Burne-Jones to the same quest.
Christina, before the end of April 1859, had utilized
the wombat in her *Goblin Market*, and Dante drew his
portrait in the illustration to that poem as published in
1862 ; and, when the wombat of Tudor House was
first domiciled there, Christina hailed him in some
Italian verses which have been published, headed by
an English distich—

> "When wombats do inspire,
> I strike my disused lyre."

Though she was not exactly gifted with the pencil of a
Burne-Jones, she had a certain knack at catching in
drawings the expression of animals ; and she made
at the Zoölogical Gardens a sketch of a wombat which
at this moment hangs framed in my dressing-room,
along with similar portraits of two squirrels and a
fennec fox.

I had known something of Mr. George Meredith—
not very much—before he joined us in the tenancy
of Tudor House ; from that time forward, October
1862, I saw him intimately and somewhat frequently
as long as he remained in the house, which may have
been for a year or probably less. He was not present
there however at all constantly—not nearly so many
days in a month as myself. I have in fact heard it
affirmed that he never once slept in the house ; this may,
I apprehend, be a mistake. He and I were always on
very good terms—no hitch has occurred between us at

any time ; but, after he discontinued his sub-tenancy,
I saw him but seldom, and for many years past it has
not been my good fortune to meet him at all. Meredith
had a far wider interest in life and society, the actual
transactions of men and women in their relations ordinary or exceptional, the interaction of characters and
motives, than either my brother or myself had ; without
this he could obviously not have been the novelist he is.
Thus, although I enjoyed his company and conversation,
I did not always fall in either with the tone of his
mind, or with the objects towards which he directed
its remarkable powers. He understood, and liked to
understand, many things to which I was mainly indifferent—to some of them, as for instance everything
connected with the ordinary politics of the day, my
brother was much more indifferent than myself. Among
inquiring minds, and people on the look out for new
talents, Meredith then already enjoyed a solid reputation. He was not however a popular writer ; and
I take it he is scarcely to be called a popular writer
even at the present day, except in the sense that the
gusto of connoisseurs has compelled the tardy but still
rather half-hearted acquiescence of " the general reader."
The books which chiefly occupied Meredith in his
Cheyne Walk days would have been the poem of
Modern Love and the novel of *Emilia in England;* I
was but slightly acquainted with the latter, and did not
(which may have been my fault) like the former, though
I recognized the uncommon ability in it. Swinburne
upheld a high estimate of both.

Mr. Meredith had (and no doubt still has) a fine
well-chiselled face, more noticeable perhaps for mould
of feature, and for the air of observant intellect, than

for the expression of indulgent fellow-feeling : an Italian would have called him " *bello* " rather than " *simpatico.*" It is the face of a man not easily hoodwinked by the shows of the world. My brother was wont to say that Meredith bore a rather marked resemblance to the busts of the Emperor Hadrian ; I think he improved upon them. The early termination of his sub-tenancy in Cheyne Walk was due, not to any disagreement with any one, but, on his own part, to finding that practically he made very little use of the rooms, and, on Rossetti's part, to a perception that, as his money-affairs continued to improve, his original wish to abate the expense of house-rent had come to count for very little. It has also been alleged, and I am sure with *some* measure of truth, that Mr. Meredith, being more fastidious in such matters than Rossetti, disliked the diet in Cheyne Walk.

Swinburne remained there a good deal longer than Meredith : he must have been a resident, I think, throughout 1865, and perhaps well on into 1866. He honoured me, as I have already intimated, with the most cordial friendship ; and I think I may without vanity say that he was as ready to ask and take my advice as that of any one upon any point of practical difficulty or uncertainty. I am not here speaking of questions of literary composition, though neither need these be wholly excluded. I spent many glorious evenings in Swinburne's company—sometimes *tête à tête,* but more often along with my brother or some others ; listening to what he read of *Atalanta in Calydon,* then in course of writing, and of numerous other poems as well. Swinburne, though far too great a poet to have an uneasy itch for listeners, was none the less very

willing to read his poems to the appreciative. He is a
fine reader, and might be termed an admirable one ;
and is exactly as good now as he was in the days of his
youth. His delivery is singularly pure, every syllable
precise and perfect, in a way not too common among
Englishmen, though frequent enough with Italians.
His matchless sense of metre and rhythm controls
every line ; while the fiery fervour of his mind governs
every intonation, redressing anything that might otherwise be even excessive in his verbal exactness. It may
indeed be said that the quality of his reading is a close
counterpart to that of his writing : the impetuous
inspiration of the poet glowing through and trans-
figuring the forceful structure of the rhetorician. To
hear him for one hour was to wish that it might be
two.

If I remember right, Mr. Swinburne had quitted the
Cheyne Walk house before he published in 1866 the
much-debated and more-denounced volume (to which I
have already made a slight reference) *Poems and Ballads*
—a well-head of the most splendid poetry. I was
already however perfectly familiar with the great
majority of the compositions in that volume. I considered at the time—and had expressed my opinion to
the author—and I still consider that some things in the
book had better be excluded ; but the amount of noise
made over it, the frenzied abuse and indiscriminate
anathemas, were such as could only be forthcoming in a
land of " Scribes and Pharisees, hypocrites." Anglo-
Saxons on both sides of the Atlantic were capable of
this ; I do not imagine that any other race under the
sun would have been equally capable. While the
phials of wrath were sputtering, fizzing, and yielding

an evil odour of cant and commonplace, I offered to write for *The North American Review* a notice of this volume, and I wrote it ; but I then learned that Mr. Lowell had already expressed in that magazine his opinion of Swinburne (this would have been apropos to *Atalanta* and *Chastelard*, and not to the *Poems and Ballads*), and so an arrangement was made with the London publisher Hotten (who had taken over the *Poems and Ballads* from Moxon & Co.) that he would bring out my little essay as a pamphlet-volume. It appeared under the title of *Swinburne's Poems and Ballads, a Criticism, by William Michael Rossetti* ; and few incidents in my literary life have given me greater or more permanent satisfaction than the belief that I published on that occasion a few words of common sense when the press was reeking with uncommon nonsense on the same topic. I came in for some vituperation here and there—much less than I had expected. If any one were to read my booklet now, he would find that I was outspoken in homage to a great poet, but that I was not by any means a "dumb dog" when I thought some strictures apposite. *Tempora mutantur.* A few days before I wrote this present paragraph I had in my hands a costly volume named *The Imperial Gallery of Portraiture, edited by W. Lawler Wilson*, 1902. Here I find the following rather downright sentences : "To him (Swinburne) cannot be imputed the worst of all failings, the shame of putting great powers to a vile use. On the score of morality too no one could censure him. His works are an inspiration to do right boldly. Some of his early poems were indeed sufficiently hot-blooded ; but this is no great reproach to a young man. He has given the labour of his life to prove, to all in whom the

WILLIAM BELL SCOTT   JOHN RUSKIN   DANTE GABRIEL ROSSETTI.

TAKEN IN ROSSETTI'S GARDEN, 1864.

sense of divine beauty is vivid and exquisite, not that God punishes, but that God lives."

In connexion with the *Poems and Ballads* and the out-pourings about them, Dante Rossetti made a neat *jeu de mots* which has not, I presume, yet been in print: " Poeta nascitur, non fit . . . for publication." Possibly Mr. Swinburne heard it at the time, and I am confident he forgave it.

As I have intimated, plenty of friends and some acquaintances used to frequent the house at Cheyne Walk in the years with which I am here chiefly concerned, 1862 to 1869. There were Madox Brown, and with him every now and then his wife, two daughters, and son ; Burne-Jones and his wife ; Morris and his wife ; Scott and his wife, with at times Miss Boyd ; Ruskin (up to 1865, but scarcely at all after that date) ; Boyce ; Peter Paul Marshall ; now and again Val Prinsep, Arthur Hughes, John Seddon, Sala, and Stephens, also our warm friends of early years the Heimann family ; Browning looked in at intervals—at rarer intervals Leighton and George F. Watts. Perhaps Woolner was there a few times in the first year or two ; Holman Hunt probably not. Several others remain to be named ; but, as these are persons of whom I have as yet spoken very little or not at all, I shall reserve them for an ensuing section. Of course the women of our own family were in the house many a time—our mother and two sisters, with occasionally Charlotte and Eliza Polidori. Mr. Swinburne always treated my mother, the most unassuming and quiet-mannered of women, with a remarkable degree of considerate respect : I can still see them as they were seated one day in the studio—she in a chair, and the poet of

Atalanta close to her feet on a stool. Christina was particularly charmed and touched by these evidences of regard to our mother. She had a very high appreciation of the scope and intensity of Swinburne's poetic genius, and admired profoundly some of his writings ; others lay necessarily quite outside the range of her approval as a Christian devotee, and into these, I suppose, she never looked at all. The poet presented her with a copy of *Atalanta in Calydon* (the smaller edition) ; she read it (probably indeed she had perused it before), and she prized it most highly ; but she pasted little strips of paper over two lines in the magnificent central chorus regarding "God." If she thought Swinburne an exalted poet, he, as he has made sufficiently manifest, held the same estimate of her. It was with strong gratification that I dedicated to Swinburne the volume, which I brought out soon after Christina's death, of her theretofore unpublished or uncollected poems ; few persons would have been worthy to receive the dedication—he was the worthiest. Various critics expressed surprise and reprehension, and some opined that I had no business to dedicate to any one writings which were not my own ; Mr. Swinburne was satisfied with the transaction, and so was I, and so I have continued to this day.

Thus much for the house in Cheyne Walk, and my partial tenancy of it. The house in Albany Street remained our family residence up to midsummer 1867 ; when, consequent upon the death of my aunt Margaret Polidori in the preceding February, and the questions which thereupon arose as to our most suitable plans for the future, we removed into a much larger and better-looking house No. 56 Euston Square, which, after an interval of years, received a different name, 5 Endsleigh Gardens.

This house, with its fellows in Endsleigh Gardens, is
a very creditable specimen of the Cubitt firm's building.
In front of it is the now well-kept (but at one time very
badly kept) enclosure of Euston Square, green with turf
and trees ; from the back windows another longish
range of trees, proper to some neighbouring houses, is
to be seen. The rent was rather heavy, £125 per
annum ; but, by assigning the second floor to Eliza
Polidori and (when in London) her sister Charlotte, we
had no difficulty in meeting it. Here therefore I settled
down, with my mother and sisters, and I remained in
the house full twenty-three years, up to Michaelmas
1890. Not long after we had entered on the house the
lease of it was offered for sale, and it was bought by
Charlotte Polidori. She, dying in 1890, left it to me ;
so, just before I quitted the house, I became the lease-
holder, and I let it to the Reverend Dr. Lunn, well
known as a Nonconformist preacher, and as the organizer
of the "Grindelwald Conferences." This gentleman has
for several years past established a thriving travelling
agency to most parts of the world. Since I left the
house in 1890 I have only once re-entered it (1901),
and I found its internal arrangements a good deal
altered to meet the requirements of the travelling agency.
Some excavations in the roadway fronting Endsleigh
Gardens began almost as soon as I had left, and copious
remains of a mammoth were unearthed, as reported in
several newspapers.

Many Londoners are aware that Euston Square—
applying that name (as in 1867) to *both* sides of the
large green enclosure—consists of two façades of houses,
running north and south ; the north side being of less
attractive residential aspect and quality than the south

side. Towards 1878 some inhabitants of the south side (I was not myself concerned in the matter) thought that the decorum of this address would be enhanced by giving a new name to that side of the square : "Endsleigh Gardens" was fixed on and adopted. It happened that before this change of nomenclature had been actually carried out, a "horrid murder" termed "the Euston Square Murder" startled the town ; the corpse of a rather eccentric old lady being discovered in one of the houses on the north side of the square. Hannah Dobbs was tried in 1879 for the crime and acquitted, and no further light has been thrown upon it since then. When the south side of the square received its new name, many people fancied that the residents had not relished getting associated with "the Euston Square murder" ; this however was not the real incentive to the change, which had already been mooted and pushed forward before the murder was discovered. There were, while we resided in that house, two other vile murders perpetrated in houses quite near to us—Great Coram Street and Burton Crescent ; no one has been brought to justice in either case. In the very house which stood next to ours, No. 4 Endsleigh Gardens, a policeman was shot, and either killed or severely wounded. This was the act of a maniacal medical man from Australia. I think that he was tried, and a verdict of insanity returned.

In Endsleigh Gardens, as in Albany Street, I pursued the even tenor of my way—a very even one it was : my official employ in Somerset House from the morning till the late afternoon, and at home, in the evening, very frequently a full amount of literary work. We did not see much company in Endsleigh Gardens, but several of the persons whom I have been naming as frequenting Cheyne Walk were also at times in the former house, and others besides, known more especially to the female members of the family. That graceful and firm-handed poetess and excellent woman, Miss Jean Ingelow, may have been there once or twice ; I can at any rate recall her presence earlier in the Albany Street house. There were mutual appreciation and esteem between Miss Ingelow and Christina ; their meetings however did not at any time become frequent.

END OF VOL. I